lone

D0450547

Discover
Paris

Experience the best
of Paris

This edition written and researched by

Catherine Le Nevez,
Christopher Pitts, Nicola Williams

Discover Paris

Eiffel Tower & La Défense p47

Home to the city's signature spire and La Défense's forest of sky-scrapers.

Don't Miss Eiffel Tower

Champs-Élysées & Grands Boulevards p63

Paris' grandest avenue, department stores and the palatial opera house.

Don't Miss Arc de Triomphe

Louvre & Les Halles p85

The world's mightiest museum, market streets and the capital's cutting-edge cultural centre showcasing modern and contemporary art.

Don't Miss The Louvre, Centre Pompidou

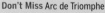

Montmartre & Northern Paris p119

The Paris of myth and films, Montmartre's hilly streets adjoin the red-light district Pigalle, home to the Moulin Rouge.

Don't Miss Sacré-Cœur

Le Marais & Bastille p139

Hip boutiques, bars and restaurants, mansion-housed museums and a celebrity-filled cemetery.

Don't Miss Cimetière du Père Lachaise

Montmartre & Northern Paris p119

Champs Élysées & Grands Boulevards p63

Eiffel Tower & La Défense p47

Louvre & Les Halles p85

The Islands p173

Le Marais & Bastille p139

St-Germain, Les Invalides & Montparnasse p211

Latin Quarter p191

The Islands p173

Paris' landmark cathedral dominates the larger Île de la Cité, while little Île St-Louis is graced with elegant buildings.

Don't Miss Notre Dame

Latin Quarter p191

The hub of academic life, filled with lively student haunts and institutions, and featuring Paris' beautiful botanic gardens.

St Germain, Les Invalides & Montparnasse p211

Literature lovers and fashionistas flock to this mythological Left Bank neighbourhood.

Don't Miss Musée d'Orsay, Jardin du Luxembourg

Contents

In Focus | ## Survival Guide

Welcome to Paris

France's romanticised capital seduces every moment of the year. Whether you're here in the springtime, the autumn, the winter (when it drizzles) or the summer (when it sizzles!), Paris' cache of artistic treasures, chic fashion sense, exquisite cuisine and majestic monuments captivate locals and visitors alike.

No matter the season, Paris has a timeless familiarity.
The Eiffel Tower's wrought-iron spire, the Arc de Triomphe standing sentinel above Paris' most glamorous avenue, the Champs-Élysées, the gargoyled Notre Dame cathedral and the art nouveau cafes spilling onto wicker-chair-lined terraces are indelibly etched in the minds of anyone who's visited the city – and in the imaginations of anyone who hasn't.

Paris' cuisine (the French word for 'kitchen') is renowned.
From cosy neighbourhood bistros to triple-Michelin-starred temples of gastronomy, you'll find every establishment prides itself on exquisite preparation and presentation of quality produce, invariably served with wine. Enticing patisseries, *boulangeries* (bakeries), *fromageries* (cheese shops) and colourful street markets are perfect for packing a picnic to take to the city's parks and gardens.

Fashion shopping is this stylish city's forte.
Paris remains at the forefront of international fashion trends, and browsing designer boutiques and flagship *haute couture* houses is a quintessential part of any visit. You'll also find uberhip concept stores and resplendent art nouveau department stores, along with a trove of vintage shops, flea markets, atmospheric bookshops, adorable children's wear, art and antique dealers, and, of course, gourmet food and wine shops galore.

Paris is one of the great art repositories of the world.
In addition to big hitting museums including the world's largest, the Louvre, there are scores of smaller museums housing collections of every imaginable genre – tangible reminders of the city's illustrious artistic legacy, which endures to this day.

66

France's romanticised capital seduces every moment of the year

99

Rodin's *The Thinker*, Musée Rodin (p225)

25
Top Experiences

25
Paris' Top
Experiences

Eiffel Tower (p52)

No one could imagine Paris today without its signature spire. But Gustave Eiffel only constructed this graceful tower – then the world's tallest, at 320m – as a temporary exhibit for the 1889 Exposition Universelle. Luckily, its acceptance and ultimate popularity (and its usefulness as a perfect platform for the transmitting antennae needed for the new science of radiotelegraphy) assured its survival beyond the World Fair, and its elegant art nouveau webbed-metal design has become the defining fixture of the city's skyline.

1

2

Sacré-Cœur (p124)

Sacré-Cœur is a place of pilgrimage in more ways than one. Staircased, ivy-clad streets wind up the hill of the fabled artists' neighbourhood of Montmartre to the dove-white domes of B silique du Sacré-Cœur. The chapel-lined basilica crowns the 130m-high Butte de Montmart (Montmartre Hill). Its lofty position provides dizzying vistas across Paris from the basilica's front steps and, above all, from up inside its main dome.

Arc de Triomphe (p68)

If anything rivals the Eiffel Tower as the symbol of Paris, it's this magnificent monument to Napoleon's 1805 victory at Austerlitz. Commissioned in 1806, the intricately sculpted triumphal arch stands sentinel in the centre of the Étoile (star), the world's largest roundabout – be sure to use the underground pedestrian tunnels to reach it! Some of the best vistas in Paris radiate from the top, including sweeping views along Paris' most glamorous avenue, the Champs-Élysées.

The Best...
Views

EIFFEL TOWER
Not only the city's most iconic building but also its highest. (p52)

NOTRE DAME
Scale the cathedral's spiralling steps for a view you'll never forget. (p178)

ARC DE TRIOMPHE
Little known fact: you can climb to the top of the arch. (p68)

TOUR MONTPARNASSE
The saving grace of this otherwise-hideous high-rise is its panoramic observation deck. (p215)

CENTRE POMPIDOU
Captivating views extend from this distinctive cultural centre's rooftop. (p96)

The Best...
Places of Worship

SACRÉ-CŒUR
Paris' landmark basilica
lords it over the city. (p124)

ÉGLISE ST-SULPICE
Featured in *The Da Vinci
Code*, it has frescoes by
Eugène Delacroix. (p220)

NOTRE DAME
The city's mighty cathedral
is without equal. (p178)

STE-CHAPELLE
Sunlight streams through
exquisite stained glass in
this hidden Gothic gem.
(p188)

MOSQUÉE DE PARIS
This 1920s art deco–
Moorish tiled mosque has
a wonderful tearoom and
hammam (steam baths)
(p197).

HENTZ JEAN/HEMIS.FR ©

The Louvre (p90)

The *Mona Lisa* and the *Venus de Milo* are just two of the priceless treasures resplendently housed inside this former royal palace, now France's first national museum. Stretching a whopping 700m along the Seine, the world's biggest museum can seem overwhelming, but there are plenty of ways to experience it, even if you don't have nine months to glance at every artwork and artefact here. One of the best is the thematic trails – from the 'Art of Eating' to 'Love in the Louvre'.

4

CENTRE POMPIDOU DESIGNED BY RENZO PIANO, RICHARD ROGERS, GIANFRANCO FRANCHINI

DEA/C. SAPPA/GETTY IMAGES ©

Centre Pompidou (p96)

This primary-coloured, inside-out building houses France's national modern and contemporary art museum, the Musée National d'Art Moderne, containing works from 1905 through to the present. The centre's cutting-edge cultural offerings include exhibition spaces, a public library, cinemas and entertainment venues. Topping it off is a spectacular rooftop panorama.

5

Musée National du Moyen Âge (p201)

Medieval weapons, suits of armour, gold and ivory aren't the only reasons to visit France's National Museum of the Middle Ages. You can also see the sublime series of late-15th-century tapestries, *The Lady with the Unicorn*; the flowering gardens planted with flowers, and France's finest civil medieval building, the Hôtel de Cluny. Sculptures at the Musée National du Moyen Âge

Musée d'Orsay (p216)

Magnificent renovations at the Musée d'Orsay display the celebrated canvases by impressionis and postimpressionist masters (including Renoir, Gauguin, Cézanne, Manet, Monet, Degas and Toulouse-Lautrec) as if they're hung in an intimate home. The grand former railway station housing the museum is still an exemplar of art nouveau architecture, of course, but France's treasured national collection of masterpieces from 1848 to 1914 are now – more than ever – th stars of the show. Edouard Manet's *La Parisienne*, shown as part of a temporary exhibition at the Musée d'Orsay

Musée Rodin (p225)

The lovely Musée Rodin is the most romantic of Paris' museums. Auguste Rodin's former workshop, the 1730-built Hôtel Biron, is filled with masterpieces like the marble monument to love, *The Kiss*, as well as works by his muse and protégé, sculptor Camille Claudel, and by other artists including Van Gogh and Renoir. The real treat, though, is the mansion's rambling sculpture garden, which provides an entrancing setting for contemplating works like *The Thinker*.

8

The Best...
Smaller Museums

MUSÉE DE L'ORANGERIE
Monet conceived a stunning cycle of his *Waterlilies* series especially for this one-time greenhouse. (p104)

MUSÉE MARMOTTAN MONET
More Monet – in fact the world's largest collection – inside an intimate hunting lodge. (p60)

MUSÉE PICASSO
An incomparable overview of Picasso's work and life. (p152)

MAISON DE VICTOR HUGO
A must for literary buffs, the writer's former apartment overlooks picturesque place des Vosges. (p146)

Parisian Cafes (p234)

Paris' cafes are the city's 'communal lounge rooms': places t[o]
eat, drink, read, write, flirt and fall in – and out – of love. Man[y]
such as Les Deux Magots, are gilded, dark-wood-panelled
belle époque treasures, where past patrons like Picasso and
Sartre still haunt the air. It's the quintessential Parisian exper[i]
ence: settle inside a cosy cafe and press pause, or perch at a[n]
outdoor cafe table and watch the parade of Parisians go abo[ut]
their daily lives...all for the price of a *café au lait*. Café Les Deux
Magots, St-Germain de Prés

The Best...
Cafes

LES DEUX MAGOTS
A must-visit address in
literary St-German des
Prés. (p234)

LE PURE CAFÉ
Still as quintessentially
Parisian as Ethan Hawke's
character found it in *Before Sunset*. (p161)

CHEZ PRUNE
The original *bobo* (bourgeois bohemian) hangout
on the banks of Canal
St-Martin. (p135)

CAFÉ LA FUSÉE
A relaxed escape from
the bustle of Centre
Pompidou. (p114)

LES DEUX MAGOTS

Cimetière du Père Lachaise (p144)

Paris is a collection of villages, and these sprawling hectares of cobbled lanes and elaborate tombs, with a population (as it were) of over one million, qualify as one in their own right. The world's most visited cemetery was founded in 1804, and initially attracted few funerals because of its distance from the city centre. The authorities responded by exhuming famous remains and resettling them here. Their marketing ploy worked and Cimetière du Père Lachaise has been Paris' most fashionable final address ever since.

Jardin des Tuileries (p104)

Filled with fountains, ponds and sculptures, the Jardin des Tuileries is a verdant oasis that offers a chance to enjoy Paris at its symmetrical best. These 28-hectare formal gardens, where Parisians paraded in all their finery in the 17th century, are now a Unesco World Heritage Site and form part of the *axe historique* (historic axis), Paris' line of monuments running from the Louvre's glass pyramid in the east to La Défense's modern, box-like Grande Arche in the west.

LONELY PLANET/GETTY IMAGES ©

12

Versailles (p244)

No wonder revolutionaries massacred the palace guard and dragged King Louis XVI and Marie Antoinette back to Paris: this monumental, 700-room palace and sprawling estate – with its fountains, gardens, ponds and canals – could not have been in starker contrast to the average Parisians' living conditions at the time. A Unesco World Heritage–listed wonder, Versailles is easily reached from central Paris; try to time your visit to catch musical fountain displays and equestrian shows.

13

Ste-Chapelle (p188)

Richly coloured biblical tales are exquisitely told with a stained-glass grace and beauty at Ste-Chapelle, the Gothic 'Holy Chapel' near Notre Dame on the Île de la Cité. A masterpiece of delicacy, with a curtain of glazing across the 1st floor of deeply coloured stained glass (marvel at that incredible deep blue), Ste-Chapelle is at its most dazzling when the sun is shining and the glass flickers in a glorious rainbow of colours.

Street Markets (p155)

Stall after stall of cheeses, punnets of raspberries, stacked baguettes, sun-ripened tomatoes, freshly lopped pigs' trotters, horsemeat sausages, spit-roasted chickens, bottles of olives and olive oils, quail and duck eggs, boxes of chanterelle mushrooms and knobbly truffles, long-clawed langoustines and prickly sea urchins on beds of crushed ice – along with belts, boots, wallets, cheap socks, chic hats, colourful scarves, striped T-shirts, wicker baskets, wind-up toys, buckets of flowers... Paris' street markets, such as the wonderful Marché Bastille, are a feast for the senses.

The Best...
Markets

MARCHÉ BASTILLE
One of the city's largest, liveliest street markets. (p155)

RUE MOUFFETARD
An old Roman road is now a sensory feast of street stalls. (p209)

MARCHÉ AUX ENFANTS ROUGES
Paris' oldest covered market, with communal tables where you can eat lunch. (p160)

MARCHÉ AUX FLEURS
Fragrant flower market. (p187)

MARCHÉ AUX PUCES DE ST-OUEN
Europe's largest flea market. (p137)

The Best...
Nights Out

PALAIS GARNIER
Paris' palatial opera house.
(p77)

MOULIN ROUGE
The cancan creator is
touristy but spectacular all
the same. (p136)

SUNSET & SUNSIDE
Respected double venue
on a street famed for its
jazz clubs. (p114)

POINT ÉPHÉMÈRE
Edgy cultural centre, club
and performance venue
booking emerging and
established DJs, artists
and bands. (p136)

REX CLUB
Paris' first dedicated
techno club is still cutting
edge. Phenomenal sound
system. (p114)

Canal St-Martin (p129)

Bordered by shaded tow-paths and traversed by iron footbridges, the charming, 4.5km-long Canal St-Martin was slated to be concreted over when barge transportation declined, until local residents rallied to save it. The quaint setting lured artists, designers and students, who set up artists' collectives, vintage and offbeat boutiques and a bevy of neo-retro cafes and bars. Enduring maritime legacies include old swing-bridges that still pivot 90 degrees when boats pass through the canal's double-locks; a canal cruise is the best way to experience Paris' lesser-known waterway.

ABOVE: HEMIS/ALAMY © ; LEFT: WALTER BIBIKOW/GETTY IMAGES ©

Parisian Dining (p58)

There's a reason that boxes of leftovers aren't done in Paris, and it has nothing to do with portion sizes. Whether you're at an unchanged-in-decades bistro, an art nouveau brasserie, a switched-on neobistro or a gastronomic extravaganza, the food and the dining experience are considered inseparable. France pioneered what is still the most influential style of cooking in the Western world and Paris is its showcase. Do as Parisians do and savour every moment.

Diners at Minipalais (p75)

Stylish Shopping (p82)

Paris, like any major city, has its international chains. But what really sets Parisian shopping apart is the incredible array of specialist shops. Candles from the world oldest candle maker, pigments from the art sup shop that developed 'K blue' with the artist, sof leather handbags made the hip Haut Marais and green-metal *bouquinist* (secondhand bookshop stalls lining the banks o the Seine are just some the goodies in store.

WIREIMAGE/GETTY IMAGES ©

Notre Dame (p178)

A vision of stained glass rose windows, flying buttresses and frightening gargoyles, Paris' glorious cathedral on the larger of the two inner-city islands is the city's geographic and spiritual heart. This Gothic wonder took nearly 200 years to build, but it would have been demolished following damage during the French Revolution had it not been for the popularity of Victor Hugo's timely novel, *The Hunchback of Notre Dame,* which sparked a petition to save the building. Climb its 422 spiralling steps for magical rooftop views.

The Best...
Street Snacks

ROAST CHESTNUTS
In the chilly winter months, warm up with *marrons chauds* (roast chestnuts) from street vendors citywide.

CRÊPES
Unlike at sit-down Breton crêperies, crêpes cooked at Parisian street stalls are rolled up and eaten on the move.

BREAD & BAKERY TREATS
Boulangeries (bakeries) are omnipresent.

ICE CREAM
Berthillon's ice cream and sorbets can't be beaten. (p183)

FELAFELS
Join the queue for scrumptious sandwiches from L'As du Felafel. (p159)

Champs-Élysées (p70)

Baron Haussmann famously reshaped the Parisian cityscape around the Arc de Triomphe, from which 12 avenues radiate like the spokes of a wheel. The most celebrated (and the scene of many major celebrations, including the final stretch of the Tour de France) is the av des Champs-Élysées, which is named for the Elysian Fields (heaven in Greek mythology). No trip to Paris is complete without strolling this broad, tree-shaded avenue lined with luxury shops, car showrooms and restaurant terraces.

RICHARD I'ANSON/GETTY IMAGES ©

The Best...
Shopping

GALERIES LAFAYETTE
France's most famous department store, crowned by a magnificent art nouveau cupola, with free fashion shows. (p82)

E DEHILLERIN
Paris' professional chefs stock up at this c 1820 cookware shop. (p115)

SHAKESPEARE & COMPANY
A 'wonderland of books', as Henry Miller described it. (p208)

ADAM MONTPARNASSE
Historic art supply shop with paints, canvases and paraphernalia galore. (p237)

DIDIER LUDOT
Couture creations of yesteryear including the timeless little black dress. (p114)

Les Catacombes
(p226)

Down below the streets of Paris, you can take a spine-tingling wander through Les Catacombes. These one-time quarries were packed with exhumed bodies relocated here due to overflowing cemeteries, and later served as the headquarters of the Resistance during WWII. Today, the skull- and bone-lined tunnels are at once horrid yet intriguing, and offer a macabre way to experience the city's history in a way that is both figuratively and literally chilling (dress warmly), but above all unique.

SCOTT STULBERG/CORBIS ©

Jardin du Luxembourg (p218)

The Jardin du Luxembourg offers a snapshot of Parisian life. Couples stroll through the chestnut groves. Children chase sailboats around the pond. Old men play rapid-fire chess at weathered tables. Students pore over books between lectures. Office workers snatch some sunshine, lounging in sage-green metal chairs. Joggers loop past stately statues. And friends meet and make plans to meet again.

Cruising on the Seine (p288)

Paris' most beautiful 'boulevard' of all is the Seine, which runs through the heart of the city. A river cruise with an operator such as the Bateaux Mouches is an idyllic way to watch the city's landmarks float past. Alternatively you can board the Batobus, which allows you to hop on and off at its eight stops: the Eiffel Tower, Musée d'Orsay, St-Germain des Prés, Notre Dame cathedral, Paris' botanic gardens the Jardin des Plantes, the Hôtel de Ville (town hall), the Louvre and the Champs-Élysées.

Gourmet Food Shops (p237)

Instead of stocking up at a supermarket, Parisians will buy their bread at a *boulangerie* (bakery), cheese at a *fromagerie* (cheese shop), meat at a *charcuterie* (specialist butcher), fruit and vegetables at street-market stalls and other delectable items from small shops specialising in everything from honey to mustard, truffles and foie gras, as well as at glorious food emporiums like La Grande Épicerie de Paris. The goods are fresher and better, and the social interaction forms part of the city's village atmosphere.

CROISSANT
1.00€
1.40€

The Best...
Tours

FAT TIRE BIKE TOURS
Friendly cycling tours around the city as well as further afield. (p288)

LEFT BANK SCOOTERS
Zoom around the capital in Parisian style aboard a scooter. (p288)

L'OPEN TOUR
Hop-on, hop-off open-topped bus tours. (p288)

PARIS GREETER
See Paris through local eyes with free walking tours led by resident volunteers. (p288)

Cooking & Wine-Tasting Courses (p241)

If dining in the city's sublime restaurants whets your appetite for cooking, there are stacks of cookery schools, from famous institutions like École Le Cordon Bleu to private Parisian home most of which include shopping and market visits. Where there's food in France, wine is never more than an arm's lengt away, and plenty of places offer wine tastings and instruction. Courses cater to all abilities, schedules and budgets. Many are run in English; confirm language requirements when you book

The Best...
For Free

CITY MUSEUMS
Free entry to permanent exhibits (temporary exhibitions command an additional fee).

NATIONAL MUSEUMS
Free on the first Sunday of the month (temporary exhibitions cost extra).

NATIONAL MONUMENTS
Some national monuments (eg Arc de Triomphe and Notre Dame towers) are free on the first Sunday of the month from November to March.

CEMETERIES
Celebrity-filled cemeteries including Père Lachaise are free to wander.

(25)

Maison de Claude Monet (p251)

The prized drawcard of tiny Giverny is the home and flower-filled garden of the seminal impressionist painter and his family from 1883 to 1926. Here Monet painted some of his most famous series, including *Décorations des Nymphéas* (Waterlilies). The house and garden are open from April to October. From early to late spring, daffodils, tulips, wisteria and irises appear, followed by poppies and lilies. By June, nasturtiums, roses and sweet peas are in blossom. Around September, there are dahlias, sunflowers and hollyhocks. Monet's garden, Giverny

Top Days in
Paris

Central Right Bank

The central Right Bank is the ideal place to kick off your Parisian trip. As well as the ancient art and artefacts in the world's largest museum, the Louvre, you'll also see ground-breaking modern and contemporary art inside the striking Centre Pompidou.

① Jardin des Tuileries (p104)

Start your day with a stroll through the elegant Jardin des Tuileries, stopping to view Monet's *Waterlilies* at the Musée de l'Orangerie and/or photography exhibits at the Jeu de Paume.

JARDIN DES TUILERIES ❂ MUSÉE DU LOUVRE
🏃 Stroll through the gardens to the Louvre.

② Musée du Louvre (p90)

Visiting the world's largest museum could easily consume a full day, but bear in mind that tickets are valid all day, so you can come and go as you please. Various tours help you maximise your time.

MUSÉE DU LOUVRE ❂ CAFÉ MARLY
🏃 Café Marly overlooks the glass pyramid.

③ Lunch at Café Marly (p112)

The Louvre's nine cafes and restaurants include the swish Café Marly.

CAFÉ MARLY ❂ JARDIN DU PALAIS ROYAL
🏃 Walk north through place du Palais Royal.

Exterior of the Centre Pompidou, designed by Renzo Piano, Richard Rogers & Gianfranco Franchini
PHOTOGRAPHER JOHN SONES SINGING BOWL MEDIA/GETTY IMAGES ©

④ Jardin du Palais Royal (p102)

Browse the colonnaded arcades of the exquisite Jardin du Palais Royal.

JARDIN DU PALAIS ROYAL ❂ ÉGLISE ST-EUSTACHE
🏃 Exit the gardens on rue St-Honoré, turn left into rue du Louvre and right on rue Coquillière.

⑤ Église St-Eustache (p103)

One of Paris' most beautiful churches, Église St-Eustache has a magnificent organ – catch a classical concert here if you can.

ÉGLISE ST-EUSTACHE ❂ CENTRE POMPIDOU
🏃 Continue east on to place Georges Pompidou.

⑥ Centre Pompidou (p96)

Head to the late-opening Centre Pompidou for amazing modern and contemporary art. For dinner, try Georges, the Centre's swishest dining option, with a spectacular view.

CENTRE POMPIDOU ❂ LE PICK-CLOPS
🏃 Follow rue Rambuteau, turning right into rue Vieille du Temple.

⑦ Le Pick-Clops (p161)

The Marais really comes into its own at night, with a cornucopia of hip clubs and bars like Le Pick-Clops.

Western & Southern Paris

It's a day of Parisian icons today – from the triumphal span of the Arc de Triomphe to the world-famous avenue, the Champs-Élysées, and, of course, the city's stunning art nouveau Eiffel Tower, with some surprises too, such as floating nightclubs.

① Arc de Triomphe (p68)

Climb the mighty Arc de Triomphe for a pinch-yourself Parisian panorama. Back down on ground level, take the time to check out the intricate sculptures and historic bronze plaques, and pay your respects to the Tomb of the Unknown Soldier.

ARC DE TRIOMPHE ➲ CHAMPS-ÉLYSÉES

🏃 Walk down the Champs-Élysées.

② Champs-Élysées (p70)

Promenade along Paris' most glamorous avenue, the Champs-Élysées, and perhaps give your credit card a workout in the adjacent Triangle d'Or (Golden Triangle), home to flagship *haute couture* fashion houses.

CHAMPS-ÉLYSÉES ➲ MUSÉE DU QUAI BRANLY

Ⓜ Franklin D Roosevelt to Alma Marceau.

③ Musée du Quai Branly (p59)

From Alma Marceau metro station, cross the Pont d'Alma and turn right along quai Branly to check out indigenous art as well as the awesome architecture of the Musée du Quai Branly.

MUSÉE DU QUAI BRANLY ➲ CAFÉ BRANLY

🏃 Head to the museum's Café Branly.

④ Lunch at Café Branly (p59)

Casual yet classy, Café Branly has ringside Tower views.

CAFÉ BRANLY ➲ PALAIS DE TOKYO

🏃 Cross the Passerelle Debilly and walk up rue de la Manutention, turning right on av du Président Wilson.

⑤ Palais de Tokyo (p54)

This stunning building takes on major temporary cutting-edge exhibits – the rooftop, for example, has been the setting for projects like the transient Hotel Everland and the see-through restaurant Nomiya.

PALAIS DE TOKYO ➲ EIFFEL TOWER

Ⓜ Iéna to Trocadéro.

⑥ Eiffel Tower (p52)

Exiting the Trocadéro metro station, walk east through the Jardins du Trocadéro for the ultimate Eiffel Tower snapshot, and cross Pont d'Iéna to the tower itself (600m total). Sunset is the best time to ascend the Eiffel Tower, to experience both the dazzling views during daylight and then the twinkling *la ville lumière* (the City of Light) by night. (Prepurchase your tickets to minimise queuing!)

EIFFEL TOWER ➲ FIRMIN LE BARBIER

🏃 Turn left on av Gustave Eiffel, then right on av de la Bourdonnais and immediately left on rue de Monttessuy.

⑦ Dinner at Firmin Le Barbier (p58)

Dining inside the Eiffel Tower itself is unforgettable. Alternatively, book ahead for fabulous bistro fare at Firmin Le Barbier.

FIRMIN LE BARBIER ➲ LE BATOFAR

Ⓜ Bir-Hakeim to Quai de la Gare.

⑧ Le Batofar (p236)

Shadow the Seine by metro to party aboard several floating nightclubs permanently moored here, including Le Batofar. Other nightlife options in this area include the Docks en Seine (aka Cité de la Mode et du Design), home to the French fashion institute, and the hot new 'creative space' Wanderlust, with the city's largest terrace.

Statue in the Jardin des Tuileries

The Islands & Left Bank

Begin the day in the heart of Paris at the city's colossal cathedral then venture across to Paris' elegant Left Bank to see impressionist masterpieces in the Musée d'Orsay, and visit the city's oldest church and its loveliest gardens.

① Notre Dame (p178)

Starting your day at the Notre Dame gives you the best chance of beating the crowds. As well as the stained-glass interior, allow an hour to climb up to the top to check out the gargoyles, and another to explore the crypt.

NOTRE DAME ❍ STE-CHAPELLE

🏃 Walk south along rue de la Cité, turning right on quai du Marché-Neuf, then right on bd du Palais.

② Ste-Chapelle (p188)

For even more beautiful stained-glasswork, don't miss the exquisite chapel Ste-Chapelle. Consecrated in 1248, its stained glass forms a curtain of glazing on the 1st floor.

STE-CHAPELLE ❍ CUISINE DE BAR

Ⓜ Cité to St-Sulpice, then walk west on rue du Vieux Colombier and left on rue du Cherche-Midi.

③ Lunch at Cuisine de Bar (p227)

This stylish lunch spot serves gourmet *tartines* (open sandwiches) on sourdough made by famous bakery Poilâne next door. Nip into Poilâne afterwards to pick up some *punitions* (crispy butter biscuits).

CUISINE DE BAR ❍ MUSÉE D'ORSAY

Ⓜ Sèvres-Babylone to Solférino, then northwest on bd St-Germain and right up rue de Bellechasse.

④ Musée d'Orsay (p216)

Visit the magnificent Musée d'Orsay, filled with impressionist masterpieces including works by Renoir, Monet, Van Gogh, Degas and dozens more.

MUSÉE D'ORSAY ❍ ST-GERMAIN DES PRÉS

Ⓜ Solférino to Sèvres-Babylone, then change lines for Mabillon.

⑤ Église St-Germain des Prés (p220)

Paris' oldest church, the Église St-Germain des Prés, sits in the heart of the buzzing St-Germain des Prés district, with chic boutiques and historic literary cafes including Les Deux Magots, just opposite the church.

ÉGLISE ST-GERMAIN DES PRÉS ❍ JARDIN DE LUXEMBOURG

🏃 Head south on rue Bonaparte to place St-Sulpice and continue on to rue Vaugirard.

⑥ Jardin du Luxembourg (p218)

Enter the lovely Jardin du Luxembourg from rue Vaugirard and stroll among its chestnut groves, paths and statues.

JARDIN DU LUXEMBOURG ❍ BOUILLON RACINE

🏃 From rue Vaugirard, turn left on rue Monsieur-le-Prince and right on rue Racine.

⑦ Dinner at Bouillon Racine (p224)

Feast on French classics at the art nouveau jewel Bouillon Racine.

BOUILLON RACINE ❍ SHAKESPEARE & COMPANY

🏃 Head east on rue Racine, turning left at bd St-Michel then right at rue de la Huchette and cross rue St-Jacques to reach tiny rue de la Bûcherie.

⑧ Shakespeare & Company (p208)

Scour the shelves of late-night bookshops like the fabled Shakespeare & Company.

Interior of the Musée d'Orsay

Northern & Eastern Paris

Montmartre's sinuous streets and steep staircases lined with crooked ivy-clad buildings are especially enchanting to meander in the early morning when tourists are few. Afterwards, explore charming Canal St-Martin and futuristic Parc de la Villette before drinking, dining and dancing in lively Bastille.

① Musée de Montmartre (p126)

Brush up on the area's fabled history at the local museum, the Musée de Montmartre. Not only was Montmartre home to seminal artists, but Renoir and Utrillo are among those who lived in this very building.

MUSÉE DE MONTMARTRE ➲ SACRÉ-CŒUR
🏃 Walk east along rue Cortot and right on rue du Mont Cenis then left on rue Azais.

② Sacré-Cœur (p124)

Head to the hilltop Sacré-Cœur basilica and, for an even more extraordinary panorama over Paris, up into the basilica's main dome. Regular metro tickets are valid on the funicular that shuttles up and down the steep Butte de Montmartre (Montmartre Hill).

SACRÉ-CŒUR ➲ LE MIROIR
🏃 At the bottom of the hill, walk west along rue Tardieu and rue Yvonne le Tace, turning left on rue des Martyrs.

③ Lunch at Le Miroir (p129)

Dining-wise Montmartre has more than its fair share of tourist traps, but locals' favourite Le Miroir offers lunch *menu* specials that offer superb quality and value, as do its wines from its own shop across the street. You'll also find wonderful food shops along the street, including award-winning *boulangerie* (bakery) Arnaud Delmontel.

LE MIROIR ➲ CANAL ST-MARTIN
Ⓜ Abbesses to Marcadet-Poissonniers, then change lines for Gare de l'Est.

④ Canal St-Martin (p129)

A postcard-perfect vision of iron footbridges, swing bridges and shaded tow paths, Canal St-Martin's banks are lined with funky cafes and boutiques. Also here are the historic Hôtel Du Nord (the setting for stories that formed the basis for the eponymous film and now a restaurant/bar) and the ubercool cultural centre Point Éphemère.

CANAL ST-MARTIN ➲ PARC DE LA VILLETTE
Ⓜ Jacques Bonsergent to Porte de Pantin.

⑤ Parc de la Villette (p128)

In addition to its striking geometric gardens, innovative Parc de la Villette has a slew of attractions including the kid-friendly Cité des Sciences museum. Sailing schedules permitting, you can take a two-and-a-half-hour cruise to Bastille with canal cruise operator Canauxrama. Alternatively, head for the metro.

PARC DE LA VILLETTE ➲ SEPTIME
Ⓜ Porte de Pantin to Oberkampf, then change lines for Charonne.

⑥ Dinner at Septime (p154)

After a pre-dinner *apéro* (aperitif) at the classic, cherry-red corner cafe Le Pure Café, head around the corner to enjoy Modern French culinary magic at Septime.

SEPTIME ➲ RUE DE LAPPE
🏃 Head west on rue de Charonne for 450m to rue de Lappe.

⑦ Rue de Lappe (p167)

The Bastille neighbourhood and its surrounds spill over with nightlife venues. A good place to start the evening off is heaving little rue de Lappe, not far from place de la Bastille, where you can salsa your socks off at the 1936 dance hall Le Balajo or simply hop between the street's buzzing bars.

Sacré-Cœur at night
PHOTOGRAPHER: BRUNO MORANDI/GETTY IMAGES ©

Month by Month

January

😊 Fashion Week

Prêt-à-porter (www.
pretparis.com), the ready-
to-wear fashion salon held
twice a year (in late January
and in September), is a
must for fashion buffs, who
flock to the Parc des Expositions at Porte de Versailles.

February

😊 Salon International de l'Agriculture

At this 10-day agricultural
fair (www.salon-agriculture.
com), produce and animals
from all over France are
turned into gourmet fare at
the Parc des Expositions,
from late February to early
March.

March

😊 Banlieues Bleues

Big-name acts perform
during the 'Suburban
Blues' jazz, blues and R&B
festival (www.banlieues
bleues.org) from mid-
March to mid-April in Paris'
northern suburbs.

April

😊 Foire du Trône

Dating back some 1000
years (!), this huge funfair
(www.foiredutrone.com)
is held on the pelouse de
Reuilly of the Bois de Vincennes from around early
April to late May.

😊 Marathon International de Paris

On your marks... The Paris
International Marathon
(www.parismarathon.
com), usually held on
the second Sunday of
April, starts on the av des
Champs-Élysées, 8e, and
finishes on av Foch, 16e, attracting more than 40,000
runners from over 100
countries.

May

◎ European Museums Night

Key museums across
Paris stay open late for the
European Museums Night
(www.nuitdesmusees.cul
ture.fr), on one Saturday/
Sunday in mid-May.

😊 French Open

The glitzy Internationaux
de France de Tennis Grand
Slam hits up from late May
to early June at Stade Roland Garros (www.roland
garros.com) at the Bois de
Boulogne, 16e.

June

😊 Fête de la Musique

This national music festival
(http://fetedelamusique.
culture.fr) welcomes in
summer on the solstice (21
June) with staged and im-
promptu live performances
of jazz, reggae, classical and
more all over the city.

◉ Gay Pride March

Late June's colourful Saturday-afternoon Marche des Fiertés (www.gaypride.fr) through the Marais to Bastille celebrates Gay Pride Day with over-the-top floats and outrageous costumes.

✪ Paris Jazz Festival

Free jazz concerts swing every Saturday and Sunday afternoon in June and July in the Parc Floral de Paris (www.parisjazzfestival.paris.fr); park entry fee applies (adult/under 25 €5/3).

⬛ July

✪ Paris Cinéma

Rare and restored films screen in selected cinemas citywide during this 12-day festival (www.pariscinema.org) in the first half of July.

◉ Bastille Day (14 July)

The capital celebrates France's national day with a morning military parade along av des Champs-Élysées accompanied by a fly-past of fighter aircraft and helicopters, and *feux d'artifice* (fireworks) lighting up the sky above the Champ de Mars by night.

✪ Paris Plages

Sand and pebble 'beaches'– complete with sun beds, umbrellas and palm trees – line the banks of the Seine from mid-July to mid-August.

✪ Tour de France

The last of 21 stages of this legendary, 3500km-long cycling event (www.letour.fr) finishes with a dash up av des Champs-Élysées on the third or fourth Sunday of July.

⬛ August

✪ Cinéma au Clair de Lune

Themed film screenings take place under the stars around town during Paris' free 'moonlight cinema'(www.forumdesimages.fr).

⬛ September

✪ Festival d'Automne

Painting, music, dance and theatre take place at venues throughout the city from mid-September to late December as part of the long-running Autumn Festival of arts (www.festival-automne.com).

◉ European Heritage Days

The third weekend in September sees Paris opens the doors of otherwise-off-limits buildings – such as embassies, corporate offices and the Palais de l'Élysée – during European Heritage Days (www.journeesdupatrimoine.culture.fr).

⬛ October

✪ Nuit Blanche

From sundown until sunrise on the first Saturday and Sunday of October, museums and recreational facilities like swimming pools stay open, along with bars and clubs, for one 'White Night' (ie 'All Nighter').

✪ Fête des Vendanges de Montmartre

The grape harvest from the Clos Montmartre in early October is followed by five days of festivities including a parade (www.fetedesvendangesdemontmartre.com).

⬛ November

✪ Africolor

From mid-November to late December, this six-week African music festival (www.africolor.com) is primarily held in surrounding suburbs, such as St-Denis, St-Ouen and Montreuil.

⬛ December

✪ New Year's Eve

Bd St-Michel (5e), place de la Bastille (11e), the Eiffel Tower (7e) and, above all, av des Champs-Élysées (8e) are the places to be to welcome in the New Year.

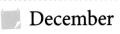

What's New

For this new edition of Discover Paris, our authors have hunted down the fresh, the transformed, the hot and the happening. These are some of our favourites. For up-to-the-minute recommendations, see lonelyplanet.com/Paris.

1 FUTURE FORUM
Since Paris' historic wholesale markets shifted out of the city centre in the 1970s, their replacement, the banal Forum des Halles shopping mall, has been a source of civic shame. But a rainforest-inspired giant glass canopy and lush, landscaped meadow-like gardens atop the subterranean mall (itself receiving a facelift) are set to restore Parisian pride from 2013, with final completion in 2016. (p102)

2 LOUVRE FLYING CARPET
The interior courtyard of the Louvre's Cour Visconti, housing the new Islamic art galleries, was crowned by a shimmering gold flying carpet roof in late 2012. (p90)

3 NOTRE DAME BELLS
As part of 2013's celebrations for Notre Dame's 850th anniversary of the start of construction, some of the cathedral's worn bells are being melted down to create nine new bells replicating the original medieval chimes. (p178)

4 MUSÉE PICASSO REOPENING
After four years of renovations, the Musée Picasso, housed inside a beautiful 17th-century Marais mansion, once again displays thousands of the master's works. (p152)

5 FASHION MUSEUM REVAMP
Yet another long-awaited 2013 reopening following renovations is Paris' fashion museum, the Musée Galliera de la Mode de la Ville de Paris, fittingly housed in a lavish Italiante palace. (p55)

6 BURGER MANIA
The burger trend sweeping Paris is, unsurprisingly, *très* gourmet. Recent openings include buzzing Blend, serving burgers with house-baked brioche buns, homemade ketchup and hand-cut meat. (p105)

7 MINIPALAIS
Art nouveau architecture, artist studio ambience and all-day dining on fare like truffled duck breast and foie gras burgers make the Grand Palais' new restaurant a maxipleasure. (p75)

8 BUS PALLADIUM REDUX
It swung in the '60s and now mythical Pigalle club Bus Palladium is rolling on again with rock, electro and funk nights, acoustic concerts and a vintage-cool restaurant. (p136)

9 PIC'S PARISIAN DEBUT
France's only triple-Michelin-starred female chef, Anne-Sophie Pic, is preparing to open at 20 rue du Louvre, 1er: watch this space. (www.anne-sophie-pic.com)

Get Inspired

🖋 Books

○ **The Flâneur: A Stroll Through the Paradoxes of Paris** (Edmund White) White muses about his beloved adopted city.

○ **Les Misérables** (Victor Hugo) Epic novel tracing convict Jean Valjean through the battles of early-19th-century Paris.

○ **Life: A User's Manual** (Georges Perec) Intricate tale of Parisian life told through characters inhabiting an apartment block between 1833 and 1975.

○ **Down and Out in Paris and London** (George Orwell) Follows Eric Blair's (aka Orwell's) days as a downtrodden hotel dishwasher.

🎞 Films

○ **Le Fabuleux Destin d'Amélie Poulain** (Amélie) Feel-good fable about Montmartre cafe waitress Amélie Poulain.

○ **La Môme** (La Vie en Rose) Acclaimed biopic of Édith Piaf, uncannily portrayed by Marion Cotillard.

○ **Last Tango in Paris** Marlon Brando steams up the screen.

🎵 Music

○ **She: the Best of Charles Aznavour** (Charles Aznavour) Hits from 'France's Frank Sinatra' including 'La Bohème' and 'The Old Fashioned Way'.

○ **Anthologie** (Serge Gainsbourg) Famous tracks include 'Le Poinçonneur des Lilas' and 'Je t'aime...Moi Non Plus', a duet with Brigitte Bardot.

○ **Le Voyage dans la Lune** (AIR) The seventh album from electronica duo AIR (for *Amour, Imagination, Rêve*' meaning 'Love, Imagination, Dream').

○ **La Nouvelle Chanson Française** (Various Artists) Everything from traditional and cabaret to folk-electronic and Paris club sound.

🔑 Websites

○ **Paris By Mouth** (http://parisbymouth.com) Foodie heaven.

○ **My Little Paris** (www.mylittleparis.com) Little-known local treasures.

○ **Go Go** (www.gogoparis.com) Fashion, food, arts, gigs and gossip.

⏱ Short on time?

This list will give you an instant insight into the city.

Read Hemingway's classic *A Moveable Feast* recounts his early Parisian career, with priceless vignettes of fellow writers including F Scott Fitzgerald.

Watch Paris' timeless magic is palpable in Woody Allen's *Midnight in Paris*.

Listen *Live at the Paris Olympia* features Édith Piaf's' classics, including 'Milord', 'Padam... Padam' and, of course, 'Non, Je Ne Regrette Rien'.

Log on Paris Convention & Visitors Bureau (www.parisinfo.com).

Street art

Need to Know

Currency
Euro (€)

Language
French

Visas
Not required for EU citizens. Generally not required for most other nationalities for stays of up to 90 days.

Money
ATMs are everywhere. Credit cards are accepted in larger establishments. Smaller shops may not accept cards.

Mobile Phones
Check with your provider before you leave about roaming costs or ensure your phone is unlocked to use a French SIM card.

Time
Central European Time (GMT plus one hour).

Wi-Fi
There are 400 free hotspots around the city; free wi-fi is available on Paris' metro.

Tipping
Tips are included under French law, though for good service you might tip an extra 10% in restaurants. Round taxi fares up to the nearest euro.

For more information, see Survival Guide (p277).

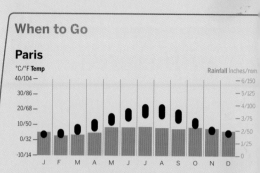

When to Go

Paris

Spring and autumn are ideal times to visit. Summer is the main tourist season, but some businesses close during August. Sights are quieter and prices lower during winter.

Advance Planning

As early as possible Book accommodation.

Two months before Book a cooking or wine-tasting course, organise opera, ballet or cabaret tickets and make reservations for high-end and/or popular restaurants for a Parisian feast.

Two weeks before Sign up for a free, local-led tour and start narrowing down your choice of museums, pre-purchasing tickets online where possible to avoid lengthy ticket queues on the ground in Paris.

Two days before Pack your comfiest pair of shoes for all that walking you'll be doing.

Your Daily Budget

Budget under €80
- Dorm beds €25–35
- Excellent self-catering supermarkets and markets
- Inexpensive public transport; discounted stand-by theatre tickets

Midrange €80–200
- Double room €110–200
- Two-course dinner with a glass of wine €20–40
- Affordable museums

Top End over €200
- Historic luxury hotels
- Gastronomic restaurants
- Designer boutiques

Arriving in Paris

Charles de Gaulle Airport Trains (RER), buses, night buses and private door-to-door shuttles to the city centre €9–€15; private door-to-door shuttles €26–€42; taxi €50–€65.

Orly Airport Trains (Orlyval then RER), buses, night buses and private door-to-door shuttles to the city centre €7–€15; private door-to-door shuttles €26–€42; taxi €40–€50.

Beauvais Airport Buses (€15) to Porte Maillot then metro (€1.70); taxi from €140 (day) and €180 (night and all day Sunday).

Gare du Nord Train Station Served by metro (€1.70) within central Paris.

Getting Around

Walking is a pleasure in Paris, but the city also has one of the most efficient and inexpensive public transport systems in the world, making getting around a breeze.

o **Metro & RER** The fastest way to get around. Runs from about 5.20am to 1.15am (around 2.15am on Friday and Saturday nights), depending on the line.

o **Bicycle** Virtually free pick-up, drop-off Vélib' bikes operate across 1800 stations citywide.

o **Bus** Good for parents with prams/strollers and people with limited mobility.

o **Boat** The Batobus is a handy hop-on, hop-off service stopping at eight key destinations along the Seine.

Sleeping

Paris has a wealth of accommodation options, but they're often *complet* (full) well in advance. Reservations are recommended any time of year, and are essential during the warmer months (April to October) and all public and school holidays. Accommodation outside central Paris is marginally cheaper, but it's almost always a false economy, as travelling into the city consumes time and money. Try to choose somewhere within Paris' 20 *arrondissements* (city districts), where you can experience Parisian life the moment you step out the door.

Useful Websites

o **Paris Hotel** (www.hotels-paris.fr) Well-organised site with lots of user reviews.

o **Paris Hotel Service** (www.parishotelservice. com) Specialises in boutique gems.

o **Paris Hotels** (www.parishotels.com) Loads of options and locations.

o **Lonely Planet** (www.lonelyplanet.com/hotels) Reviews and bookings.

What to Bring

o **Phrase book** The more French you attempt, the more rewarding your visit will be.

o **Corkscrew** For picnics complete with French wines.

o **Adaptor** Especially to charge your phone/camera to snap Parisian panoramas.

o **Bike helmet** Not supplied with Vélib' bikes, so you may want to bring your own.

o **Your appetite** France's reputation for fine food precedes it.

Be Forewarned

o **Museums** Most close Monday or Tuesday. All museums and monuments shut their doors 30 minutes to one hour before listed closing times.

o **Summer closures** Many restaurants and shops close for summer holidays, generally during August.

o **Restaurants** *Menus* (fixed-price meals) offer infinitely better value than ordering à la carte. Meals are often considerably cheaper at lunch than dinner.

o **Bars & cafes** A drink costs more sitting at a table than standing, on the terrace rather than indoors, and on a fancy square rather than a back street. Come 10pm many cafes apply a pricier *tarif de nuit* (night rate).

o **Shopping** Paris' twice-yearly *soldes* (sales) usually last around six weeks, starting in mid-January and again in mid-June.

o **Metro stations** Worth avoiding late at night: Châtelet-Les Halles and its seemingly endless corridors, Château Rouge (Montmartre), Gare du Nord, Strasbourg St-Denis, Réaumur Sébastopol and Montparnasse Bienvenüe.

o **Pickpockets** Pickpockets prey on busy places; *always* stay alert to the possibility of someone surreptitiously reaching for your pockets or bags.

Eiffel Tower & La Défense

With its hourly sparkles that illuminate the evening skyline, the Eiffel Tower needs no introduction. Heading up to its viewing platforms offers you a panorama over the whole of Paris, with the prestigious neighbourhood of Passy (the 16e *arrondissement*) stretching out along the far banks of the Seine to the west.

In the 18th and 19th centuries, Passy was home to luminaries such as Benjamin Franklin and Balzac. Defined by its sober, elegant buildings from the Haussmann era, it was only annexed to the city in 1860.

Passy boasts some fabulous museums, both big-hitters and a host of smaller collections devoted to everything from Balzac to fashion, crystal, wine and sub-Saharan art. At the city's western edge is the leafy refuge of the Bois de Boulogne. Beyond this lies the high-rise business district of La Défense, home to some great urban art.

CARLOS GOTAY/GETTY IMAGES ©

Eiffel Tower & La Défense Highlights

Eiffel Tower (p52)

Almost any time is a good time to visit the tower (except in inclement weather when views are diminished or high winds force it to shut). But the best time to ascend this famous landmark – more Parisian than Paris itself – is at dusk for day- and night-time views of the glittering city. Celebrate making it to the top at the tower's sparkling-new champagne bar.

1

2 ## Musée du Quai Branly (p59)

Like in all good Paris museums, the collection of indigenous artwork at th Musée du Quai Branly – the brainchil of former French President Jacques Chirac – is as controversial as it is innovative. Check out its 'vertical livi garden', which scales the exterior of the structure, before heading inside t contemplate anthropological artefact from every continent except Europe.

NATHALIE DARBELLAY/CORBIS © ARCHITECT JEAN NOUVEL

ARNAUD CHICUREL/HEMIS/CORBIS©

Bois de Boulogne (p61)

The leafy Bois de Boulogne is where city-dwellers head to escape the concrete, whether on bikes, skates or by *footing* (jogging). Other activities and attractions include paddling row boats around the lake, the delightful Jardin d'Acclimatation amusement park for littlies, the Stade Roland Garros and its adjacent tennis museum, and the stunning new Frank Gehry–designed fine-arts centre Fondation Louis Vuitton pour la Création. Bagatelle park, Bois de Boulogne

Cité de l'Architecture et du Patrimoine (p55)

Wander past cathedral portals, gargoyles and intricate scale models at the Cité de l'Architecture et du Patrimoine. This colossal 23,000-sq-metre space overlooking the Jardins du Trocadéro houses a comprehensive collection of elements of French architecture and heritage. It's an education and a delight, and the views of the Eiffel Tower from the windows are equally monumental.

Musée Marmottan Monet (p60)

Take a trip out to the Musée Marmottan Monet, on the edge of the Bois de Boulogne, to see the world's largest collection of Monet canvases. Some of the masterpieces to look out for include *La Barque* (1887), *Cathédrale de Rouen* (1892), *Londres, le Parlement* (1901) and the various *Nymphéas* (Waterlilies; many of these canvases were smaller studies for the works in the Musée de l'Orangerie).

Eiffel Tower & La Défense Walk

The ultimate symbol of Paris, the Eiffel Tower, is never far from view on this walk, but you'll also explore a little-known artificial island in the middle of the Seine, and see one of the city's innovative vertical gardens at the Musée du Quai Branly.

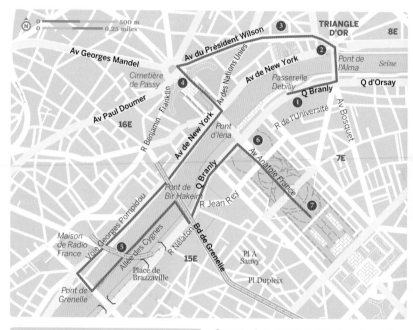

WALK FACTS

- **Start** Musée du Quai Branly
- **Finish** Parc du Champ de Mars
- **Distance** 5km
- **Duration** 2½ hours

① Musée du Quai Branly

Facing the Seine at the **Musée du Quai Branly** (p59) is a *mur végétal* (vegetation wall; ie a vertical garden) designed by Patrick Blanc, with some 15,000 low-light foliage plants on a surface of 800 sq metres. They're held in place by a frame of metal, PVC and non-biodegradable felt, but no soil. The museum itself, showcasing indigenous art from Oceania, Asia, Africa and the Americas, is in a striking building designed by Jean Nouvel.

② Flame of Liberty Memorial

Walk east along quai Branly and cross the Pont de l'Alma to place de l'Alma. Near the end of bridge, the bronze **Flame of Liberty Memorial** (p55) is a replica of the Statue of Liberty's flame. You'll see floral tributes for Diana, Princess of Wales, who died in a car accident here in 1997.

③ Musée Galliera de la Mode de la Ville de Paris

Walk west along av du Président Wilson. On your left you'll pass the modern art museum the **Musée d'Art Moderne de la Ville de Paris** (p55), then the **Palais de Tokyo** (p54), built for the 1937 Exposition Universelle and now hosting contemporary art installations. On your right, set back behind lavish gardens in the 19th-century Palais Galliera, is Paris' fashion museum, the **Musée Galliera de la Mode de la Ville de Paris** (p55).

④ Palais de Chaillot

Continue to place du Trocadéro et du 11 Novembre to the **Palais de Chaillot**. The two curved, colonnaded wings of this palace and the terrace in between them afford an exceptional panorama of the Eiffel Tower. The eastern wing houses the excellent architectural museum the **Cité de l'Architecture et du Patrimoine** (p55).

⑤ Île aux Cygnes

From the Palais de Chaillot's terrace, descend the steps and walk through the Jardins du Trocadéro; on your left you'll see the kid-pleasing **Cinéaqua aquarium** (p55) and cinemas. Continue to the river and turn right to cross the Pont de Grenelle's eastern side. Descend to the artificially created island **Île aux Cygnes** (Isle of Swans), formed in 1827 to protect the river port, and measuring just 850m long by 11m wide. On the western side of the bridge is a 11.5m-high replica of the Statue of Liberty, inaugurated in 1889. Walk east along the **Allée des Cygnes** – the tree-lined walkway that runs the length of the island.

⑥ Eiffel Tower

Ascend the steps on Pont de Bir Hakeim and turn right to cross to the Left Bank. West of the Musée du Quai Branly, the **Eiffel Tower** (p52) is at its most monumental as you stand beneath it.

⑦ Parc du Champ de Mars

From the tower, stroll the lawns of the **Parc du Champ de Mars** (p54), perhaps stopping for an ultrascenic picnic.

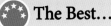 The Best...

PLACES TO EAT

Firmin Le Barbier Intimate bistro a five-minute walk from the Eiffel Tower. (p58)

Tokyo Eat The funkiest dining option in the otherwise sedate west. (p58)

L'Astrance Triple Michelin-starred gastronomic extravaganza. (p58)

58 Tour Eiffel Affordable dining inside the Eiffel Tower under the direction of Alain Ducasse. (p60)

MUSEUMS

Musée du Quai Branly Indigenous art, artefacts, music and more from every continent bar Europe. (p59)

Cité de l'Architecture et du Patrimoine Huge space with exhibits covering Paris' architectural history and its future. (p55)

Musée Marmottan Monet The world's largest collection of Monet's works. (p60)

Musée Guimet des Arts Asiatiques France's foremost repository of Asian art. (p55)

SPORTS & ACTIVITIES

Bois de Boulogne Bike rides, row boats and more. (p61)

Roland Garros France's premier tennis stadium, with an extravagant tennis museum. (p61)

Tokyo Eat (p58), in the Palais du Tokyo
HEMIS/ALAMY ©

Don't Miss
Eiffel Tower

There are many ways to experience the Eiffel Tower, from an evening ascent amid the lights to a meal in one of its two restaurants, and even though some 6.7 million people come annually, few would dispute the fact that each visit is unique. Like many Parisian icons, it has gone from being roundly criticised by city residents to much loved.

Map p56

01 44 11 23 23

www.tour-eiffel.fr

lift to 3rd fl adult/12-24yr/4-12yr €14/12.50/9.50, lift to 2nd fl €8.50/7/4, stairs to 2nd fl €5/3.50/3

lifts & stairs 9am-midnight mid-Jun–Aug, lifts 9.30am-11pm, stairs 9.30am-6pm Sep–mid-June

M Bir Hakeim or RER Champ de Mars–Tour Eiffel

Top Floor

Views from the wind-buffeted top floor (276m) can stretch up to 60km on a clear day, though at this height the panoramas are more sweeping than detailed. Celebrate your ascent with a glass of bubbly from the champagne bar while you try to pick out the monuments below, or check out Gustave Eiffel's restored top-level office, where lifelike wax models of Eiffel and his daughter Claire greet Thomas Edison.

In order to access the top floor, you'll need to take a separate lift on the 2nd level. Note that it will close in the event of heavy winds.

2nd Floor

Views from the 2nd floor (115m) are generally considered to be the best, as they are impressively high but still close enough to see the details of the city below. Telescopes and panoramic maps placed around the tower pinpoint locations in Paris and beyond. Other sights to look out for include the story windows, which give a nuts-and-bolts overview of the lifts' mechanics, and the vision well, which allows you to gaze down (and down, and d-o-w-n) through glass panels to the ground. Also up here is the Michelin-starred restaurant Le Jules Verne, now run by Alain Ducasse.

1st Floor

The 1st floor (57m), which should be finishing the tail end of a massive redevelopment project by the time you read this, has the most space but the least impressive views, which makes it a prime location for its new museum-like layout. Glass floors, interactive history exhibits, and an immersion film are some of the new features that you can expect to find as you learn more about the tower's ingenious design.

If you're visiting Paris during the winter holidays, definitely check to see if the ice-skating rink has been set up here; it's usually open from mid-December to mid-January and is free for visitors (skates included). Also on this level is the restaurant 58 Tour Eiffel and simpler dining options.

Ticket Purchases & Queueing Strategies

Highly recommended is the online booking system that allows you to buy your tickets in advance, thus avoiding the monumental queues at the ticket office. Note that you need to be able to print out your tickets to use this service or have your ticket on a smart-phone screen (eg Blackberry or iPhone) that can be read by the scanner at the entrance. If you can't reserve your tickets ahead of time, expect waits of well over an hour in high season.

Another option for avoiding long queues (and for working off that last meal) is to take the stairs. These are accessed at the south pillar: the climb consists of 360 steps to the 1st level and another 360 steps to the 2nd pillar. You cannot reserve stair tickets online.

Finally, if you have reservations for either restaurant, you are granted direct access to the lifts.

Nightly Sparkles

Every hour on the hour, the entire tower sparkles for five minutes with 20,000 gold-toned lights. First installed for Paris' millennium celebration in 2000, it took 25 mountain climbers five months to install the bulbs and 40km of electrical cords. For the best view of the light show, head across the Seine to the Jardins du Trocadéro.

Discover Eiffel Tower & La Défense

Getting There & Away

- **Metro** Line 6 runs south from Charles de Gaulle–Étoile past the Eiffel Tower (views are superb from the elevated section); line 9 runs southwest from the Champs-Élysées.

- **RER** RER A runs west to La Défense; RER C runs east–west along the Left Bank, with a stop at the Eiffel Tower.

- **Bus** One of Paris' most scenic bus routes, bus 69 runs from the Champ du Mars (Eiffel Tower) along the Left Bank, crosses the Seine at the Louvre and then continues east to Père Lachaise.

- **Bicycle** For bike rental, a convenient station is located in front of the Musée du Quai Branly.

- **Boat** Batobus stop Eiffel Tower

Grande Arche de la Défense (p58)
JOSE FUSTE RAGA © ARCHITECT JOHANN OTTO VON SPRECKELSEN

⊙ Sights

Eiffel Tower & 16e

Parc du Champ de Mars   Park
(Map p56; Ⓜ Champ de Mars–Tour Eiffel or École Militaire) At the base of the Eiffel Tower, the grassy Champ de Mars was originally used as a parade ground for cadets from the 18th-century **École Militaire** (Military Academy; Map p56), at the southeastern end of the park, which counts Napoleon Bonaparte among its graduates.

Also here are **puppet shows** (Map p56; ☎ 01 48 56 01 44; allée du Général Margueritte, 7e; admission €3.50; Ⓜ École Militaire).

Musée Dapper   Art Museum
(Map p56; www.dapper.com.fr; 35 rue Paul Valéry, 16e; adult/senior/under 26yr €6/4/free; ⊙ 11am-7pm, closed Tue & Thu; Ⓜ Victor Hugo) Focused on African and Caribbean art, this jewel of a museum is an invitation to leave Paris behind for an hour or two. Although exhibits rotate throughout the year, expect to find a superb collection of ritual and festival masks and costumes accompanied by several video presentations in each room. The ever-active auditorium sponsors cultural events year-round, from concerts to storytelling and films.

Palais de Tokyo   Art Museum
(Map p56; www.palaisdetokyo.com; 13 av du Président Wilson, 16e; adult/18-25yr/under 18yr €8/6/free; ⊙ noon-midnight Tue-Sun; Ⓜ Iéna) The Tokyo Palace, created for the 1937 Exposition Universelle and now a contemporary art space, has no permanent collection. Instead, its shell-like interior is the stark backdrop for rotating, interactive art installations.

Cité de l'Architecture et du Patrimoine
Architecture Museum

(Map p56; www.citechaillot.fr; 1 place du Trocadéro et du 11 Novembre, 16e; adult/18-25yr/under18yr €8/5/free; ⏰11am-7pm Wed-Mon, to 9pm Thu; Ⓜ Trocadéro) In the eastern wing of the **Palais de Chaillot**, directly across from the Eiffel Tower, is this standout museum devoted to French architecture and heritage. The burgundy walls and skylit rooms here showcase 350 plaster casts taken from the country's greatest monuments, a collection whose seeds were sown following the desecration of many buildings during the French Revolution.

FREE Musée d'Art Moderne de la Ville de Paris
Art Museum

(Map p56; www.mam.paris.fr; 11 av du Président Wilson, 16e; permanent collections free; ⏰10am-6pm Tue-Sun, to 10pm Thu; Ⓜ Iéna) The permanent collection at the city's modern-art museum displays works representative of just about every major artistic movement of the 20th and nascent 21st centuries, but the main reason for a trip here is to check out one of the cutting-edge temporary exhibits.

Musée Galliera de la Mode de la Ville de Paris
Fashion Museum

(Map p56; www.galliera.paris.fr; 10 av Pierre 1er de Serbie, 16e; ⏰10am-6pm Tue-Sun; Ⓜ Iéna) Paris' Fashion Museum, housed in the 19th-century Palais Galliera, warehouses some 100,000 outfits and accessories – from canes and umbrellas to fans and gloves – from the 18th century to the present day. The sumptuous Italianate palace and gardens dating from the mid-19th century are worth a visit in themselves. The museum has been undergoing renovations but should be open by the time you read this.

Cinéaqua
Aquarium

(Map p56; www.cineaqua.com; av des Nations Unies, 16e; adult/child €20/13; ⏰10am-7pm; Ⓜ Trocadéro) On the eastern side of the Jardins du Trocadéro is Paris' largest aquarium. It's not the best you'll ever see, but it is a decent rainy-day destination for families, with a shark tank and some 500 species of fish on display. There are also, somewhat oddly, three cinemas inside (only one of which shows ocean-related films), though non-French-speaking kids will need to be old enough to read subtitles, as almost everything is dubbed into French.

Flame of Liberty Memorial
Monument

(Map p56; place de l'Alma; Ⓜ Alma-Marceau) This bronze sculpture, a replica of the one topping the Statue of Liberty, was placed here in 1987 on the centenary of the launch of the *International Herald Tribune*, as a symbol of friendship between France and the USA. The sculpture is located on the place de l'Alma, near the end of the Pont de l'Alma bridge. On 31 August 1997 in the place d'Alma underpass, Diana, Princess of Wales, was killed in a devastating car accident along with her companion, Dodi Fayed, and their chauffeur, Henri Paul.

Musée Guimet des Arts Asiatiques
Art Museum

(Map p56; www.museeguimet.fr; 6 place d'Iéna, 16e; adult/18-25yr/child €7.50/5.50/free; ⏰10am-6pm Wed-Mon; Ⓜ Iéna) France's foremost Asian arts museum, the Musée Guimet has a superb collection of sculptures, paintings and religious articles that originated in the vast stretch of land between Afghanistan and Japan.

Part of the collection, comprising Buddhist paintings and sculptures, is housed in the nearby **Galeries du Panthéon Bouddhique du Japon et de la Chine** (Map p56; 19 av d'Iéna, 16e). Don't miss the wonderful Japanese garden here.

La Défense

Architecture buffs will have a field day in Paris' high-rise business district. Begun in the 1950s, today La Défense counts more than 100 buildings, housing three-quarters of France's largest corporations.

More than just office space, La Défense is also an open-air art gallery. Calder, Miró, Agam, César and Torricini are among the international artists behind the colourful and often surprising sculptures and murals that pepper the central 1km-long promenade. Pick up a detailed map at the Espace-Info information centre at the

Eiffel Tower & 16e

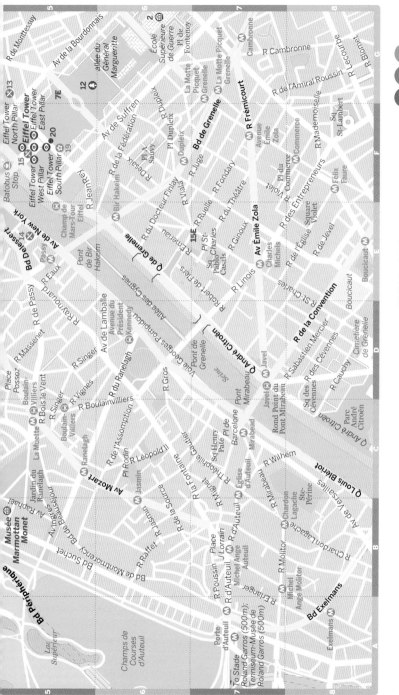

Lac Supérieur

Champs de Courses d'Auteuil

To Stade Roland Garros (500m); Tennseum-Musée de Roland Garros (500m)

Bd Périphérique

Bd Suchet

Bd de Montmorency

R Raffet

R Poussin

R d'Auteuil

Porte d'Auteuil Ⓜ

J Lorrain

Michel Ange Auteuil Ⓜ

R Erlanger

Michel Ange Molitor Ⓜ

Bd Exelmans

Exelmans Ⓜ

Musée Marmottan Monet

Av Raphaël

Jardin du Ranelagh

Av Ingres

Bd de Beauséjour

Av de Montmorency

Place Possoz

R Massenet

La Muette Ⓜ

Boulainvilliers Ⓡ

R Singer

R Vignes

R du Ranelagh

R Singer

R Bois le Vent

Ranelagh Ⓜ

R de l'Assomption

Av Mozart

Jasmin Ⓜ

R Rodin

Pl Rodin

R de la Fontaine

R Théophile Gautier

R Michel

Sq Henry Paté

R d'Auteuil

R de la Source

Pl Léopold II

Place J Lorrain

Pl de Barcelone

Église d'Auteuil Ⓜ

Mirabeau Ⓜ

Chardon Lagache Ⓜ

R Molitor

R Mirabeau

Ste-Périne

R Wilhem

Av de Versailles

Q Louis Blériot

R Chardon Lagache

Q André Citroën

Parc André Citroën

Cimetière de Grenelle

Boucicaut

Boucicaut Ⓜ

Sq des Cévennes

R des Cévennes

R Cauchy

R Sébastien Mercer

R de la Convention

R St-Charles

R de Javel

R de l'Église

Square Violet

R de Javel

Javel Ⓜ

Javel Ⓡ

Pont Mirabeau

Rond Point du Pont Mirabeau

Voie Georges Pompidou

Pont de Grenelle

Allée des Cygnes

R Gros

Av de Lamballe

Avenue du Président Kennedy Ⓜ

Q de Grenelle

R Linois

R Ginoux

R Charles Michels

Charles Michels Ⓜ

Pl St-Charles

R St-Entienau

Pl St-Pablo Casals

R Robert de Flers

15E

Av Émile Zola Ⓜ

Avenue Émile Zola

Commerce Ⓜ

R Commerce

Pl du Commerce

R Violet

R des Entrepreneurs

R Mademoiselle

Félix Faure Ⓜ

Sq St-Lambert

R Lecourbe

R Biomat

R Cambronne

Cambronne Ⓜ

R de l'Amiral Roussin

La Motte Picquet Grenelle Ⓜ

La Motte Picquet Grenelle Ⓜ

Bd de Grenelle

R Frémicourt Ⓜ

Pl de Fontenoy

École Supérieure de Guerre

Ⓖ 2

Av de la Bourdonnais

R de Monttessuy

allée du Général Marguerite

7E

12 🏛

Eiffel Tower North Pillar ✕13

Eiffel Tower Ⓞ

Eiffel Tower West Pillar Ⓞ

15 Ⓞ Eiffel Tower East Pillar

Eiffel Tower South Pillar ● 20

19

Batobus Stop 🛥

Bd D Pelesert

Av de New York

✕ 14

Passy Ⓜ

R Eaux

R Raynouard

R de Passy

Champ de Mars-Tour Eiffel

Pont de Bir Hakeim

Bir Hakeim Ⓜ

R Jean Rey

Av de Suffren

R de la Fédération

R Duplex

R A Sauvy

Pl A Sauvy

Pl Duplex

Duplex Ⓜ

R Duplex

R Juge

R Desaix

R du Docteur Finlay

R Viala

R du Théâtre

R Fondary

R Ruelle

Seine

Q André Citroën

57

Eiffel Tower & 16e

Musée de la Défense (www.ladefense.fr; 15 place de la Défense; ⏰10am-6pm Sun-Fri, to 7pm Sat; Ⓜ La Défense).

Grande Arche
de la Défense   Landmark

(1 Parvis de la Défense; Ⓜ La Défense) La Défense's landmark edifice is the white marble Grande Arche, a striking cubelike structure built in the 1980s and now home to government and business offices. The arch marks the western end of the *axe historique* (historic axis).

Access to the roof has been suspended indefinitely for security reasons.

⚔ Eating

This neighbourhood is best known for its monuments and museums and, conveniently, there are a number of good restaurants located in the sights themselves.

Firmin Le Barbier   Bistro €€

(Map p56; ☏01 45 51 21 55; www.firminlebarbier. fr; 20 rue de Montteessuy, 7e; mains €22; ⏰lunch Sun only, dinner Tue-Sun; Ⓜ Pont de l'Alma) This discreet brick-walled bistro was opened by a retired surgeon turned gourmet, and his passion for a good meal is apparent in everything from the personable service to the wine list. The menu is traditional French (sirloin steak with polenta, decadent bœuf bourguignon), while the modern interior is bright and cheery and even benefits from an open kitchen – a rarity in smaller Parisian restaurants.

Tokyo Eat   Fusion €€

(Map p56; ☏01 47 20 00 29; www.palaisdetokyo. com; 13 av du Président Wilson, 16e; lunch menu €20, mains €12-28; ⏰noon-1am Tue-Sun; Ⓜ Iéna) Tokyo Eat is the artsy canteen attached to the modern-art museum Palais de Tokyo. Much like the museum itself, the setting is very industrially chic, with colourful flying saucers hovering above the tables and changing art exhibits in the street-facing windows.

L'Astrance   Gastronomic €€€

(Map p56; ☏01 40 50 84 40; 4 rue Beethoven, 16e; lunch/dinner menus €70/210; ⏰Tue-Fri; Ⓜ Passy) It's been over a decade now since Pascal Barbot's dazzling cuisine at the three-star L'Astrance made its debut, but it has shown no signs of losing its

GARDEL BERTRAND/GETTY IMAGES © ARCHITECT JEAN NOUVEL

☑ Don't Miss
Musée du Quai Branly

No other museum in Paris provides such inspiration for travellers, armchair anthropologists and those who simply appreciate the beauty of traditional craftsmanship. A tribute to the incredible diversity of human culture, the Musée du Quai Branly presents an overview of indigenous and folk art from around the world.

The museum showcases an impressive array of masks, carvings, weapons, jewellery and more, all displayed in a refreshingly unique interior without rooms or high walls.

The **Oceania section** features some remarkable carvings from Papua New Guinea and the surrounding islands, including façade masks, daggers, jewellery, hair pieces and several ancestor skulls. Other cultures well represented include Maori and Australian Aborigines.

The **Asian collection** includes clothing, jewellery and textiles from ethnic minorities from India to Vietnam, though one of the most striking articles on display is an Evenk shaman cloak from eastern Siberia. Also worth looking for are the intricate cured-leather Chinese shadow puppets and the Tibetan thangkas (Buddhist paintings on silk scrolls).

The **Africa collection** is particularly strong on musical instruments and masks, but there are other unusual pieces here, such as the life-sized 11th-century sculpture of a hermaphrodite (Mali), which greets visitors with a raised arm. One of the more notable masks on display is a Krou mask from the Ivory Coast, said to have influenced Picasso.

Look for highlights from the great civilisations in the **Americas collection** – the Mayas, Aztecs and Incas – as well as objects from lesser-known peoples, such as the grizzly totem pole (Tsimshian) or the crazily expressive Kiiappaat masks (Greenland).

NEED TO KNOW
Map p56; www.quaibranly.fr; 37 quai Branly, 7e; adult/child €8.50/free; ☺11am-7pm Tue, Wed & Sun, 11am-9pm Thu-Sat; Ⓜ Alma-Marceau or RER Pont de l'Alma

ROBERT HOLMES/CORBIS ©

✓ Don't Miss
Musée Marmottan Monet

Housed in the duc de Valmy's former hunting lodge (well, let's call it a mansion), this intimate museum houses the world's largest collection of Monet paintings and sketches, beginning with paintings such as the seminal *Impression Soleil Levant* (1873) and *Promenade près d'Argenteuil* (1875), passing through numerous waterlily studies, before moving on to the rest of the collection, which is considerably more abstract and dates from the early 1900s.

Temporary exhibitions, included in the admission price and always excellent, are generally shown either in the basement or on 1st floor. Also on display are a handful of canvases by Renoir, Pissarro, Gauguin and Morisot, and a collection of 15th- and 16th-century illuminations, which are quite lovely if somewhat out of place.

NEED TO KNOW
Map p56; ☏01 44 96 50 33; www.marmottan.com; 2 rue Louis Boilly, 16e; adult/7-25yr €10/5; ⏰10am-6pm Tue-Sun, to 9pm Thu; Ⓜ La Muette

cutting edge. Look beyond the complicated descriptions on the menu – what you should expect are teasers of taste that you never even knew existed, and a presentation that is an art unto itself.

A culinary experience unique to Paris, you'll need to reserve two months in advance (one month for lunch).

58 Tour Eiffel   Brasserie €€€
(Map p56; ☏01 45 55 20 04; www.restaurants toureiffel.com; 1st level, Champ de Mars, 7e; lunch menus €18-23, dinner menus €67-150; ⏰11.30am-4.30pm & 6.30-11pm; Ⓜ Bir Hakeim or RER Champ de Mars–Tour Eiffel) If you're intrigued by the idea of a meal in the Tower the 58 Tour Eiffel is a pretty good choice. It may not be the caviar and black truffles of **Le Jules Verne** (Map p56; ☏01 45 55 61 44;

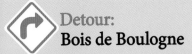

Detour:
Bois de Boulogne

The 845-hectare Bois de Boulogne owes its informal layout to Baron Haussmann, who, inspired by London's Hyde Park, planted 400,000 trees here.

Along with various gardens and other sights, the park has 15km of cycle paths and 28km of bridle paths through 125 hectares of forested land.Be warned that the area becomes a distinctly adult playground after dark, especially along the Allée de Longchamp, where all kinds of prostitutes cruise for clients.

The Bois de Boulogne is served by metro lines 1 (Porte Maillot, Les Sablons), 2 (Porte Dauphine), 9 (Michel-Ange-Auteuil) and 10 (Michel-Ange-Auteuil, Porte d'Auteuil), and the RER C (Avenue Foch, Avenue Henri Martin).

Paris Cycles (Map p56; ☏ 01 47 47 76 50; per hr €5; ☺10am-7pm mid-Apr-mid-Oct) rents bikes on av du Mahatma Gandhi, across from the Porte Sablons entrance to the Jardin d'Acclimatation, and near the Pavillon Royal (av Foch).

Families flock to **Jardin d'Acclimatation** (Map p56; www.jardindacclimatation.fr; av du Mahatma Gandhi; admission €2.90, activity tickets €2.90, under 3yr free; ☺10am-7pm Apr-Sep, to 6pm Oct-Mar; Ⓜ Les Sablons), a great amusement park with puppet shows, boat rides, a small water park, pony rides, art exhibits and sometimes special movies.

Rowing boats (Map p56; per hr €15; ☺10am-6pm mid-Mar-mid-Oct; Ⓜ Av Henri Martin) can be hired at Lac Inférieur, the largest of the Bois' lakes and ponds.

The world's most extravagant tennis museum, the **Tenniseum-Musée de Roland Garros** (www.fft.fr; 2 av Gordon Bennett; adult/child €7.50/4, with stadium visit €15/10; ☺10am-6pm Tue-Sun; Ⓜ Porte d'Auteuil) traces the sport's 500-year history. Tours of the stadium take place at 11am and 3pm in English; reservations are required.

Designed by Frank Gehry, this fine-arts centre **Fondation Louis Vuitton pour la Création** (Map p56; www.fondationlouisvuitton.fr) is expected to open in late 2012.

Champ de Mars; ☺lunch & dinner; Champ de Mars-Tour Eiffel or Bir Hakeim) on the 2nd level, but Alain Ducasse did sign off on the menu, ensuring that this is much more than just another tourist cafeteria.

For lunch, go first to the restaurant's outside kiosk (near the north pillar); for dinner, reserve online or by telephone.

Les Ombres   Modern French €€€
(Map p56; ☏ 01 47 53 68 00; www.lesombres restaurant.com; 27 quai Branly, 7e; lunches €26-38, dinners €65; ☺daily; Ⓜ Iéna or RER Pont de l'Alma) Paris gained not only a museum in the Musée du Quai Branly but also this glass-enclosed rooftop restaurant on the 5th floor. Named the 'Shadows' for the patterns cast by the Eiffel Tower's webbed ironwork, the dramatic views are complemented by the kitchen's creations, such as gambas (prawns) with black rice and fennel, or sea bream in a parmesan crust.

Stop by between 3pm and 5pm to sample pastry chef Pascal Chanceau's decadent afternoon-tea menu, or in the evening when the tower is all a-glitter.

Le Petit Rétro   Bistro €€
(Map p56; ☏ 01 44 05 06 05; www.petitretro.fr; 5 rue Mesnil, 16e; mains €15-29, menus €25 (lunch only), €30 & €35; ☺lunch & dinner to 10.30pm Mon-Fri; Ⓜ Victor Hugo) From the gorgeous 'Petit Rétro' emblazoned on the zinc bar to the art nouveau tile tiles, this is a handsome old-style bistro. It serves up classic French fare year-round, such as blood sausage with apples and honey, and blanquette de veau (veal in a butter and cream sauce).

Marché Président Wilson   Market
(Map p56; av du Président Wilson, 16e; ☺7am-2.30pm Wed & Sat; Ⓜ Iéna or Alma-Marceau) This open-air market is the most convenient in the neighbourhood.

61

Champs-Élysées & Grands Boulevards

The Champs-Élysées and Grands Boulevards area is grandiose in layout and it's possible to play an epic game of connect the dots here. The main landmarks – the Arc de Triomphe, place de la Concorde, place de la Madeleine and the Opéra – are all joined by majestic boulevards, each lined with harmonious rows of Haussmann-era buildings.

Fans of *haute couture* à la Dior, Chanel, Louis Vuitton et al will find themselves pulled into the Triangle d'Or (Golden Triangle), which neighbours the Champs-Élysées. Further east along the Grands Boulevards are the historic and more affordable *grands magasins* (department stores) like Le Printemps and Galeries Lafayette.

The vestiges of the 1900 World's Fair – the Grand Palais and Petit Palais (along with the bridge Pont Alexandre III) – play host to a variety of excellent exhibits. Entertainment, too, has a strong tradition, most notably at the famed 19th-century opera house, the Palais Garnier.

Arc de Triomphe (p68)

Champs-Élysées & Grands Boulevards Highlights

Arc de Triomphe (p68)

Climb to the top of Paris' signature arch and gasp at the breathtaking, bird's-eye view of the *axe historique* (historic axis), extending from the Louvre's Grande Pyramide through the Jardin des Tuileries and along the av des Champs-Élysées to the Arc de Triomphe, then west all the way to the modern Grande Arche in the skyscraper district of La Défense.

Grand Palais (p71)

It's worth reserving ahead to catch exhibitions at the stunning art nouveau Grand Palais, erected for the 1900 Exposition Universelle (World's Fair), especially for big-name shows in the Galeries Nationales. Advance reservations are also highly recommended for one of Paris' most exciting restaurants, the Grand Palais' architecturally and culinarily stunning Minipalais. Temporary exhibition at the Grand Palais by Daniel Buren

Palais Garnier (p77)

By day, take a tour – guided or DIY – of this classic example of opulent, Second-Empire architecture, the 19th-century Palais Garnier. By night the original home of Parisian opera focuses on ballet, theatre and dance – book tickets in advance and pack your finery for an unforgettable performance by the Opéra National de Paris' affiliated orchestra and ballet companies.

YANG LIU/CORBIS ©

BRUCE YUANYUE BI/GETTY IMAGES ©

Champs-Élysées (p70)

Over-the-top, grandiose and even kind of kitsch, you can't leave Paris without strolling the av des Champs-Élysées. A wide, overwhelming and bustling commercial artery full of enormous big-name shops and clogged traffic, it's anchored by the Arc de Triomphe at one end and place de la Concorde – the enormous square where Louis XVI and thousands more were guillotined – at the other. Obelisk on the place de la Concorde

Galeries Lafayette (p82)

Get the inside edge on Parisian fashion while shopping beneath the stained-glass dome of the capital's best-known and most resplendent department store. The free Friday-afternoon fashion shows (advance bookings required) and the panoramic views from the rooftop terrace will sweep you off your feet, as will the contemporary art gallery and a cocktail or stylish bite at one of the on-site eateries.

Champs-Élysées & Grands Boulevards Walk

This glamorous walk takes you from the Arc de Triomphe along the famed av des Champs-Élysées, ending at the opulent Palais Garnier opera house.

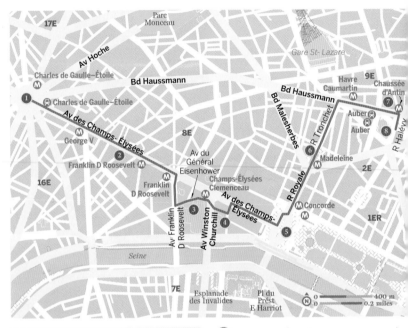

1 Arc de Triomphe

The city's sense of grandeur peeks beneath the soaring **Arc de Triomphe** (p68), the mighty arch commissioned by Napoleon in 1806 in Roman triumphal style. Just don't try to cross the traffic-choked Étoile ('star') roundabout above ground – use the subterranean pedestrian tunnels. For great views from the arch, climb to the top.

2 Champs-Élysées

A dozen avenues radiate out from the Étoile but none is more famous than the **av des Champs-Élysées** (p70). Take your time strolling this broad, tree-shaded avenue past car showrooms and luxury shops such as Louis Vuitton's flagship store at 101 av des Champs-Élysées, which has a free contemporary art gallery, the **Louis Vuitton Espace Culturel**, at the top.

3 Grand Palais

Parkland unfolds in front of you at the Rond Point Champs-Élysées Marcel Dassault roundabout; turn right (south) here on av Franklin D Roosevelt then left on av du Général Eisenhower to find the vast

glass-roofed **Grand Palais** (p71). In addition to major gallery spaces, it houses the children's science museum the **Palais de la Découverte**, with excellent temporary exhibits (such as moving lifelike dinosaurs) as well as a hands-on, interactive permanent collection focusing on astronomy, biology, physics and the like.

4 Petit Palais

Heading south across av Winston Churchill, the smaller but equally striking art nouveau **Petit Palais** (p71) was also built for the 1900 World Fair. Today it houses the **Musée des Beaux-Arts de la Ville de Paris**, the city's fine arts museum.

5 Place de la Concorde

Beyond the Petit Palais, turn right to rejoin the Champs-Élysées and continue east to **place de la Concorde** (p70), the vast square between the Champs-Élysées and the Jardin des Tuileries. Paris spreads out around you, with views taking in the Eiffel Tower and Seine. In the centre, the pink granite obelisk stands on the site of a French Revolution guillotine.

6 Place de la Madeleine

Head left on rue Royal to **place de la Madeleine** (p72). The Greek-temple-style **Église de la Madeleine** dominates the centre, while the place itself is home to some of the city's finest gourmet shops, as well as the **Marché aux Fleurs Madeleine**, a colourful flower market trading since 1832.

7 Galeries Lafayette

Continue north along rue Tronchet and right onto bd Haussmann. On your left you'll see the grands magasins (department stores) **Le Printemps** (p82), followed by **Galeries Lafayette** (p82), topped by a stained-glass dome – be sure to head inside and up to Galeries Lafayette's rooftop for a fabulous, free panorama over Paris.

8 Palais Garnier

Turn right on rue Halévy to reach the entrance to Paris' resplendent **Palais Garnier** opera house (p77).

 **The Best...**

PLACES TO EAT

Le Hide Smart, affordable French cuisine including decadent desserts. (p73)

Makoto Aoki The name suggests otherwise, but this is traditional French *haute cuisine*. (p73)

Le Boudoir Beguiling decor and bistro cuisine. (p73)

Le J'Go Spirited Southwest French cuisine and wines. (p75)

ENTERTAINMENT

Palais Garnier Paris' palatial 19th-century opera house is where the fabled Phantom of the Opera lurked. (p78)

Au Limonaire Perfect little Parisian wine bar with traditional French *chansons*. (p79)

Salle Pleyel Classical concerts and recitals in art deco surrounds. (p79)

PLACES TO SHOP

Galeries Lafayette This quintessential department store has fabulous fashions beneath a dramatic cupola. (p82)

Le Printemps Grand Parisian department store. (p82)

Triangle d'Or Go on a *haute couture* treasure hunt in Paris' 'Golden Triangle'.

Place de la Madeleine Garlanded by gourmet food shops. (p82)

Interior of the Galeries Lafayette (p82)
TOM BONAVENTURE/GETTY IMAGES ©

☑️ Don't Miss
Arc de Triomphe

Napoleon's armies never did march through the Arc de Triomphe showered in honour, but the monument has nonetheless come to stand as the very symbol of French patriotism. The Tomb of the Unknown Soldier and the names of the numerous generals engraved onto the arch's inner walls pay homage to those who have fought and died for France. It's not for nationalistic sentiments, however, that so many visitors huff up the narrow, spiralling staircase every day. Rather it's the sublime panoramas from the top, which extend out over the Paris skyline.

Map p74

www.monuments
-nationaux.fr

place Charles de
Gaulle

adult/18-25yr
€9.50/6

⊙10am-10.30pm, t⟨
11pm Apr-Sep

Ⓜ Charles de Gaulle-
Étoile

Napoleon's Arch

The arch was first commissioned in 1806, following Napoleon's victory at Austerlitz the year before. At the time, the victory seemed like a watershed moment that confirmed the tactical supremacy of the French army, but a mere decade later Napoleon had already fallen from power and his empire had crumbled. The Arc de Triomphe, however, was never fully abandoned and in 1836, after a series of starts and stops under the restored monarchy, the project was finally completed. In 1840 Napoleon's remains were returned to France and passed under the arch before being interred at Invalides.

Today, the military parade commemorating France's national Bastille Day (14 July) kicks off from the arch (adorned by a billowing tricolour).

Beneath the Arch

Beneath the arch at ground level lies the tomb of the Unknown Soldier. Honouring the 1.3 million French soldiers who lost their lives in WWI, the Unknown Soldier was laid to rest in 1921, beneath an eternal flame that is rekindled daily at 6.30pm.

Also here are a number of bronze plaques laid into the ground. Take the time to try to decipher some: these mark significant moments in modern French history, such as the proclamation of the Third French Republic (4 September 1870) or the return of Alsace and Lorraine to French rule (11 November 1918). The most notable plaque is the text from Charles de Gaulle's famous London broadcast on 18 June 1940, which sparked the French Resistance to life.

The Sculptures

The arch is adorned with four main sculptures, six panels in relief and a frieze running beneath the top. Each was designed by a different artist; the most famous sculpture is the one to the right as you approach from the Champs-Élysées: La Marseillaise (Departure of the Volunteers of 1792). Sculpted by François Rude, it depicts soldiers of all ages gathering beneath the wings of victory, en route to drive back the invading armies of Prussia and Austria. The higher panels depict a series of important victories for the Revolutionary and imperial French armies, from Egypt to Austerlitz, while the detailed frieze is divided into two sections: the *Departure of the Armies* and the *Return of the Armies*. Don't miss the multimedia section beneath the viewing platform, which provides more detail and historical background for each of the sculptures.

Viewing Platform

Climb the 284 steps up to the viewing platform at the top of the 50m-high arch and you'll be suitably rewarded with magnificent panoramas over western Paris. From here, a dozen broad avenues – many of them named after Napoleonic victories and illustrious generals – radiate out towards every compass point. The Arc de Triomphe is the highest point in the line of monuments known as the *axe historique* (historic axis; also called the grand axis); it offers views that swoop east down the Champs-Élysées to the gold-tipped obelisk at place de la Concorde (and beyond to the Louvre's glass pyramid), and west to the skyscraper district of La Défense, where the colossal Grande Arche marks the *axe*'s western terminus.

Tunnels

Tickets to the Arc de Triomphe viewing platform are sold in the underground passageway that surfaces on the even-numbered side of av des Champs-Élysées. It is the only sane way to get to the base of the arch and is *not* linked to nearby metro tunnels.

Discover Champs-Élysées & Grands Boulevards

🔀 Getting There & Away

○ **Metro** Line 1, which follows the Champs-Élysées below ground, is the most useful, followed by lines 8 and 9, which serve the Grands Boulevards.

○ **RER** RER A stops at Auber (Opéra) and Charles de Gaulle-Étoile.

○ **Bicycle** Bike-hire stations line the upper part of the Champs-Élysées.

○ **Boat** Batobus stop Champs-Élysées

◎ Sights

Champs-Élysées

Avenue des Champs-Élysées   Landmark

(Map p74; Ⓜ Charles de Gaulle–Étoile, George V, Franklin D Roosevelt or Champs-Élysées-Clemenceau) If the Eiffel Tower is Paris, then the Champs-Élysées is *la belle France* in all it grandeur and glamour. First laid out in th 17th century, the broad avenue today is where presidents and soldiers strut their stuff on Bastille Day, the Tour de France holds its final sprint and, most important ly, where the country parties when it has reason to celebrate.

It's also one of the globe's most sought-after addresses, which you'll undoubtedly notice as you stroll down the avenue: many of the world's biggest brands have opened up showrooms here looking to promote their prestige. Part of the *axe historique* (historic axis), the Champs-Élysées links place de la Concorde with the Arc de Triomphe.

Place de la Concorde   City Square

(Map p74; Ⓜ Concorde) With its majestic vistas in just about every direction – the Arc de Tri omphe, the Assemblée Nationale (the lower house of Parliament) an even a rare swath of open sky above place de la Concorde is one of Paris' most impressive squares. It was first laid out in 1755 and originally named after King Louis XV; however, its associations with royalty meant that it would eventually go on to take centre stage during the Revolution.

Pedestrians on the Champs-Élysées
ATLANTIDE PHOTOTRAVEL/CORBIS ©

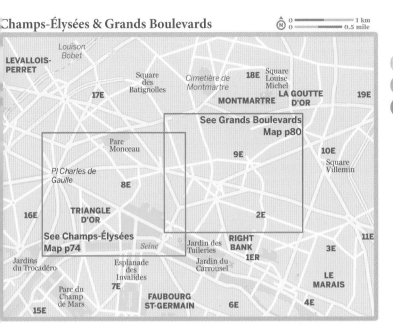

Louis XVI was the first to be guillotined here in 1793; over the next two years, 1343 more people, including Marie Antoinette, Danton and Robespierre, all lost their heads here as well. The square was given its present name after the Reign of Terror in the hope that it would become a place of peace and harmony. In the centre, atop the site of one of the former guillotines, stands a 3300-year-old Egyptian obelisk engraved with hieroglyphics. It originally stood in the Temple of Ramses at Thebes (now Luxor) and was presented to France in 1831.

Grand Palais   Art Gallery

(Map p74; www.grandpalais.fr; 3 av du Général Eisenhower; adult/13-25yr/under 13yr €12/8/free; ⊙10am-10pm Wed-Mon, to 8pm Thu; Ⓜ Champs-Élysées-Clemenceau) Erected for the 1900 Exposition Universelle (World Fair), the Grand Palais today houses several exhibition spaces and a restaurant (Minipalais) beneath its huge 8.5-ton art nouveau glass roof. Some of Paris' biggest shows (Renoir, Chagall, Turner) are held in the Galeries Nationales, lasting three to four months.

Other exhibit spaces include the imaginative Nef – which plays host to concerts, art installations, a seasonal amusement park and horse shows – and several other minor galleries. Reserving a ticket online for any show is strongly advised.

Also here is the children's science museum, the **Palais de la Découverte** (Map p74; www.palais-decouverte.fr; av Franklin D Roosevelt, 8e; adult/senior & 6-25yr/under 6yr €8/6/free; ⊙9.30am-6pm Tue-Sat, 10am-7pm Sun; Ⓜ Champs-Élysées-Clemenceau).

FREE Petit Palais   Art Museum

(Map p74; www.petitpalais.paris.fr; av Winston Churchill; permanent collections free; ⊙10am-6pm Tue-Sun; Ⓜ Champs-Élysées-Clemenceau) Like the Grand Palais opposite, this architectural stunner was also built for the 1900 Exposition Universelle, and is home to the Paris municipality's Museum of Fine Arts.

Grands Boulevards

Place de la Madeleine
City Square

(Map p80; M Madeleine) Ringed by fine-food shops, place de la Madeleine is named after the 19th-century neoclassical church at its centre, the **Église de la Madeleine** (Church of St Mary Magdalene; Map p80; www.eglise-lamadeleine.com; 9.30am-7pm). Constructed in the style of a massive Greek temple, what is now simply called 'La Madeleine' was consecrated in 1842 after almost a century of design changes and construction delays.

The monumental staircase on the south side affords one of the city's most quintessential Parisian panoramas: down rue Royale to place de la Concorde and its obelisk and across the Seine to the Assemblée Nationale. The gold dome of the Invalides appears in the background.

The church is a popular venue for classical-music concerts (some free).

La Pinacothèque
Art Museum

(Map p80; www.pinacotheque.com; 28 place de la Madeleine, 8e; adult/12-25yr/under 12yr €10/8/free; 10.30am-6pm daily, to 9pm Wed & Fri; M Madeleine) The top private museum in Paris, La Pinacothèque organises three to four major exhibits per year. Its nonlinear approach to art history, with exhibits that range from Mayan masks to retrospectives covering the work of artists such as Edvard Munch, has shaken up the otherwise rigid Paris art world and won over residents used to more formal presentations elsewhere.

Although the focus here is primarily on temporary exhibits, be sure to visit the permanent collection as well. Displayed thematically, it presents artwork rarely seen side by side in most other museums.

FREE Musée du Parfum
Perfume Museum

(Map p80; www.fragonard.com; 9 rue Scribe, 2e; 9am-6pm Mon-Sat, to 5pm Sun; M Opéra) If the art of perfume-making entices, stop by this collection of copper distillery vats and antique flacons and test your nose on a few basic scents. It's run by the parfumerie Fragonard and located in a beautiful old *hôtel particulier* (private mansion); free guided visits are available in multiple languages. A separate wing is a short distance south in the **Théâtre-Musée des Capucines** (Map p80; 39 blvd des Capucines; 9am-6pm Mon-Sat; M Opéra).

Eating

The area around the Champs-Élysées is known for its big-name chefs (Alain

---

The Unsung Museums of Paris

Marc Restellini, director of the excellent **La Pinacothèque**, filled us in on his favourite art museums in Paris.

Musée d'Art Moderne de la Ville de Paris (p55) An intelligent museum with high-quality, original exhibits, it carries out its mission as a modern-art museum with courage.

Musée Dapper (p54) The greatest collection of African art in the world, imbued with a magical setting. It's a small museum, but when you leave it's as if returning from an incredible journey.

Musée Jacquemart-André (p127) The second major private museum in Paris along with La Pinacothèque, it stages real art-history exhibits that are both original and daring.

Ducasse, Pierre Gagnaire) and culinary icons (Taillevent), but there are a few under-the-radar restaurants here too, where the Parisians who live and work in the area actually dine on a regular basis. For a more diverse selection, head east to the Grands Boulevards, where you'll find everything from hole-in-the-wall wine bars to organic cafes.

Champs-Élysées

Le Hide Traditional French €€

(Map p74; 01 45 74 15 81; www.lehide.fr; 10 rue du Général Lanrezac, 17e; menus from €24; lunch Mon-Fri, dinner Mon-Sat; Charles de Gaulle–Étoile) A reader favourite, Le Hide is a tiny neighbourhood bistro serving scrumptious traditional French fare: snails, baked shoulder of lamb with pumpkin purée or monkfish in lemon butter. Unsurprisingly, this place fills up faster than you can scamper down the steps at the nearby Arc de Triomphe. Reserve well in advance.

Ladurée Patisserie €

(Map p74; www.laduree.fr; 75 av des Champs-Élysées, 8e; pastries from €1.50; 7.30am-11pm; George V) One of the oldest patisseries in Paris, Ladurée has been around since 1862. The tearoom here is the classiest spot to indulge your sweet tooth on the Champs; alternatively, pick up some pastries to go – from croissants to its trademark *macarons*, it's all quite heavenly.

Makoto
Aoki Traditional French €€€

(Map p74; 01 43 59 29 24; 19 rue Jean Mermoz, 8e; lunch menu €22, mains €34-38; lunch Mon-Fri, dinner Mon-Sat; Franklin D Roosevelt) In an *arrondissement* known for grandiose dining rooms and superstar chefs who are often elsewhere, this intimate neighbourhood favourite is a real find. Don't let the name confuse you – the chef, although Japanese, is an *haute cuisine* perfectionist who trained with Alain Senderens and Lucas Carton. Lunch might include an extravagant bacon-morel brioche; dinner a heavenly risotto with John Dory or truffles.

Le Boudoir Traditional French €€€

(Map p74; 01 43 59 25 29; www.boudoirparis.fr; 25 rue du Colisée, 8e; lunch menus €25, mains €25-29; lunch Mon-Fri, dinner Tue-Sat;

73

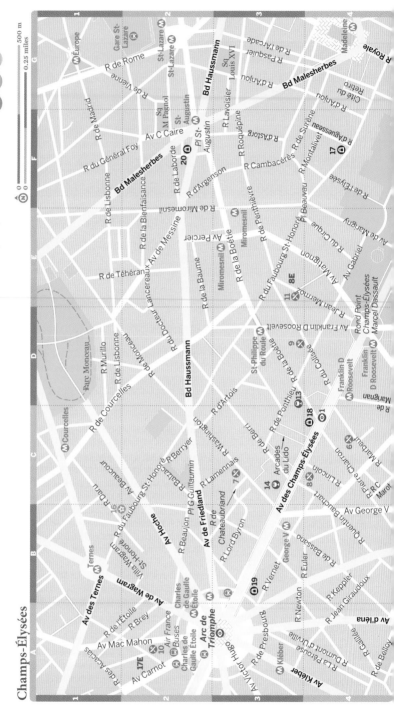

Champs-Élysées

M St-Philippe du Roule or Franklin D Roosevelt) Spread across two floors, the quirky salons here – Marie Antoinette, Palme d'Or, le Fumoir – are individual works of art with a style that befits the name. Expect classy bistro fare (quail stuffed with dried fruit and foie gras, chateaubriand steak with chestnut purée) prepared by chef Arnaud Nicolas, a recipient of France's top culinary honour.

Aubrac Corner Burgers €

(Map p74; www.aubrac-corner.com; 37 rue Marbeuf, 8e; sandwiches from €5, burgers from €9; ⏱7.30am-6.30pm Mon-Sat; M Franklin D Roosevelt) Burgers? On the Champs-Élysées? It might not sound all that French, but rest assured, this isn't fast food – it's actually the gourmet deli of a famous steakhouse. The burgers come with bowls of fries or *aligot* (mashed potatoes with melted cheese); take it all downstairs into the hidden wine cellar, a welcome refuge from the nonstop commotion outside.

Minipalais Modern French €€

(Map p74; ☎01 42 56 42 42; www.minipalais.com; av Winston Churchill, 8e; lunch menus €28, mains €15-35; ⏱10am-1am; M Champs-Élysées-Clemenceau or Invalides) Set inside the fabulous Grand Palais, the Minipalais resembles an artist's studio on a colossal scale, with unvarnished hardwood floors, industrial lights suspended from ceiling beams and a handful of plaster casts on display. Its sizzling success, however, means that the crowd is anything but bohemian; dress to impress for a taste of the lauded modern cuisine.

Grands Boulevards

Le J'Go Southwest French €€

(Map p80; ☎01 40 22 09 09; www.lejgo.com; 4 rue Drouot, 9e; lunch/dinner menus €16/35; ⏱Mon-Sat; M Richelieu Drouot) This contemporary Toulouse-style bistro is meant to transport you away to southwestern France for a spell (perfect on a grey Parisian day). Its bright yellow walls are decorated with bull-fighting posters and the flavourful regional cooking is based around the rotisserie – not to mention

Champs-Élysées

other Gascogne standards like cassoulet and foie gras.

For the full experience, it's best to go in a small group with time to spare: the roasting takes a minimum 20 minutes, which gives you the opportunity to sample its choice selection of sunny southern wines.

🍃 SuperNature   Organic €
(Map p80; 📞01 47 70 21 03; www.super-nature. fr; 12 rue de Trévise, 9e; mains €13, menu €15.80; ⊙lunch Mon-Fri, brunch Sun; Ⓜ Cadet or Grands Boulevards) A funky organic cafe, Supernature has some clever creations on the menu, like curried split-pea soup and a cantaloupe, pumpkin seed and feta salad. Though there are plenty of veggie options available, it's not all legumes – this is France after all – and you can still order a healthy cheeseburger with sprouts if so inclined.

A takeaway branch two doors down (at no 8) serves sandwiches, salads and thick slices of sweet potato and gorgonzola quiche.

Chez Plume   Rotisserie €
(Map p80; 6 rue des Martyrs, 9e; dishes €4.50-8.50; ⊙10am-3pm Tue-Sun, 5.30-8.30pm Tue-Sat; Ⓜ Notre Dame de Lorette) This gourmet rotisserie specialises in free-range chickens from southwest France, prepared in a variety of fashions: simply roasted, as a crumble, or even in a quiche or sandwich. It's wonderfully casual: add a side or two (potatoes, polenta, seasonal veggies) and pull up a counter seat.

Le Zinc des Cavistes   Bar, Cafe €
(Map p80; 📞01 47 70 88 64; 5 rue du Faubourg Montmartre, 9e; lunch menus €16, mains €11-19; ⊙8am-10.30pm; Ⓜ Grands Boulevards) Don't tell the masses standing dutifully in the Chartier queue that there's a much better restaurant right next door – your formerly friendly waiter will probably run off screaming. A local favourite, Le Zinc des Cavistes is as good for a full-blown meal (duck confit, salads) as it is for sampling new vintages.

🍷 Drinking & Nightlife

Champs-Élysées

Charlie Birdy   Pub
(Map p74; 124 rue de la Boétie, 8e; ⊙noon-5am; Ⓜ Franklin D Roosevelt) This kick-back brick-walled pub just off the Champs

YANG LIU/CORBIS ©

✓ Don't Miss
Palais Garnier

Few other Paris monuments have provided artistic inspiration in the way that the Palais Garnier has. From Degas' ballerinas to Gaston Leroux' *Phantom of the Opera* and Chagall's ceiling, the layers of myth painted on gradually over the decades have bestowed a particular air of mystery and drama to its ornate interior. Designed in 1860 by Charles Garnier (then an unknown 35-year-old architect), the opera house was part of Baron Haussmann's massive urban renovation project.

The opera is open to visits during the day, and the building is a fascinating place to explore if you're not already taking in a show here. Highlights include the opulent Grand Staircase, the library-museum (1st floor) and the horseshoe-shaped auditorium (2nd floor), with its extravagant gilded interior and red velvet seats. Above the massive chandelier is Chagall's gorgeous ceiling mural (1964), which depicts scenes from 14 operas.

Visits are generally unguided, though three days a week you can reserve a spot on an English-language guided tour. Staff advise showing up at least 30 minutes ahead of time. Check the website for updated schedules.

NEED TO KNOW

Map p80; 📞08 25 05 44 05; www.operadeparis.fr; cnr rues Scribe & Auber; unguided tour adult/10-25yr/under 10yr €9/6/free, guided tour €13.50/9.50/6.50; 🕙10am-4.30pm; Ⓜ Opéra

Élysées is easily the most inviting spot in the neighbourhood for a drink. The usual array of bar food is served; DJs hit the decks on weekend nights.

Queen
Club

(Map p74; ☏ 01 53 89 08 90; www.queen.fr; 102 av des Champs-Élysées, 8e; admission €20; ⏰ 11.30pm-10am; Ⓜ George V) Once the king (as it were) of gay discos in Paris, Le Queen now reigns supreme with a very mixed crowd, though it still has a mostly gay Disco Queen on Monday. While right on the Champs-Élysées, it's not as difficult to get into as it used to be – and not nearly as inaccessible as the other nearby clubs.

ShowCase
Club

(Map p74; www.showcase.fr; Port des Champs Élysées, 8e; ⏰ 11.30pm-dawn Fri & Sat; Ⓜ Invalides or Champs Élysées-Clemenceau) This gigantic electro club has solved the neighbour-versus-noise problem that haunts so many other Parisian nightlife

spots: it's secreted away beneath a bridg alongside the Seine. Unlike many of the other exclusive backstreet clubs along the Champs, the Showcase can pack 'em in (up to 1500 clubbers) and is less stringent about its door policy, though you'll still want to look like a star.

Grands Boulevards

Au Général La Fayette
Brasserie

(Map p80; 52 rue La Fayette, 9e; ⏰ 10am-3am; Ⓜ Le Peletier) With its archetypal belle époque decor and special beers on offer, this old-style brasserie is a dependable stop for an afternoon coffee or evening drink.

✪ Entertainment

Palais Garnier
Opera

(Map p80; ☏ 08 92 89 90 90; www.operadeparis. fr; place de l'Opéra, 9e; Ⓜ Opéra) The city's original opera house is smaller than its

Left: Domes of Le Printemps (p82); **Below:** Interior of ShowCase nightclub

Bastille counterpart, but boasts perfect acoustics. Due to its odd shape, however, some seats have limited or no visibility. Ticket prices and conditions (including last-minute discounts) are available at the **box office** (Map p80; cnr rues Scribe & Auber; ☉11am-6.30pm Mon-Sat).

Au Limonaire
Live Music

(Map p80; ☎01 45 23 33 33; http://limonaire. free.fr; 18 cité Bergère, 9e; ☉7pm-midnight; Ⓜ Grands Boulevards) This little wine bar is one of the best places to listen to traditional French *chansons* and local singer-songwriters. Performances begin at 10pm Tuesday to Saturday and 7pm on Sunday. Entry is free, the wine is good and dinner is served (*plat du jour* €7). Reservations are recommended if you plan on dining.

Salle Pleyel
Classical

(Map p74; ☎01 42 56 13 13; www.sallepleyel. fr; 252 rue du Faubourg St-Honoré, 8e; ☉box office noon-7pm Mon-Sat, to 8pm on day of performance; Ⓜ Ternes) This highly regarded hall dating from the 1920s hosts many of Paris' finest classical-music recitals and concerts, including those by the celebrated **Orchestre de Paris** (www. orchestredeparis.com).

Kiosque Théâtre Madeleine
Discount Tickets

(Map p80; opposite 15 place de la Madeleine, 8e; ☉12.30-8pm Tue-Sat, to 4pm Sun; Ⓜ Madeleine) Pick up half-price tickets for same-day performances of ballet, opera and music at this outdoor kiosk. Grab a copy of *Pariscope* from a newsstand to help you choose what you want to see, then make your request. Figure on paying €24 on average, though it can be cheaper.

Grands Boulevards

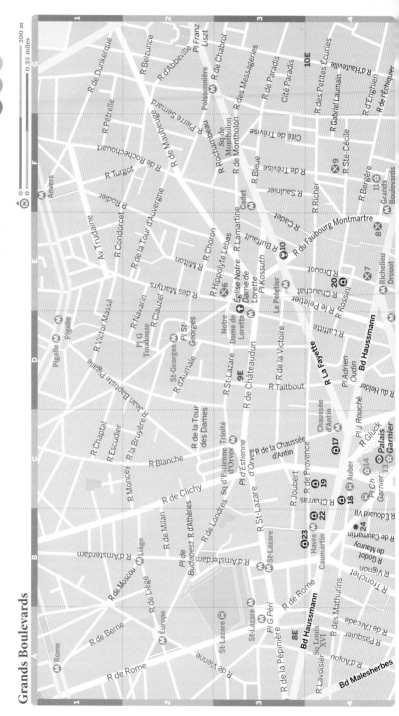

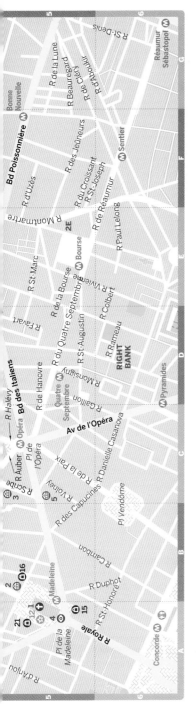

🔒 Shopping

A stroll around the legendary **Triangle d'Or** (Golden Triangle; bordered by avs Georges V, Champs-Élysées and Montaigne, 8e) constitutes the walk of fame of top French fashion. Rubbing shoulders with the world's top international designers are Paris' most influential French fashion houses like Chanel and Dior.

The area around Opéra and the Grands Boulevards is where you'll find department stores such as Galeries Lafayette.

Guerlain   Perfume
(Map p74; www.guerlain.com; 68 av des Champs-Élysées, 8e; ⊙10.30am-8pm Mon-Sat, noon-7pm Sun; MFranklin D Roosevelt) Guerlain is Paris' most famous parfumerie, and its shop (dating from 1912) is one of the most beautiful in the city. With its shimmering mirror and marble art deco interior, it's a reminder of the former glory of the Champs-Élysées. For total indulgence, make an appointment at its decadent **spa** (☎01 45 62 11 21).

Les Caves Augé   Food, Drink
(Map p74; www.cavesauge.com; 116 bd Haussmann, 8e; ⊙Mon-Sat; MSt-Augustin) Head here if you trust the taste of Marcel Proust, who was a regular customer. This fantastic wine shop, founded in 1850, has bottles stacked in every conceivable nook and cranny. The shop organises tastings every other Saturday (see website), where you can meet local winemakers from different regions.

Chloé   Fashion
(Map p74; 54 rue du Faubourg St-Honoré, 8e; ⊙Mon-Sat; MChamps-Élysées-Clemenceau) Bold prints, bohemian layers and uneven hemlines have given street cred to this 1950s-established Parisian label.

Lancel   Accessories
(Map p74; 127 av des Champs-Élysées, 8e; ⊙daily; MCharles de Gaulle–Étoile) Open racks of luscious totes fill this handbag designer's gleaming premises.

81

Grands Boulevards

Galeries Lafayette
Department Store

(Map p80; www.galerieslafayette.com; 40 bd Haussmann, 9e; ⊙9.30am-8pm Mon-Sat, to 9pm Thu; Ⓜ Auber or Chaussée d'Antin) Probably the best known of the big Parisian department stores, Galeries Lafayette is spread across three buildings: the main store (the historic dome of which turned 100 in 2012), the **men's store** (Map p80) and the **home design store** (Map p80).

You can check out modern art in the **gallery** (1st fl; ⊙11am-7pm Mon-Sat), take in a **fashion show** (🕿 bookings 01 42 82 30 25; ⊙Mar-Jul & Sep-Dec) at 3pm on Fridays, or ascend to the rooftop for a windswept Parisian panorama (free). When your legs need a break, head to one of the many restaurants and cafes inside – top picks include Angélina and the champagne bar on the 1st floor, **Lafayette Organic** (soups, salads and sandwiches) on the 3rd floor, **Sichuan Panda** on the 6th floor and the rooftop restaurant.

On the 1st floor of the men's store is Lafayette Gourmet, an entire floor dedicated to the art of pleasing the palate.

Le Printemps
Department Store

(Map p80; www.printemps.com; 64 bd Haussmann, 9e; ⊙9.30am-8pm Mon-Sat, to 10pm Thu; Ⓜ Havre Caumartin) This is actually three separate stores – **Le Printemps de la Mode** (women's fashion), **Le Printemps de l'Homme** (Map p80) (for men) and Le Printemps de la Beauté et Maison (for beauty and household goods) – offering a staggering display of perfume, cosmetics and accessories, as well as established and up-and-coming designer wear.

Place de la Madeleine
Food, Drink

(Map p80; place de la Madeleine, 8e; Ⓜ Madeleine) Ultragourmet food shops are the treat here; if you feel your knees start to go all wobbly in front of a display window, you know you're in the right place. The most notable names include truffle dealers **La Maison de la Truffe** (Map p80; 🕿 01 42 65 53 22; www.maison -de-la-truffe.com; 19 place de la Madeleine;

Chanel display in the showroom of the Hôtel Drouot auction house

BENOIT TESSIER/REUTERS/CORBIS ©

10am-10pm Mon-Sat; M Madeleine); luxury food shop Hédiard; mustard specialist **Boutique Maille** (Map p80; 📞 01 40 15 06 00; www.maille.com; 6 place de la Madeleine; ⏰ 10am-7pm Mon-Sat; M Madeleine); and Paris' most famous caterer, **Fauchon** (Map p80; 📞 01 70 39 38 00; www.fauchon.fr; 26 & 30 place de la Madeleine; ⏰ 8.30am-7pm Mon-Sat; M Madeleine), selling incredibly mouth-watering delicacies, from foie gras to jams, chocolates and pastries.

Hôtel Drouot   Art, Antiques
(Map p80; www.drouot.com; 7-9 rue Drouot, 9e; ⏰ 11am-6pm; M Richelieu Drouot) Selling everything from antiques and jewellery to rare books and art, Paris' most established auction house has been in business for more than a century. Viewings are from 11am to 6pm the day before and from 11am to noon the morning of the auction.

Louvre & Les Halles

Carving its way through the city, Paris' *axe historique* (historic axis) passes through the Jardin des Tuileries and the Arc de Triomphe du Carrousel before reaching IM Pei's glass pyramid at the world's largest museum, the Louvre. Many smaller museums and galleries also cluster around this art lovers' Holy Grail.

Shoppers crowd along rue de Rivoli, which has beautiful cloisters along its western end, and congregate within the Forum des Halles – the underground mall that supplanted the city's ancient marketplace and is undergoing a major renaissance. The original markets' spirit lives on in Les Halles' lively backstreets, such as rue Montorgueil.

The bright blue and red Centre Pompidou attracts art aficionados with its amazing hoard of modern art. Outside, place Georges Pompidou is a hub for buskers, while place Igor Stravinsky's mechanical fountains are a riot of outlandish creations.

View from the Centre Pompidou (p96)
JOHN SONES SINGING BOWL MEDIA/GETTY IMAGES ©

Louvre & Les Halles Highlights

Louvre (p90)

The Musée du Louvre, the mother of all museums, houses Western art from the Middle Age to about 1848, as well as the works of ancient civilisations that formed the starting point for Western art – all under one seemingly endless roof. Successive French governments have amassed works from all over Europe, including collections of Assyrian, Etruscan, Greek, Coptic and Islamic art and antiquities.

Centre Pompidou (p96)

The Centre Pompidou, a kind of Louvr for the 21st century, offers a day of culture and amusement for the whol family. From the modern and conter porary masterpieces at its fabulous National Museum of Modern Art to the whimsical mechanical fountains and the buskers performing in the adjacent square, this is where art an fun fuse together seamlessly.

Jardin du Palais Royal (p102)

With pristine lawns, designer fashion shops, galleries, sculptures and history (the French Revolution effectively started at a cafe here), the gardens of this former royal palace are a perfect hang-out spot for a warm day. Don't miss the sculpture at the southern end of the garden: legend says if you can toss a coin onto one of the columns, your wish will come true. Sculpture by Daniel Buren in the Jardin du Palais Royal

RICHARD I'ANSON/GETTY IMAGES ©

3

4

Église St-Eustache (p103)

One of the least-known (and most beautiful) churches in Paris, the Église St-Eustache is also one of the best examples of early Renaissance style on the Right Bank, with a magnificent mix of Flamboyant Gothic and neoclassical architectural features. Don't miss the colossal organ inside, which you can catch in action during recitals.

PAR ÉTIENNE CAZIN/GETTY IMAGES ©

5

Jardin des Tuileries (p104)

The Jardin des Tuileries' verdant oasis is a great place to recharge your batteries and enjoy Paris at its symmetrical best. While wandering, you can admire its exquisite sculptures, including Rodin's *The Kiss* and Louise Bourgeois' delicate *Welcoming Hands*. Within the gardens, the Musée de l'Orangerie is an exquisite space in which to enjoy Monet's *Decorations des Nymphéas* (Waterlilies). La Montagne by Aristide Maillol

Louvre & Les Halles Walk

Exploring the immense Musée du Louvre takes as many hours as you have free after finishing this walk at the museum's cobbled square courtyard, the Cour Carrée. But there's much more to see in this neighbourhood, including glorious gardens, churches and centuries-old towers.

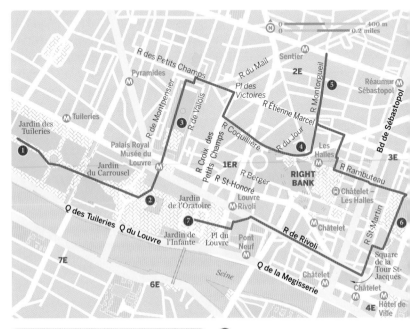

1 Jardin des Tuileries

With the Parisian panorama of the **place de la Concorde** (p70) behind you, step into the Unesco World Heritage–listed **Jardin des Tuileries** (p104). On your left is the **Jeu de Paume** photography gallery, while on your right, a 19th-century greenhouse now contains the **Musée de l'Orangerie** (p104), showcasing Monet's enormous *Waterlilies*.

2 Louvre Grande Pyramide

Promenade through the Tuileries past the Arc de Triomphe du Carrousel to the **Grande Pyramide** (p92). Egypt's original pyramid builders couldn't have imagined this 21m-high glass wonder, which has been the Musée du Louvre's main entrance since 1989.

3 Jardin du Palais Royal

Turn left at the pyramid and cross rue de Rivoli, past the **Palais Royal-Musée du Louvre metro entrance**, featuring two crown-shaped cupolas (one representing the day, the other night) consisting of 800 pieces of red, blue, amber and violet glass. Enter the exquisite **Jardin du Palais Royal** (p102), and browse its colonnaded arcades.

④ Église St-Eustache

Exit next to the historic restaurant **Le Grand Véfour** (p110) onto rue de Beaujolais, turn left into Passage du Perron and right onto rue des Petits Champs. Continue to place des Victoires, with its equestrian **Louis XIV Memorial**. Turn right on rue Croix des Petits Champs and left into rue Coquillière past enduring brasserie **Au Pied de Cochon** (p111). On your right is the subterranean shopping mall the **Forum des Halles** (p102), currently undergoing a massive, much-needed makeover, while up ahead **Église St-Eustache** (p103) is one of the city's most beautiful churches.

⑤ Rue Montorgueil

A splinter of the former *halles* (markets), **rue Montorgueil** was previously the oyster market. Grocery and speciality street stalls set up daily, except Monday. Look out for patisserie **Stohrer** at No 51, which opened in 1730, with pastel murals added in 1864 by Paul Baudry (who also decorated the Palais Garnier's Grand Foyer); and, at the northern end (rue des Petite Carreaux), horse-meat butcher **J Davin** at No 9.

⑥ Centre Pompidou

From rue Montorgueil, head down rue Étienne Marcel, passing the Gothic **Tour Jean sans Peur** (p105), turning right on rue Pierre Lescot then left again on rue Rambuteau to find the extraordinary **Centre Pompidou** (p96). The inside-out-designed building is such a sight in its own right that it's easy to forget that it houses France's foremost contemporary and modern art museum, the **Musée National d'Art Moderne** (p97).

⑦ Cour Carrée

Cross the fountain-filled **place Igor Stravinsky** and head south to rue de Rivoli and turn right – on your left you'll see the Flamboyant Gothic **Tour St-Jacques** (p105). Take rue Parrault to the place du Louvre. At the **Église Saint-Germain-l'Auxerrois**, cross the place du Louvre and enter the grand Louvre courtyard, the **Cour Carrée**.

 **The Best…**

Le Grand Rex cinema (p117)
XAVIER RICHER/GETTY IMAGES ©

Don't Miss
The Louvre

Few art galleries are as prized or as daunting as the Musée du Louvre, Paris' pièce de résistance. Showcasing 5000 works of art, it would take nine months to glance at every piece, making advance planning essential.

Map p100

☎ 01 40 20 53 17

www.louvre.fr

rue de Rivoli & quai des Tuileries, 1er

permanent/ temporary collection €11/12, both €15, under 18yr free

⏱ 9am-6pm Mon, Thu, Sat & Sun, to 9.45pm Wed & Fri

M Palais Royal– Musée du Louvre

Palais du Louvre

Philippe-Auguste had this vast fortress built on the Seine's right bank (constructed 1190–1202). In the 16th century it became a royal residence and after the Revolution, in 1793, it was turned it into a national museum. Its booty was no more than 2500 paintings and objets d'art.

Over the centuries, French governments have gradually amassed the paintings, sculptures and artefacts displayed today. The 'Grand Louvre' project, inaugurated by the late President Mitterrand in 1989, doubled the museum's exhibition space, and both new and renovated galleries have since opened devoted to objets d'art such as the **crown jewels of Louis XV** (Room 66, 1st floor, Denon). The official opening, at the end of 2012, of new Islamic art galleries in the restored **Cour Visconti** was moment of national pride for French art and architecture lovers. The interior courtyard, unkempt and abandoned for years, has been topped with an elegant, shimmering gold 'flying carpet' roof, evocative of a veil fluttering in the wind, designed by Italian architects Mario Bellini and Rudy Ricciotti.

Mona Lisa

Easily the Louvre's most admired work (and world's most famous painting) is Leonardo da Vinci's *La Joconde* (in French; *La Gioconda* in Italian), the lady with that enigmatic smile known as *Mona Lisa* (Room 6, 1st floor, Denon). For centuries admirers speculated on everything from the possibility that the subject was mourning the death of a loved one to the possibility that she might have been in love or in bed with her portraitist.

Mona (*monna* in Italian) is a contraction of madonna, and Gioconda is the feminine form of the surname Giocondo. Canadian scientists used infrared technology to peer through paint layers and confirm *Mona Lisa*'s identity as Lisa Gherardini (1479–1542), wife of Florentine merchant Francesco de Giocondo. Scientists also discovered her dress was covered in a transparent gauze

I've been working at the Louvre for five years, so I'm quite new in this old house! It's an everyday pleasure to work here, enjoying the palace, the gardens and, of course, the artworks.

1 THE DEPARTMENT OF ISLAMIC ART

The design and installation of these new galleries is the museum's largest expansion project since IM Pei created the Pyramid 20 years ago. The new department is home to one of the most exceptional collections of Islamic art in the world, owing to its geographic diversity (from Spain to India), the historical periods covered (from the 8th to the 19th century) and the wide variety of materials and techniques represented. It's simply magnificent, both the architecture and the artworks.

2 PORTRAIT OF THE MARQUISE DE POMPADOUR BY MAURICE-QUENTIN DELATOUR (DEPARTMENT OF THE 18TH CENTURY)

What impress me the most in this portrait is the technique: using only pastel pencils heightened with gouache, Delatour successfully reinvents the style of official portraits. The sumptuousness of her clothing is also a delight, and a perfect representation of a French-style dress of the 18th century.

3 EBIH-IL, THE SUPERINTENDENT OF MARI (DEPARTMENT OF MESOPOTAMIA)

I love this statuette, made of translucent alabaster. The bust is sculpted in a subtle way – and the eyes! Made of lapis lazuli, they look at you in a very gentle and calm way. It inspires serenity and wisdom in me, and it's the favorite artwork of my little son.

4 *JEUNE FILLE EN BUSTE* BY PIERRE-NARCISSE GUERIN (DEPARTMENT OF PAINTING)

I love the modernity and the freshness of this young lady, with her short hair, hiding her breasts. The light on her pearly skin is very smooth. This painting is seated in a calm part of the museum, so you can stay for a while in front of this very beautiful portrait.

91

Queue-Dodging

Avoid queues outside the Grande Pyramide by using the Porte des Lions entrance (closed Tuesday and Friday) or the Carrousel du Louvre entrance at 99 rue de Rivoli. Another top queue-dodging technique is to buy tickets in advance, online or from the machines in the Carrousel du Louvre.

veil typically worn in early-16th-century Italy by pregnant or new mothers; it's surmised that the work was painted to commemorate the birth of her second son around 1503, when she was aged about 24.

Antiquity to Renaissance

The palace rambles through three wings: the **Sully Wing** creates the four sides of the **Cour Carrée** (literally 'square court-yard') at the eastern end of the complex; the **Denon Wing** stretches 800m along the Seine to the south; and the northern **Richelieu Wing** skirts rue de Rivoli.

One of the most famous works from antiquity is the cross-legged *Squatted Scribe* (Room 22, 1st floor, Sully), a painted limestone statue with rock-crystal inlaid eyes dating from c 2620–2500 BC. Measuring 53.7cm tall, the unknown figure is depicted holding a papyrus scroll in his left hand; he's thought to have been holding a brush in his right hand that has since disappeared. Equally compelling is the *Code of Hammurabi* (Room 3, ground floor, Richelieu), and the armless duo of the **Venus de Milo** (Room 16, ground floor, Sully) and the **Winged Victory of Samothrace** (top of Daru staircase, 1st floor, Denon).

The eastern side of the Sully Wing's ground and 1st floors house the Louvre's astonishing cache of Pharaonic Egyptian treasures. Don't miss the mummy of a man from the Ptolemaic period (Room 15, ground floor, Sully) and the funerary figurine of pharaoh Ramesses IV (Room 13, ground floor, Sully). From the Renaissance, Michelangelo's marble masterpiece *The Dying Slave* (Room 4, ground floor, Denon) and works by Raphael, Botticelli and Titian (1st floor, Denon) draw big crowds.

Northern European & French Painting

The 2nd floor of the Richelieu Wing allows for a quieter meander through the Louvre's inspirational collection of Flemish and Dutch paintings spearheaded by works by Peter Paul Rubens and Pieter Bruegel the Elder.

Trails & Tours

Self-guided thematic trails (1½ hours to three hours) range from Louvre masterpieces to the art of eating. There's also several trails for kids (hunt lions, galloping horses). Download trail brochures in advance from the website. Alternatively, rent a **Nintendo 3DS multimedia guide** (adult/child €5/3) at ticket desks or machines in the Hall Napoléon. More formal, English-language **guided tours** (☑01 40 20 51 77; ☉ 11am & 2pm Wed-Mon except 1st Sun of month) depart from the Hall Napoléon. Reserve a spot up to 14 days in advance or sign up on arrival at the museum.

The Pyramid: Inside & Out

Almost as dazzling as the masterpieces inside is the 21m-high glass pyramid designed by Chinese-born American architect IM Pei that bedecks the main entrance to the Louvre in a dazzling crown of shimmering sunbeams and glass. Beneath Pei's **Grande Pyramide** is the **Hall Napoléon**, a split-level public area comprising a temporary exhibition hall, bookshop, souvenir store, cafe and auditoriums for lectures and films. To revel in another Pei pyramid of equally dramatic dimensions, head towards the **Carrousel du Louvre** (www.carrouseldu louvre.com; rue de Rivoli; ☉10am-8pm) a busy shopping mall that loops underground from the Grande Pyramide to the Arc de Triomphe du Carrousel (p99) – its centrepiece is Pei's **Pyramide Inversée** (inverted glass pyramid).

Top: The *Mona Lisa* by Leonardo da Vinci

Bottom: Staircase in the Musée du Louvre

WILL SALTER/GETTY IMAGES ©

The Louvre

A HALF-DAY TOUR

Successfully visiting the Louvre is a fine art. Its complex labyrinth of galleries and staircases spiralling three wings and four floors renders discovery a snakes-and-ladders experience. Initiate yourself with this three-hour itinerary – a playful mix of *Mona Lisa* obvious and up-to-the-minute unexpected.

Arriving by the stunning main entrance, pick up colour-coded floor plans at the lower-ground-floor **information desk 1** beneath IM Pei's glass pyramid, ride the escalator up to the Sully Wing and swap passport for multimedia guide (there are limited descriptions in the galleries) at the wing entrance.

The Louvre is as much about spectacular architecture as masterly art. To appreciate this zip up and down Sully's Escalier Henri II to admire **Venus de Milo 2**, then up parallel Escalier Henri IV to the palatial displays in **Cour Khorsabad 3**. Cross room 1 to find the escalator up to the 1st floor and staircase-as-art **L'Esprit d'Escalier 4**. Next traverse 25 consecutive galleries (thank you, floor plan!) to flip conventional contemplation on its head with Cy Twombly's **The Ceiling 5**, and the hypnotic **Winged Victory of Samothrace sculpture 6** – just two rooms away – which brazenly insists on being admired from all angles. End with the impossibly famous **The Raft of Medusa 7**, **Mona Lisa 8** and **Virgin & Child 9**.

TOP TIPS

» **Floor Plans** Don't even consider entering the Louvre's maze of galleries without a *Plan/Information Louvre* brochure, free from the information desk in the Hall Napoléon

» **Crowd dodgers** The Denon Wing is always packed; visit on late nights Wednesday or Friday or trade Denon in for the notably quieter Richelieu Wing

» **2nd floor** Not for first-timers: save its more specialist works for subsequent visits

Mission Mona Lisa

If you just want to venerate the Louvre's most famous lady, use the Porte des Lions entrance (closed Tuesday and Friday), from where it's a five-minute walk. Go up one flight of stairs and through rooms 26, 14 and 13 to the Grande Galerie and adjoining room 6.

L'Esprit d'Escalier
Escalier Lefuel, Richelieu
Discover the 'Spirit of the Staircase' through François Morellet's contemporary stained glass, which casts new light on old stone. **DETOUR»** Napoleon III's gorgeous gilt apartments.

Rue de Rivoli Entrance

Jardin du Carrousel

Galerie du Carrousel Entrances

Porte des Lions Entrance

The Raft of the Medusa
Room 77, 1st Floor, Denon
Decipher the politics behind French romanticism in Théodore Géricault's *Raft of the Medusa*.

TERRY SMITH IMAGES/ALAMY ©

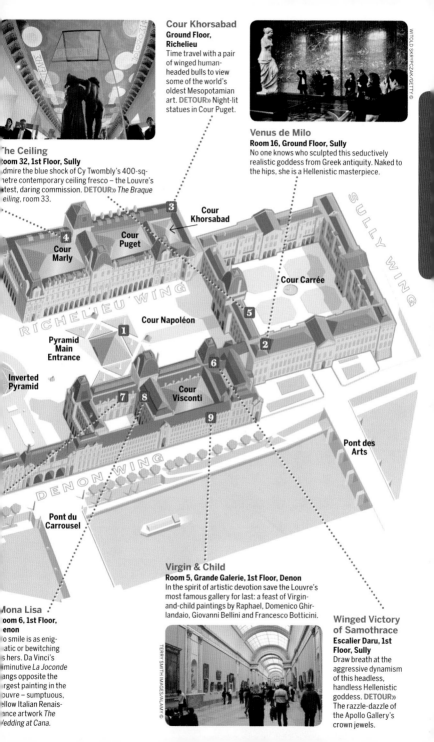

Cour Khorsabad
Ground Floor, Richelieu
Time travel with a pair of winged human-headed bulls to view some of the world's oldest Mesopotamian art. **DETOUR»** Night-lit statues in Cour Puget.

Venus de Milo
Room 16, Ground Floor, Sully
No one knows who sculpted this seductively realistic goddess from Greek antiquity. Naked to the hips, she is a Hellenistic masterpiece.

The Ceiling
Room 32, 1st Floor, Sully
Admire the blue shock of Cy Twombly's 400-sq-metre contemporary ceiling fresco – the Louvre's latest, daring commission. **DETOUR»** *The Braque Ceiling*, room 33.

Cour Khorsabad

Cour Puget

Cour Marly

Cour Carrée

Cour Napoléon

Pyramid Main Entrance

Inverted Pyramid

Cour Visconti

Pont des Arts

RICHELIEU WING

SULLY WING

DENON WING

Pont du Carrousel

Virgin & Child
Room 5, Grande Galerie, 1st Floor, Denon
In the spirit of artistic devotion save the Louvre's most famous gallery for last: a feast of Virgin-and-child paintings by Raphael, Domenico Ghirlandaio, Giovanni Bellini and Francesco Botticini.

Mona Lisa
Room 6, 1st Floor, Denon
No smile is as enigmatic or bewitching as hers. Da Vinci's diminutive *La Joconde* hangs opposite the largest painting in the Louvre – sumptuous, yellow Italian Renaissance artwork *The Wedding at Cana.*

Winged Victory of Samothrace
Escalier Daru, 1st Floor, Sully
Draw breath at the aggressive dynamism of this headless, handless Hellenistic goddess. **DETOUR»** The razzle-dazzle of the Apollo Gallery's crown jewels.

✅ Don't Miss
Centre Pompidou

The Centre Pompidou has amazed and delighted visitors ever since it opened in 1977, not just for its outstanding collection of modern art but also for its radical architectural statement. The dynamic and vibrant arts centre delights and enthrals with its irresistible cocktail of galleries and exhibitions, hands-on workshops, dance performances, free wi-fi hotspot, bookshop, design boutique, cinemas and other entertainment venues.

Map p108

☎ 01 44 78 12 33

www.centre
pompidou.fr

place Georges
Pompidou, 1er

museum,
exhibitions &
panorama adult/
child €13/free

⊗ 11am-9pm Wed-
Mon

Ⓜ Rambuteau

Musée National d'Art Moderne

France's national collection of modern art – almost 75,000 works in all – fills the airy, well-lit galleries of the National Museum of Modern Art covering two complete floors of the Pompidou. All the major movements and artists from 1905 to 1960 are well represented on the 5th floor, including Fauvist Matisse (don't miss his cut-outs *Deux danseurs*; 1937–38), cubists Braque and Picasso, and surrealists Max Ernst, Dali, Miró and Man Ray.

One floor down, works created after 1960 take centre stage. Highlights include *Ten Lizes* (1963) by pop art–wizard Andy Warhol and Yves Klein's monochromes including a 1960 marine-blue work that gave rise to the term 'Klein blue').

Every genre – sculpture, photography, painting, design, installation art and so on – gets a look in, and the museum also has an **Espace des Collections Nouveaux Médias et Film** where visitors can discover 40 years of image and sound experimentation and art.

Blockbuster temporary exhibitions, generally arranged around the work of a single artist in galleries on the 6th floor, complete the modern-art museum's prestigious and exciting repertoire.

Architecture & Views

Former French President Georges Pompidou wanted an ultracontemporary artistic hub and he got it: competition-winning architects Renzo Piano and Richard Rogers designed the building inside out, with features like plumbing, pipes and electrical cables forming part of the external façade. The building was completed in 1977.

Viewed from a distance, the Centre's primary-coloured, boxlike form amid a sea of muted grey Parisian rooftops makes it look like a child's Meccano set abandoned on someone's elegant living-room rug. Although the building is just six storeys high, the city's low-rise cityscape means stupendous views extend from its roof (reached by external escalators). Rooftop admission is included in museum and exhibition admission – or

buy a panorama ticket just for the **roof** (admission €3; ⊙11am-11pm Wed-Mon).

Children's Gallery

Interactive art exhibitions fill the fabulous children's gallery on the 1st floor. There are also regular workshops for kids aged six to 10 years (in French only; check the website for details), and a great website, www.junior.centrepompidou.fr (in English and French), which is loaded with inspirational activities to fire kids' creativity.

Tours & Guides

Guided tours are only in French (the information desk on the ground floor has details), but the gap is easily filled by the excellent **multimedia guide (adult/under 13yr €5/3)**, which explains 62 works of art in the Musée National d'Art Moderne in detail on a 1½-hour trail. There is also a shorter 45-minute tour; another covering the unique architecture of the Centre Pompidou; and one created with kids in mind.

Outdoor Entertainment

The full monty Pompidou experience is as much about hanging out in the busy streets and squares around it, packed with souvenir shops and people, as absorbing the centre's contents. Fun-packed place Georges Pompidou and its nearby pedestrian streets attract bags of buskers, musicians, jugglers and mime artists. Don't miss place Igor Stravinsky with its fanciful mechanical fountains of skeletons, hearts, treble clefs and a big pair of ruby-red lips.

Dining Options

Georges (☏01 44 78 47 99; 6th fl, Centre Pompidou; starters €20, mains €40; ⊙lunch & dinner Wed-Mon), on the 6th floor, is the chic dining option. The inexpensive mezzanine cafe on the 1st floor is unmemorable: walk instead to **Café La Fusée** (p114) or **Café Beaubourg** (100 rue St-Martin, 3e) for an affordable meal or well-deserved, postmuseum aperitif.

Discover Louvre & Les Halles

Getting There & Away

○ **Metro & RER** The Louvre has two metro stations: Palais Royal–Musée du Louvre (lines 1 and 7) and Louvre Rivoli (line 1). Numerous metro and RER lines converge at Paris' main hub, Châtelet–Les Halles.

○ **Bus** Major bus lines include the 27 from rue de Rivoli (for bd St-Michel and place d'Italie) and the 69 near the Louvre Rivoli metro (for Invalides and Eiffel Tower).

○ **Bicycle** Stations at 1 place Ste-Marguerite de Navarre and 2 rue de Turbigo are best placed for the Châtelet–Les Halles metro/ RER hub; for the Louvre pedal to/from stations at 165 rue St-Honoré or 2 rue d'Alger next to the Tuileries metro station.

○ **Boat** Batobus stop Louvre.

Arc de Triomphe du Carrousel

Sights

History and culture meet head on along the banks of the Seine. It was in this same neighbourhood that Louis VI created *halles* (markets) in 1137 for merchants who converged on the city centre to sell their wares, and for over 800 years they were, in the words of Émile Zola, the 'belly of Paris'. The wholesalers were moved lox, stock and cabbage out to the suburbs in 1971.

Les Arts Décoratifs   Art Museum

(Map p100; www.lesartsdecoratifs.fr; 107 rue de Rivoli, 1er; adult/18-25yr/under 18yr €9.50/8/ free; ⊙11am-6pm Tue-Sun; Ⓜ Palais Royal– Musée du Louvre) A trio of privately administered museums collectively known as the Decorative Arts sit in the Rohan Wing of the vast Palais du Louvre. Admission includes entry to all three. Temporary exhibitions, open until 9pm on Thursday, command an additional fee.

The **Musée des Arts Décoratifs** (Applied Arts Museum) displays furniture, jewellery and such objets d'art as ceramics and glassware from the Middle Ages and the Renaissance through the art nouveau and art deco periods to modern times.

The much smaller **Musée de la Publicité** (Advertising Museum) has some 100,000 posters in its collection dating as far back as the 13th century, and innumerable promotional materials touting everything from 19th-century elixirs to early radio advertisements for Air France, as well as electronic publicity. Only certain items are exhibited at any one time; most of the remaining space is given over to special exhibitions.

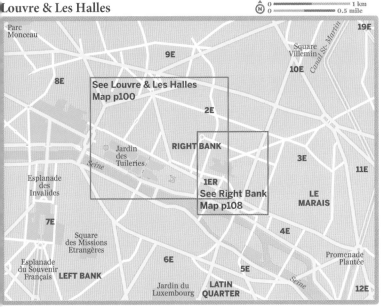

Haute couture (high fashion) creations by the likes of Chanel and Jean-Paul Gaultier can be ogled at in the **Musée de la Mode et du Textile** (Museum of Fashion & Textiles), home to some 16,000 costumes from the 16th century to present day. Most of the outfits are warehoused, however, and are only displayed during themed exhibitions.

Arc de Triomphe du Carrousel   Monument

(Map p100; place du Carrousel, 1er; **M** Palais Royal–Musée du Louvre) This triumphal arch, erected by Napoleon to celebrate his battlefield successes of 1805, sits with aplomb in the **Jardin du Carrousel**, the gardens immediately next to the Louvre. The arch was once crowned by the ancient Greek sculpture called *The Horses of St Mark's*, 'borrowed' from the portico of St Mark's Basilica in Venice by Napoleon but returned after his defeat at Waterloo in 1815.

The quadriga (the two-wheeled chariot drawn by four horses) that replaced it was added in 1828 and celebrates the return of the Bourbons to the French throne after Napoleon's downfall. The sides of the arch are adorned with depictions of Napoleonic victories and eight pink-marble columns, atop of each stands a soldier of the emperor's Grande Armée.

Place Vendôme   City Square

(Map p100; **M** Tuileries or Opéra) Octagonal place Vendôme and the arcaded and colonnaded buildings around it were constructed between 1687 and 1721. In March 1796 Napoleon married Josephine, Viscountess Beauharnais, in the building at No 3. Today the buildings surrounding the square house the posh Hôtel Ritz Paris (closed for renovations until 2014) and some of the city's most fashionable boutiques.

The 43.5m-tall **Colonne Vendôme** (Map p100) in the centre of the square consists of a stone core wrapped in a 160m-long bronze spiral made from hundreds of Austrian and Russian cannons captured by Napoleon at the Battle of Austerlitz in 1805. The statue on top depicts Napoleon in classical Roman dress.

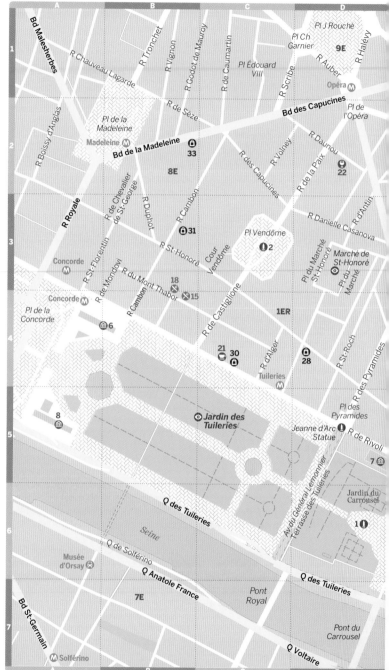

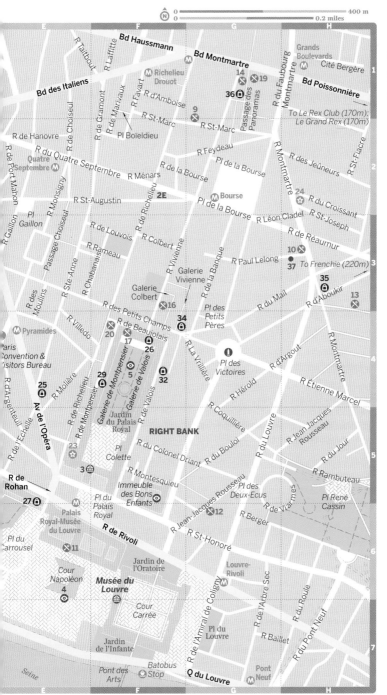

Louvre & Les Halles

Jardin du Palais Royal   Garden

(Map p100; 2 place Colette, 1er; ⊙7.30am-10pm Apr & May, 7am-11pm Jun-Aug, 7am-9.30pm Sep, 7.30am-8.30pm Oct-Mar; Ⓜ Palais Royal–Musée du Louvre) This elegant urban space is fronted by the neoclassical **Palais Royal** (Royal Palace; closed to the public), constructed in 1624 by Cardinal Richelieu but mostly dating from the late 18th century. Louis XIV hung out here the 1640s and today it is the governmental **Conseil d'État** (State Council; Map p100).

Jardin du Palais Royal is a perfect spot to sit, contemplate, picnic between box hedges and shop in the trio of arcades that frame the garden so beautifully: the upmarket **Galerie de Valois** (east); **Galerie de Montpensier** (west), where the Revolution broke out on a warm mid-July day just three years after the galleries opened in the Café du Foy; and tiny **Galerie Beaujolais**, crossed by **Passage du Perron**, above which writer Colette (1873–1954) lived out the last dozen years of her life.

The far southern end of the square is polka-dotted with the controversial black and-white striped columns of various heights by sculptor **Daniel Buren**. It was started in 1986, interrupted by irate Parisians and finished – following the intervention of the Ministry of Culture an Communication – in 1995.

Forum des Halles   Shopping Mall

(Map p108; www.forumdeshalles.com; 1 rue Pierre Lescot, 1er; ⊙shops 10am-8pm Mon-Sat; Ⓜ Les Halles or RER Châtelet–Les Halles) Tragically, the Forum des Halles is no longer a market, but rather an unspeakably ugly, four-level, underground shopping centre. It was constructed in 1970s glass-and-chrome style after Paris' main wholesale food market dating to the early 12th century was moved to the southern suburb of Rungis, near Orly.

ESCUDERO PATRICK/GETTY IMAGES ©

✓ Don't Miss
Église St-Eustache

Just north of the gardens snuggling up to the city's old marketplace, now the soulless Forum des Halles, is one of the most beautiful churches in Paris. Majestic, architecturally magnificent and musically outstanding, St-Eustache has made souls soar for centuries.

Tales of spiritual pomp and circumstance are plentiful. Richelieu and Molière were baptised here (Molière was also married here), Louis XIV celebrated his first Holy Communion in the church, and Voltaire is buried here. Mozart chose St-Eustache for the funeral mass of his mother and in 1855 Berlioz's *Te Deum* premiered here – the church's acoustics are extraordinary.

Built between 1532 and 1637, the church is primarily Gothic, although a neoclassical façade was added on the western side in the mid-18th century. Inside, contemplate the stained glass and paintings, many donated by guilds and merchants from the nearby Les Halles. Highlights include several works by Rubens in the side chapels, the colourful bas-relief of Parisian market porters (1969) by British sculptor Raymond Mason, and the exquisite altarpiece – bronze with white gold leaf (1990) – completed by 31-year-old American artist Keith Haring weeks before his death. Outside the church is a gigantic sculpture of a head and hand entitled *L'Écoute* (Listen; 1986) by Henri de Miller.

France's largest organ, above the church's western entrance, has 101 stops and 8000 pipes dating from 1854. Organ recitals at 5.30pm on Sunday are a must for music lovers, as is June's Festival des 36 Heures de St-Eustache – 36 hours of nonstop music embracing a symphony of genres, including world music, choral and jazz.

NEED TO KNOW

Map p20; www.st-eustache.org; 2 impasse St-Eustache, 1er; admission free; ⊘9.30am-7pm Mon-Fri, 10am-7pm Sat, 9am-7pm Sun; Ⓜ Les Halles

FRANCES-WYSOCKI FRANCES-WYSOCKI/GETTY IMAGES ©

Jardin des Tuileries

This quintessentially Parisian, Seine-side garden was laid out by André Le Nôtre, garden architect of gardens at Versailles, in 1664. The 28-hectare expanse of manicured green quickly became a fashionable spot for parading one's finery, and is much loved today by city joggers and Sunday-afternoon strollers. A funfair sets up here in midsummer. Look out for Louise Bourgeois' *The Welcoming Hands* (1996) facing place de la Concorde.

The 16th-century Palais des Tuileries stood at the garden's western end until 1871 when it was burnt down during the Revolution. Two remarkable art galleries mark the spot today.

Set in an 19th-century orangery built to shelter the garden's orange trees in winter, the **Musée de l'Orangerie** (Map p100; www.musee-orangerie.fr; quai des Tuileries & rue de Rivoli; adult/child €7.50/5.50; ⊙9am-6pm Wed-Mon; ⓂTuileries or Concorde) is a treat. It exhibits important impressionist works, including a series of Monet's *Decorations des Nymphéas* (Waterlilies) in two huge oval rooms purpose-built in 1927 on the artist's instructions. Works by Cézanne, Matisse, Picasso, Renoir, Sisley, Soutine and Utrillo complete the gallery's outstanding playlist. A combination ticket covering admission to the Musée d'Orsay costs €14.

The wonderfully airy **Jeu de Paume** (Map p100; ☎01 47 03 12 50; www.jeudepaume. org; 1 place de la Concorde, 8e; adult/18-25yr/under 18yr €7.50/5/free; ⊙noon-9pm Tue, noon-7pm Wed-Fri, 10am-7pm Sat & Sun; ⓂConcorde) gallery in the erstwhile *jeu de paume* (real, or royal, tennis court) is all that remains of the Palais des Tuileries. It stages innovative photography exhibitions.

Map p100; ⊙7am-7.30pm, later in summer; ⓂTuileries or Concorde

The upside is that dramatic change
(or the better) is afoot. The dodgy
(dark and dated arbours topping the
underground shopping mall have been
demolished, and cranes, diggers and
an army of builders are busy at work
creating **La Canopée** – a thoroughly
contemporary, glass-topped, curvilinear
building by architects Patrick Berger and
Jacques Anziutti, inspired by the natural
shade canopy of a rainforest. Spilling out
from the translucent, leaflike rooftop will
be state-of-the-art gardens by landscape
designer David Mangin with *pétanque*
(a variant on the game of bowls) courts
and chess tables, a central patio and
pedestrian walkways. Final completion is
slated for 2016.

The mall itself will receive a relatively
light renovation in stages; hence business
should continue more or less as usual,
with minimal disruption to city's largest
metro/RER hub. Follow the project at
www.parisleshalles.fr or pop into the
information centre on **place Jean du
Bellay**, a pretty square pierced by the
Fontaine des Innocents (1549).

Tour Jean sans Peur — Tower

(Map p108; www.tourjeansanspeur.com; 20 rue
Etienne Marcel, 1er; adult/7-18yr €5/3; ⏰ 1.30-
6pm Wed-Sun Apr-early Nov, 1.30-6pm Wed, Sat
& Sun early Nov-Mar; M Étienne Marcel) This
Gothic, 29m-high tower called Tower of
John the Fearless was built by the Duke of
Bourgogne so he could take refuge from
his enemies at the top. Part of a splendid
mansion in the early 15th century, it is
one of the very few examples of feudal
military architecture extant in Paris.
Climb 140 steps up the spiral staircase to
the top turret.

Tour St-Jacques — Tower

(Map p108; square de la Tour St-Jacques, 1er;
M Châtelet) Just north of place du Châtelet,
the Flamboyant Gothic, 52m-high St
James Tower is all that remains of the
Église St-Jacques la Boucherie, built by
the powerful butchers guild in 1523 as
a starting point for pilgrims setting out
for the shrine of St James at Santiago de
Compostela in Spain.

The church was demolished by the
Revolutionary Directory in 1797, but the
sand-coloured bell tower, perfectly clean,
was spared so that it could be used
to drop globules of molten lead in the
manufacture of shot.

Eating

Beef Club — Steak €€

(Map p108; ☎ 09 54 37 13 65; 58 rue Jean-
Jacques Rousseau, 1er; mains €20-45; ⏰ dinner
Tue-Sat; M Les Halles) Packed out ever
since it threw its first T-bone on the grill
in spring 2012, this beefy address is all
about steak, prepared to sweet perfection
by legendary Paris butcher Yves-Marie Le
Bourdonnec. The vibe is hip New York and
the downstairs cellar bar, the Ballroom du
Beef Club, shakes a mean cocktail (€12 to
€15) courtesy of the cool guys from the
Experimental Cocktail Club.

Frenchie — Bistro €€

(☎ 01 40 39 96 19; www.frenchie-restaurant.
com; 5-6 rue du Nil, 2e; menus €34, €38 & €45;
⏰ dinner Mon-Fri; M Sentier) Tucked down an
alley you wouldn't venture down otherwise, this bijou bistro with wooden tables
and old stone walls is iconic. Frenchie
is always packed and for good reason:
excellent-value dishes are modern,

Burger Mania

The burger trend sweeping Paris
is, unsurprisingly, *très* gourmet.
Sizzling new openings include
Blend (Map p108; www.blendhamburger.
com; 44 rue d'Argout, 2e; burgers €10,
lunch menus €15 & €17; ⏰ lunch & dinner
Mon-Sat; M Sentier), on happening
little rue d'Argout, serving burgers
with house-baked brioche buns,
homemade ketchup and hand-cut
meat from celebrity butcher Yves-
Marie Le Bourdonnec of Beef Club.

market-driven (the menu changes daily with a choice of two dishes by course) and prepared with just the right dose of unpretentious creative flair by French chef Gregory Marchand.

The only hiccup is snagging a table: reserve for one of two sittings (7pm or 9.30pm) two months in advance, arrive at 7pm and pray for a cancellation or – failing that – share tapas-style small plates with friends across the street at **Frenchie Bar à Vin**. No reservations – write your name on the sheet of paper strung outside, loiter in the alley and wait for your name to be called.

Claus   Breakfast €
(Map p100; ☎ 01 42 33 55 10; www.clausparis.com; 14 rue Jean-Jacques Rousseau, 1er; breakfast €13-18, lunch €19; ⏰ 7.30am-6pm Mon-Fri, 9.30am-5pm Sat & Sun; Ⓜ Étienne Marcel) Dubbed the 'haute-couture breakfast specialist' in Parisian foodie circles, this inspired épicerie du petit-dej (breakfast grocery shop) has everything you could possibly desire for the ultimate gourmet breakfast and brunch –

organic mueslis and cereals, fresh juices, jams, honey and so on.

Breakfast or brunch on site, shop at Claus to create your own or ask for a luxury breakfast hamper to be delivered to your door. Its lunchtime salads, soups and tarts are equally tasty.

Spring   Modern French €€
(Map p108; ☎ 01 45 96 05 72; www.spring paris.fr; 6 rue Bailleul, 1er; lunch/dinner menus €44/76; ⏰ lunch & dinner Wed-Fri, dinner Tue-Sat; Ⓜ Palais Royal–Musée du Louvre) Spring has no printed menu, meaning hungry gourmets put their appetites in the hands of the chef and allow multilingual waiting staff to reveal what's cooking as each course is served.

At lunchtime, nip to the **Spring Épicerie** (Map p108; 52 rue de l'Arbre Sec, 1er, 1er; ⏰ noon-8pm Tue-Sat), a tiny wine shop that serves steaming bowls of market-inspired, 'hungry worker-style' bouillon du poule (chicken soup; €12) loaded with veg, a poached farm egg, herbs and so on. Eat at a bar stool or on the trot.

Left: Café Marly (p112); **Below:** Cheese souffle
(LEFT) LONELY PLANET/GETTY IMAGES ©; (BELOW) CLAY MCLACHLAN/GETTY IMAGES ©

L'Ardoise   Bistro €€

(Map p100; ☎ 01 42 96 28 18; www.
ardoise-paris.com; 28 rue du Mont Thabor,
1er; menus €35; ⏱ lunch Tue-Sat, dinner Tue-Sun;
Ⓜ Concorde or Tuileries) This is a lovely little
bistro with no menu as such (*ardoise*
means 'blackboard', which is all there
is), but who cares? The food – fricassee
of corn-fed chicken with morels, pork
cheeks in ginger, hare in black pepper,
prepared dextrously by chef Pierre Jay
(ex-Tour d'Argent) – is superb. The menu
changes every three weeks and the three-
course *prix fixe* (set menu) offers good
value.

Le Soufflé   Traditional French €€

(Map p100; ☎ 01 42 60 27 19; www.lesouffle.fr;
36 rue du Mont Thabor, 1er; lunch/dinner menus
€25/35; ⏱ lunch & dinner Mon-Sat; Ⓜ Concorde
or Tuileries) The faintly vintage, aqua-blue
façade of this concept kitchen is reas-
suringly befitting of the timeless French
classic it serves inside – the soufflé. The
light fluffy dish served in white ramekins

comes in dozens of different flavours,
both savoury and sweet; *andouillette* (pig
intestine sausage) is the top choice for
fearless gourmets.

Racines   Wine Bar €€

(Map p100; ☎ 01 40 13 06 41; 8 Passage des
Panoramas, 2e; mains €15-30; ⏱ lunch & dinner
Mon-Fri; Ⓜ Grands Boulevards or Bourse) Sitting snugly inside a former 19th-century
marchand de vin (wine merchant's; look
up to admire the lovely old gold letter-
ing above the door), Racines (meaning
'Roots') is an address that shouts Paris
at every turn. Shelves of wine bottles
curtain the windows, the old patterned
floor smacks of feasting and merriment,
and the menu chalked on the *ardoise*
(blackboard) is a straightforward choice
of three starters, three mains and a trio of
desserts, deeply rooted in the best local
produce.

107

Right Bank Area

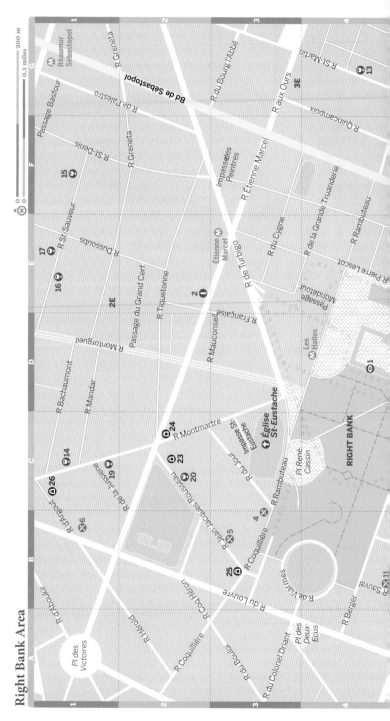

0.1 miles
200 m

A Pl des Victoires

R d'Aboukir
R Hérold
R Coquillière
R du Colonel Driant

B
R du Louvre
R Coq Héron
R de Viarmes
R Sauval
R Berger
Pl des Deux-Écus

C
R Bachaumont
R Mandar
R de la Jussienne
R du Jour
R Jean-Jacques Rousseau
R Rambuteau
R Coquillière
Pl René Cassin

D
R Montorgueil
R Maúconseil
Passage du Grand Cerf
Église St-Eustache
Impasse St-Eustache
Les Halles

E
R St-Sauveur
R Dussoubs
R Tiquetonne
R Française
Étienne Marcel
R de Turbigo
Passage Mondétour
R Pierre Lescot

F
R St-Denis
R Greneta
Passage Basfour
R de Palestro
Impasse des Peintres
R Étienne Marcel
R du Cygne
R de la Grande-Truanderie

G
Réaumur Sébastopol
R Greneta
Bd de Sébastopol
R du Bourg l'Abbé
R aux Ours
R Quincampoix
R St-Martin
R Rambuteau

2E
3E

RIGHT BANK

6
26
14
19
23
20
24
25
5
4
1
16
17
15
2
13
11

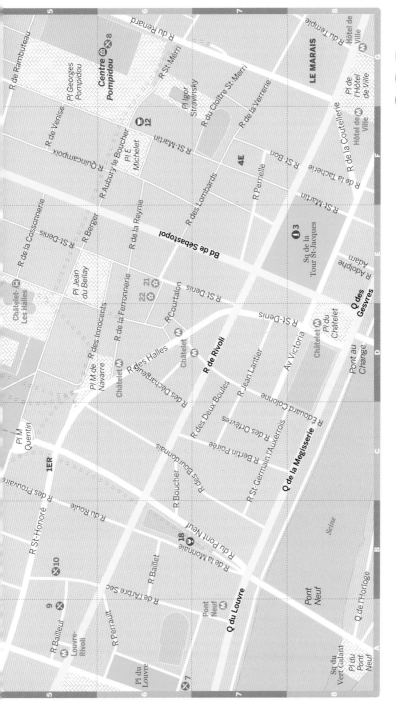

R de Rambuteau

R du Renard

Centre Pompidou 🏛️ ✕ 8

Pl Georges Pompidou

R St-Merri

LE MARAIS

R du Temple

Hôtel de

Ⓜ Hôtel de Ville

R de Venise

Pl Igor Stravinsky

R du Cloître-St-Merri

R de la Verrerie

R Aubry-le-Boucher

Pl E Michelet

⓵ 12

R de la Coutellerie

Pl de l'Hôtel de Ville

Hôtel de Ⓜ Ville

R Quincampoix

R St-Martin

4E

R St-Bon

R de la Tacherie

R de la Cossonnerie

R Berger

R de la Reynie

R des Lombards

R Perrielle

R St-Martin

Châtelet-Ⓜ Les Halles

R St-Denis

Bd de Sébastopol

⓵ 3

R Adolphe Adam

Pl Jean du Bellay

R de la Ferronnerie

R Courtalon

Sq de la Tour St-Jacques

R des Innocents

22 21 ✕❸

R St-Denis

Q des Gesvres

Pl M de Navarre

R des Halles

Châtelet Ⓜ

R de Rivoli

R St-Denis

Châtelet Ⓜ

Pl du Châtelet

Pl M Quentin

Châtelet Ⓜ

R des Déchargeurs

Av Victoria

Pont au Change

1ER

R des Deux Boules

R Jean Lantier

R du Pont Neuf

R St-Honoré

R des Prouvaires

R du Roule

R des Orfèvres

R Édouard Colonne

R Bertin Poirée

R St-Germain l'Auxerrois

Q de la Mégisserie

Q de l'Horloge

R Boucher

R des Bourdonnais

✕ 10

R Bailleul

Ⓜ Louvre-Rivoli

9 ✕

R Perrault

R de l'Arbre Sec

R Baillet

R de la Monnaie

R du Pont Neuf

18 ⓵

Pont Neuf

Q du Louvre

Seine

Pont Neuf

Pl du Louvre

✕ 7

Sq du Vert Galant

Pl du Pont Neuf

Right Bank Area

An impressive choice of organic and natural *vins* makes the wine list stand out.

Passage 53   Modern French €€€

(Map p100; ☎01 42 33 04 35; www.passage53. com; 53 Passage des Panoramas, 2e; lunch/dinner menus €60/110; ☉lunch & dinner Tue-Sat; Ⓜ Grands Boulevards or Bourse) No address inside Passage des Panoramas contrasts more dramatically with the outside hustle and bustle than this elegant restaurant at No 53. An oasis of calm and tranquillity (with window blinds pulled firmly down when closed), this gastronomic address is an ode to the only the best French produce – worked to perfection in a series of tasting courses by Japanese chef Shinichi Sato. Advance reservations recommended.

Yam'Tcha   Fusion €€€

(Map p108; ☎01 40 26 08 07; www.yamtcha. com; 4 rue Sauval, 1er; lunch/dinner menus from €50/85; ☉lunch Wed-Sun, dinner Wed-Sat; Ⓜ Louvre Rivoli) Adeline Grattard's ingeniously fused French and Chinese flavours recently earned the female chef a Michelin star. Pair dishes on the frequently

changing menu with wine or exotic teas. Book well ahead.

Le Grand Véfour   Traditional French €€€

(Map p100; ☎01 42 96 56 27; www.grand-vefour. com; 17 rue de Beaujolais, 1er; lunch/dinner menus €96/282; ☉lunch Mon-Fri, dinner Mon-Thu; Ⓜ Pyramides) This 18th-century jewel on the northern edge of the Jardin du Palais Royal has been a dining favourite of the Parisian elite since 1784; just look at who gets their names ascribed to each table – from Napoleon to Victor Hugo and Colette (who lived next door). The food is tip-top; expect a voyage of discovery in one of the most beautiful restaurants in the world.

Le Grand Colbert   Traditional French €€

(Map p100; ☎01 42 86 87 88; www.legrandcol bert.fr; 2-4 rue Vivienne, 2e; lunch menus €25.50 & €32.50; ☉noon-1am; Ⓜ Pyramides) This former workers' *cafétéria* transformed into a fin de siècle showcase is more relaxed than many similarly restored restaurants and is a convenient spot for lunch after visiting the neighbouring covered shopping arcades – the daily *formule ardoise* (blackboard fixed menu; €16) chalked on the board is good value – or cruising the streets at night (last orders: midnight).

Don't expect gastronomic miracles, but portions are big and service is friendly. Sunday ushers in a pricier €41 *menu*.

Bioboa   Organic €€

(Map p100; ☎ 01 40 28 02 83; www.bioboa. fr; 93 rue Montmartre, 2e; 2-/3-course lunch menu €21/26, mains €16-24; ☺ 9am-midnight Mon-Sat; Ⓜ Sentier or Bourse) Potted olive trees salute the entrance to this organic food cafe, a lovely space with retro mirrors, violet walls and funky collection of lampshades mixing a dozen and one fabrics, textures and materials. Order an apple and kiwifruit juice, kick back in an armchair and revel in a menu that mixes organic farm meats with a generous dose of tasty vegetarian dishes.

Don't miss the restaurant's adjoining, small but select *épicerie* (grocery store).

La Mauvaise Réputation   Modern French €€

(Map p100; ☎ 01 42 36 92 44; www.lamauvaise reputation.fr; 28 rue Léopold-Bellan, 2e; lunch menus €17-21, dinner menus €35; ☺ lunch Tue-Fri & Sun, dinner Tue-Sat; Ⓜ Sentier) The name alone – Bad Reputation (yep, also a Georges Brassens album) – immediately makes you want to poke your nose in and see what's happening behind that bright orange canopy and oyster-grey façade just footsteps from busy rue Montorgueil.

The answer is great bistro cooking and warm engaging service in a catchy designer space with coloured spots on the wall and fresh flowers on each table.

Aux Lyonnais   Lyonnais €€

(Map p100; ☎ 01 42 96 65 04; www.auxlyonnais. com; 32 rue St-Marc, 2e; lunch menu €30, mains €20-27; ☺ lunch & dinner Tue-Fri, dinner Sat; Ⓜ Richelieu-Drouot) This is where top French chef Alain Ducasse (who has three Michelin stars at his restaurant over at the Plaza Athénée) and his followers

'slum' it. The venue is an art nouveau masterpiece that feels more real than movie set and the food is perfectly restructured Lyonnais classics.

L'Arbre à Cannelle   Bistro €

(Map p100; ☎ 01 45 08 55 87; www.arbre-a -cannelle.fr; 57 Passage des Panoramas, 2e; mains €13.50-15.90; ☺ lunch Mon & Tue, lunch & dinner Wed-Sat; Ⓜ Grands Boulevards or Bourse) Tucked inside one of the Right Bank's most vibrant early-19th-century *passages couverts* (covered arcades), the 'Cinnamon Tree' is as much about ogling at original 19th-century decor – check that ceiling, man! – as feasting on good-value bistro fare. More delicate appetites will appreciate the tasty selection of salads, savoury tarts and quiches. Predictably, the place gets packed at lunchtime.

Au Pied de Cochon   Brasserie €€

(Map p108; ☎ 01 40 13 77 00; www.pieddeco chon.com; 6 rue Coquillère, 1er; lunch menu

The City's Most Famous Hot Chocolate

Clink china with lunching ladies, their posturing poodles and half the students from Tokyo University at **Angelina** (Map p100; 226 rue de Rivoli, 1er; ☺ daily; Ⓜ Tuileries), a grand dame of a tearoom dating from 1903. Breakfast, lunch and weekend brunch are all served here, against a fresco backdrop of belle époque Nice, but it is the superthick, decadently sickening 'African' hot chocolate (€7.20), served with a pot of whipped cream and carafe of water, that prompts the constant queue for a table at Angelina. Buy it bottled to take home from Angelina's small boutique. There is also a branch at **Versailles** (p204).

A Hidden Kitchen

So successful were their apartment-held dinners that American duo Braden and Laura shut their Hidden Kitchen supper club and opened the hidden, hyped restaurant **Verjus** (Map p100; [J]01 42 97 54 40; www.verjusparis.com; 52 rue de Richelieu, 1er; 4-/6-course tasting menus €55/70, with wine pairings €85/110; ⊙dinner Mon-Fri; [M]Bourse or Palais Royal–Musée du Louvre). Cuisine is contemporary and international (eg monkfish with apple and Tabasco broth).

Alternatively, Braden and Laura's pocket-sized wine bar **Verjus Bar à Vin** (Map p100; 47 rue de Montpensier, 1er; ⊙6-11pm Mon-Fri; [M]Bourse or Palais Royal-Musée du Louvre) cooks up superb and affordable food like fried buttermilk chicken.

€18.50, mains €18.60-24.35; ⊙24hr; [M]Les Halles) This venerable establishment, which once satisfied the appetites of both market porters and theatre-goers with its famous onion soup and *pieds de cochon* (grilled pig's trotters), has become more uniformly upmarket and touristy since Les Halles was moved to the suburbs.

But it still opens round the clock seven days a week (as it has since the end of WWII), and its pig's trotters, tails, ears and snouts are definitely worth writing a postcard home about. Children's *menu* €7.90.

Café Marly
Cafe €€

(Map p100; [J]01 46 26 06 60; www.maison thierrycostes.com; 93 rue de Rivoli, 1er; mains €18-39; ⊙8am-2am; [M]Palais Royal–Musée du Louvre) This chic venue facing the Louvre's inner courtyard serves contemporary French fare throughout the day under the palace colonnades. Views of the glass pyramid are priceless.

Cojean
Sandwiches, Salads €

(Map p108; www.cojean.fr; 3 place du Louvre, 1er; sandwiches €6-7; ⊙10am-4pm Mon-Fri, 11am-6pm Sat; [☎]; [M]Palais Royal–Musée du Louvre) Across the street from the Louvre, this stylish sandwich and salad bar promises a quick lunch for less than €10 beneath the splendour of an elegant moulded period ceiling.

Branches include one near the **Champs-Élysées** (Map p74; www.cojean.fr; 25 rue Washington, 8e; salads €4.80-7, sandwiches €5-6; ⊙Mon-Fri 10am-4pm; [☎]; [M]George V).

☕ Drinking & Nightlife

Experimental Cocktail Club
Cocktail Bar

(Map p108; www.experimentalcocktailclub. com; 37 rue St-Saveur, 2e; ⊙daily; [M]Réaumur-Sebastopol) Called ECC by trendies, this fabulous speakeasy with grey façade and old-beamed ceiling is effortlessly hip. Oozing spirit and soul, the cocktail bar – with retro-chic decor by American interior designer Cuoco Black and sister bars in London and New York – is a sophisticated flashback to those *années folles* (crazy years) of prohibition New York.

Cocktails (€12 to €15) are individual and fabulous, and DJs set the space partying until dawn at weekends. The same guys are behind the equally hip Ballroom cocktail bar in the cellar of the New Yorker-style **Beef Club** (p105).

Jefrey's
Cocktail Bar

(Map p108; www.jefreys.fr; 14 rue St-Saveur, 2e; ⊙Tue-Sat; [M]Réaumur-Sebastopol) Oh how dandy this trendy drawing room with wooden façade, leather Chester-fields and old-fashioned gramophone is! Gentlemen's club in soul, yes, but creative cocktails are shaken for both him and her, and never more so during happy hour (7pm to 10.30pm Tuesday and Thurday) when cocktails (€11 to €13) dip to €9.

Favourites include I Wanna be This Drink (rum, strawberry juice, fresh

Rue Montmartre

Rue Montmartre's appealing places to sip *café* or cocktails include the heritage-listed, hole-in-the-wall gem **Christ Inn's Bistrot** (Map p108; ☎01 42 36 07 56; 15 rue Montmartre, 1er; ⏱Tue-Sat; Ⓜ Les Halles), with railway-carriage-style slatted wooden seats and belle époque tiles featuring market scenes of Les Halles. Equally 'vintage' is **Le Tambour** (Map p108; ☎01 42 33 06 90; 41 rue Montmartre, 2e; ⏱8am-6am; Ⓜ Étienne Marcel or Sentier), beloved for its insomniac-friendly hours (food until 3.30am or 4am), recycled street furniture and old metro maps.

raspberries and balsamic vinegar caramel) and the Grand Marnier–based Cucumber Cooler. Well-aged whisky and other spirits are another reason to drink chez Jefrey's.

Kong   Bar
(Map p108; www.kong.fr; 1 rue du Pont Neuf, 1er; ⏱daily; Ⓜ Pont Neuf) Late nights at this Philippe Starck–designed riot of iridescent champagne-coloured vinyl booths, Japanese cartoon cut-outs and garden gnome stools see Paris' glam young set guzzling Dom Pérignon, nibbling on tapas-style platters (mains €20 to €40) and shaking their designer-clad booty on the tables.

If you can, try to snag a table *à l'étage* (upstairs) in the part-glass-roofed terrace-gallery, where light floods across the giant geisha swooning horizontal across

Interior details at Kong
MODERN DESIGN/ALAMY ©

the ceiling, and stunning river views (particularly at sunset) make you swoon. Smokers will appreciate the *fumoir* (a tiny heated room with no windows or ceiling) accessible from here.

Harry's New York Bar   Cocktail Bar
(Map p100; www.harrysbar.fr; 5 rue Daunou, 2e; ⏱daily; Ⓜ Opéra) One of the most popular American-style bars in the prewar years, Harry's once welcomed writers like F Scott Fitzgerald and Ernest Hemingway, who no doubt sampled the bar's unique cocktail and creation: the Bloody Mary. The Cuban mahogany interior dates from the mid-19th century and was brought over from a Manhattan bar in 1911.

There's a basement piano bar called Ivories where Gershwin supposedly composed *An American in Paris* and, for the peckish, old-school hot dogs and generous club sandwiches to snack on. The advertisement for Harry's that occasionally appears in the papers still reads 'Tell the Taxi Driver Sank Roo Doe Noo' and is copyrighted.

Ô Chateau
Wine Bar

(Map p108; www.o-chateau.com; 68 rue Jean-Jacques Rousseau, 1er; ⏱4pm-midnight, Tue-Sat; MLes Halles or Étienne Marcel) Wine aficionados can thank this young, fun, cosmopolitan *bar à vin* for bringing affordable tasting on tap to Paris. Sit at the long trendy bar and savour your pick of 40-odd *grands vins* served by the glass (500-odd by the bottle!). Or sign up in advance for a guided cellar tasting in English over lunch (€75), dinner (€100) or with six *grands crus* and cheese (€120).

Ô Chateau also runs **wine-tasting courses** (p117).

Depur
Bar

(Map p108; www.depur.fr; 4bis rue St-Saveur, 2e; ⏱daily; 📶; MÉtienne Marcel or Sentier) It's glitzy and chic, a definite after-dark dress-up. But what really gives this hybrid bar-restaurant wow-factor is its courtyard terrace – covered in winter, open and star-topped in summer. Cocktails are shaken from 5pm.

Café La Fusée
Bar

(Map p108; 168 rue St-Martin, 3e; ⏱daily; MRambuteau or Étienne Marcel) A short walk from the Pompidou, the Rocket is a lively, laid-back hang-out with red-and-white striped awning strung with fairy lights outside, and paint-peeling, tobacco-coloured walls evoking 101 great nights out inside. Its wine selection by the glass (€2.70 to €5.50) is notably good.

⭐ Entertainment

Comédie Française
Theatre

(Map p100; www.comedie-francaise.fr; place Colette, 1er; MPalais Royal–Musée du Louvre) Founded in 1680 under Louis XIV, the 'French Comedy' theatre bases its repertoire on the works of classic French playwrights.

Jazz Duo

Rue des Lombards, 2e, is the street to swing by for live jazz.

Le Baiser Salé (Map p108; www.lebaisersale.com; 58 rue des Lombards, 2e; ⏱daily; MChâtelet) Known for its Afro and Latin jazz, and jazz fusion concerts, the Salty Kiss combines big names and unknown artists. The place has a relaxed vibe, with sets starting at 7.30pm and 10pm.

Sunset & Sunside (Map p108; www.sunset-sunside.com; 60 rue des Lombards, 1er; ⏱daily; MChâtelet) Two venues in one at this trendy, well-respected club: electric jazz, fusion and the odd salsa session downstairs; acoustics and concerts upstairs.

Le Rex Club
Nightclub

(www.rexclub.com; 5 bd Poissonnière, 2e; ⏱Wed-Sat; MBonne Nouvelle) Attached to the art deco Grand Rex cinema, this is Paris' premier house and techno venue where some of the world's hottest DJs strut their stuff on a 70-speaker, multidiffusion sound system.

Social Club
Club

(Map p100; www.parissocialclub.com; 142 rue Montmartre, 2e; ⏱Wed-Sun; MGrands Boulevards) These subterranean rooms showcasing electro, hip hop, funk and live acts are a magnet for clubbers who take their music seriously. Across the street at No 146 is the cafe where French socialist Jean Jaurès was assassinated in 1914.

🔒 Shopping

Didier Ludot
Fashion

(Map p100; www.didierludot.fr; 19-20 & 23-24 Galerie de Montpensier, 1er; MPalais Royal–Musée du Louvre) In the rag trade since 1975, collector Didier Ludot sells the city's finest couture creations of yesteryear in his exclusive twinset of boutiques, hosts

YVAN TRAVERT/GETTY IMAGES ©

exhibitions, and has published a book portraying the evolution of the little black dress, brilliantly brought to life in his boutique that sells just that, **La Petite Robe Noire** (Map p100; 125 Galerie de Valois, 1er; M Palais Royal-Musée du Louvre).

E Dehillerin   Homewares
(Map p108; www.dehillerin.com; 18-20 rue Coquil-lière, 1er; ⏲9-12.30pm & 2-6pm Mon & Wed-Fri, 8am-6pm Tue & Sat; M Les Halles) Founded in 1820, this extraordinary two-level store – think old-fashioned warehouse rather than shiny chic boutique – carries an incredible selection of professional-quality *matériel de cuisine* (kitchenware). Poultry scissors, turbot poacher, old-fashioned copper pot or Eiffel Tower–shaped cake tin – it's all here.

Colette   Concept Store
(Map p100; www.colette.fr; 213 rue St-Honoré, 1er; M Tuileries) Uber-hip is an understatement. Ogle at designer fashion on the 1st floor, and streetwear, limited-edition sneakers, art books, music, gadgets and other hi-tech, inventive and/or plain unusual items on the ground floor. End with a drink in the basement 'water bar' and pick up free design magazines and flyers for

some of the city's hippest happenings by the door upon leaving.

Passage des Panoramas   Shopping Arcade
(Map p100; 10 rue St-Marc, 2e; M Bourse) Built in 1800, this is the oldest covered arcade in Paris and the first to be lit by gas (1817). It's a bit faded around the edges now, but retains a real 19th-century charm with several outstanding eateries, a theatre from where spectators would come out to shop during the interval, and autograph dealer Arnaud Magistry (at No 60).

Room Service   Fashion
(Map p108; www.roomservice.fr; 52 rue d'Argout, 2e; M Les Halles) *'Atelier Vintage'* (vintage workshop) is the thrust of this chic boutique that reinvents vintage pieces as new. Scarves, headpieces, sequins, bangles and beads casually strung up to be admired...the place oozes the femininity and refinement of an old-fashioned Parisian boudoir.

2WS   Fashion
(Map p108; www.2ws.fr; 68 rue Jean-Jacques Rousseau, 1er; M Étienne Marcel) As much

115

about street art as wear, this fashion boutique with rough concrete floor and industrial fittings is hip. DJs spin tunes Saturday afternoons, and tank tops, reverse sweatshirts and jumpsuits are the backbone of its lifestyle range for men, women and kids.

Galignani
Books

(Map p100; http://galignani.com; 224 rue de Rivoli, 1er; **M**Concorde) Proudly claiming to be the 'first English bookshop established on the continent', this ode to literature stocks French and English books and is the best spot in Paris for picking up just-published titles.

Antoine
Fashion

(Map p100; 10 av de l'Opéra, 1er; ⏰10.30am-3pm & 4-6.30pm Mon-Sat; **M**Pyramides or Palais Royal–Musée du Louvre) Antoine has been the Parisian master of bespoke canes, umbrellas, fans and gloves since 1745.

Jamin Puech
Fashion

(Map p100; www.jamin-puech.com; 26 rue Cambon, 1er; **M**Concorde) Among Paris' most creative handbag designers, Jamin Puech is known for its bold mix of colours, fabrics, leathers and textures – lots of beads, pompoms, shells, feathers and so on. Its Cocotte handbag starred in *Sex in the City 2*.

Comptoir de la Gastronomie
Food, Drink

(Map p108; www.comptoir-gastronomie.com; 34 rue Montmartre, 1er; ⏰6am-8pm Mon, 9am-8pm Tue-Sat; **M**Les Halles) This elegant *épicerie fine* (specialist grocer) stocks a scrumptious array of gourmet goods to take away; it adjoins a striking art nouveau dining room dating to 1894.

Librairie Gourmande
Books

(Map p100; www.librairie-gourmande.fr; 92 rue Montmartre, 1er; ⏰11am-7pm Mon-Sat; **M**Sentier) The city's leading bookshop dedicated to things culinary and gourmet.

Lavinia
Food, Drink

(Map p100; www.lavinia.com; 3 bd de la Madeleine, 8e; **M**Madeleine) Among the largest and most exclusive drinks shops is this bastion of booze with a top collection of *eaux-de-vie* (fruit brandies).

Exterior of E Dehillerin (p115)

Backstage at the Flicks

A trip to 1932 art deco cinematic icon **Le Grand Rex** (www.legrandrex.com; 1 bd Poissonnière, 2e; tour adult/child €9.80/8; ⊙tours 10am-7pm Wed-Sun; M Bonne Nouvelle) is like no other trip to the flicks. Screenings aside, the cinema runs 50-minute behind-the-scene tours (English soundtracks available) during which visitors – tracked by a sensor slung around their neck – are whisked right up (via a lift) behind the giant screen, tour a soundstage and get to have fun in a recording studio. Whizz-bang special effects along the way will stun adults and kids alike.

Legrand Filles & Fils   Food, Drink
(Map p100; www.caves-legrand.com; 1 rue de la Banque, 2e; M Pyramides) This shop, tucked inside Galerie Vivienne since 1880, sells fine wine and all the accoutrements: corkscrews, tasting glasses, decanters etc. It also has a fancy wine bar, *école du vin* (wine school) and *éspace dégustation* with several tastings a month; check its website for details.

Boîtes à Musique
Anna Joliet   Gifts, Souvenirs
(Map p100; www.boitesamusique-paris.com; Passage du Perron, 1er; M Pyramides) This wonderful shop at the northern end of the Jardin du Palais Royal special-ises in music boxes, new and old, from Switzerland.

🏃 Sports & Activities

Young, fun-charged company **Ô Chateau** (p114) offers the full range of tastings and experiences in a 17th-century vaulted stone cellar near the Louvre. Tastings start from €30 for one hour (three wines) through to grands crus master classes (€120); there are also lunches, dinners, champagne cruises and excursions.

Les Coulisses du Chef   Cooking
(Map p100; ✆ 01 40 26 14 00; www.coursde cuisineparis.com; 2nd fl, 7 rue Paul Lelong, 2e; M Bourse) Popular courses for beginners. three-hour courses (€100) often special-ise in a theme such as sauces or soufflés. Classes for children aged seven and up cost €30.

Montmartre & Northern Paris

A wellspring of Parisian myth, Montmartre has always stood apart. From its days as a simple village on the hill to its place at the centre of the bohemian lifestyle immortalised by Toulouse-Lautrec and other artists in the late 19th and early 20th centuries, the area has repeatedly woven itself into the city's collective imagination.

Today, of course, the area thrives on busloads of tourists, who come to climb the cascading steps up to Sacré-Cœur and wander through the alluring narrow hillside lanes. But even with the all the souvenir kitsch and milling crowds, it's hard not to appreciate the views looking out over Paris, or to find some romance relaxing in a backstreet cafe.

Back down at the foot of the hill is the rough-and-ready charm of the city's red-light district, a mix of erotica shops, striptease parlours, trendy nightspots and cabarets. If you take the time to wander, you'll find some unusual, less-touristy areas.

The Moulin Rouge (p136)
COURTESY OF MOULIN ROUGE®

Montmartre & Northern Paris Highlights

Sacré-Cœur (p124)

Once you've climbed the Butte de Montmartre (Montmartre Hill) and then the terraced ste of this very Parisian icon, climb a further 234 spiralling steps up inside the main dome – on clear day, the view from the top is spectacular. Inside the basilica, the glittering mosaics an chapel-lined crypt illuminated by flickering candles also merit a look.

Parc de la Vilette (p128)

Catch a performance at the Parc de la Villette, the city's largest cultural playground. Events span world, rock and classical music concerts, art exhibits outdoor cinema, circuses and mode dance, while venues include the wonderful old Grande Halle (formerl a slaughterhouse – the Parisian catt market was located here from 1867 to 1974) and giant yurt-like Cabaret Sauvage.

OLIVIER CIRENDINI/GETTY IMAGES ©

Musée Jacquemart-André (p127)

Step back into 19th-century opulence at this elegant residence-turned-museum. In addition to the exquisite furnishings and artworks, don't miss the Jardin d'Hiver (Winter Garden), with its marble statuary, tropical plants and double-helix staircase; the delightful *fumoir* (the erstwhile smoking room) filled with exotic objects; and the *salon de thé* (tearoom) – one of the most beautiful in the city.

MASSIMO LISTRI/CORBIS ©

CREDIT: JONATHAN SMITH/GETTY IMAGES ©

Basilique de St-Denis (p129)

For 1200 years the hallowed burial place of French royalty, St-Denis today is a vibrant multicultural suburb situated just a short metro ride north of Paris' 18e *arrondissement*. The ornate royal tombs, adorned with some truly remarkable sculptures, and the magnificent Basilique de St-Denis, whose construction dates from around 1136, are well worth the trip.

Cité des Sciences (p128)

If you only have time to visit one museum *en famille* (as a family), make it the Cité des Sciences. Here, kids from ages two and up can explore a variety of interactive exhibits including the brilliant Cité des Enfants' construction site, a TV studio, robots, and water-based physics experiments, all designed for children. Book sessions in advance to avoid grappling with gravely disappointed kids.

Montmartre & Northern Paris Walk

For centuries Montmartre was a country village filled with moulins (mills) that supplied Paris with flour. After it was incorporated into the capital in 1860, its picturesque charm and low rents attracted painters and writers, especially during its late 19th- and early 20th-century heyday.

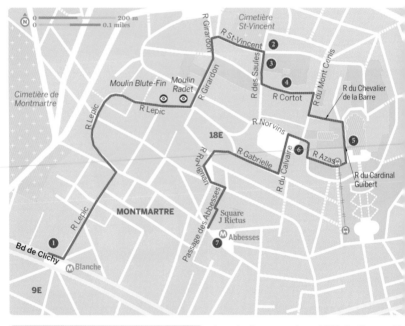

WALK FACTS

- **Start** Moulin Rouge
- **End** Metro Abbesses
- **Distance** 2.5km
- **Duration** Two hours

1 Moulin Rouge

Just west of rue Lepic you'll see the legendary **Moulin Rouge** (p136) cabaret beneath its trademark red windmill – it first opened as a dance hall in 1889. Uphill at 15 rue Lepic is **Café des Deux Moulins**, where Amélie worked in the eponymous film. Theo Van Gogh owned the house at **54 rue Lepic**; his brother, the artist Vincent, stayed here for two years from 1886. Further north two original windmills remain, the **Moulin Blute-Fin** and, about 100m east, the **Moulin Radet**. The Debray family, who owned both, turned them into a popular open-air dance hall Le Moulin de la Galette in the 19th century, which Renoir immortalised in his 1876 tableau *Le Bal du Moulin de la Galette* (displayed at the Musée d'Orsay).

2 Au Lapin Agile

Continue north into rue Girardon; descending the stairs you'll see **Cimetière St-Vincent**, the final resting place of artist Maurice Utrillo. Just over rue des Saules is the celebrated cabaret **Au Lapin Agile** (p136), whose name comes from *Le Lapin* *à Gill*, caricaturist André Gill's mural of a rabbit jumping out of a cooking pot on the western exterior wall.

③ Clos Montmartre

Opposite Au Lapin Agile is the **Clos Montmartre** vineyard, planted in 1933 to thwart real-estate development. Across rue des Saules is **La Maison Rose**, the famous subject of an Utrillo painting.

④ Musée de Montmartre

Turn left on rue Cortot; the **Musée de Montmartre** (p126) occupies Montmartre's oldest building, a 17th-century manor once home to painters Renoir, Utrillo and Raoul Dufy.

⑤ Sacré-Cœur

At the end of rue Cortot turn right (south) onto rue du Mont Cenis, left onto (tiny) rue de Chevalier de la Barre then right onto rue du Cardinal Guibert: the entrance to Paris' landmark basilica **Sacré-Cœur** (p124) is just south.

⑥ Place du Tertre

From the basilica follow rue Azaïs west, then turn north to the **Église St-Pierre de Montmartre**, built on the site of a Roman temple. Across from the church is the **place du Tertre** (p126). Cossack soldiers allegedly first introduced the term *bistro* (Russian for 'quickly') into French at No 6 (La Mère Catherine) in 1814. On Christmas Eve, 1898, Louis Renault's first car was driven up the Butte to Place du Tertre, marking the start of the French auto industry. Just off the southwestern side of the square is rue Poulbot, leading to the **Dalí Espace Montmartre** (p126).

⑦ Abbesses metro entrance

From place du Calvaire take the steps into rue Gabrielle, turning right (west) to reach place Émile Goudeau. Take the steps down and follow rue des Abbesses south into place des Abbesses. The glass-canopied **Abbesses metro entrance** is the finest remaining example designed by Hector Guimard.

⭐ The Best...

PLACES TO EAT

Vivant Where else will you get to dine in a century-old exotic bird shop? (p133)

Cul de Poule Countryside produce meets city savvy at this neobistro. (p129)

Le Verre Volé Idyllic wine bar dining. (p133)

Le Miroir Stylish, creative bistro fare. (p129)

PLACES TO DRINK

La Fourmi This Pigalle stalwart has a dynamic energy both day and night. (p135)

Chez Prune Canal St-Martin's original and still coolest cafe. (p135)

ENTERTAINMENT

Parc de la Villette A host of venues, both indoors and out. (p128)

Point Éphemère Ubercool cultural centre, club and performance venue. (p136)

Diners at Le Verre Volé (p133)
DIRECTPHOTO.ORG/ALAMY ©

☑

Don't Miss
Sacré-Cœur

Although some may poke fun at Sacré-Cœur's unsubtle design, the view from its parvis is one of those perfect Paris postcards. More than just a basilica, Sacré-Cœur is a veritable experience, from the musicians performing on the steps to the groups of friends picnicking on the hillside park. Touristy, yes. But beneath it all, the golden heart of Sacré-Cœur still shines.

Map p130

www.sacre-coeur
-montmartre.com

place du Parvis du
Sacré Cœur

Basilica dome
admission €5, cash
only

⊙6am-10.30pm,
dome 9am-7pm
Apr-Sep, to 5.30pm
Oct-Mar

Ⓜ Anvers

The Basilica

It may appear to be a place of peacefulness and worship today, but in truth Sacré-Cœur's foundations were laid amid bloodshed and controversy. Its construction began in 1876, in the wake of France's humiliating defeat to Prussia and the chaotic Paris Commune, when workers overthrew the reactionary government and took over the city. The resulting battle for control was essentially a civil war, ending with mass executions, exiles and rampant destruction.

In this context, the construction of an enormous basilica to expiate the city's sins seemed like a gesture of peace and forgiveness – indeed, the seven million French francs needed to construct the church came solely from the contributions of local Catholics. Unfortunately, the Montmartre location was no coincidence: the conservative old guard desperately wanted to assert their power in what was then a hotbed of revolution. The battle between the two camps – Catholic versus secular, royalists versus republican – raged on, and it wasn't until 1919 that Sacré-Cœur was finally consecrated, even then standing in utter contrast to the bohemian lifestyle that surrounded it.

While criticism of its design and white travertine stone has continued throughout the decades (one poet called it a giant baby's bottle for angels), the interior is enlivened by the glittering apse mosaic *Christ in Majesty*, designed by Luc-Olivier Merson in 1922 and one of the largest in the world.

The Dome

Outside, some 234 spiralling steps lead you to the basilica's dome, which affords one of Paris' most spectacular panoramas; they say you can see for 30km on a clear day. Weighing in at 19 tonnes, the bell called La Savoyarde in the tower above is the largest in France. The chapel-lined crypt, visited in conjunction with the dome, is huge but not very interesting.

You can avoid some of the climb up to the basilica with the short but useful **funicular railway** or the **tourist train**, which leaves from place Blanche.

A Place of Pilgrimage

In a sense, atonement here has never stopped: a prayer 'cycle' that began in 1835 before the basilica's completion still continues round the clock, with perpetual adoration of the Blessed Sacrament continually on display above the high altar. The basilica's travertine stone exudes calcite, ensuring it remains white despite weathering and pollution.

WWII

In 1944, 13 Allied bombs were dropped on Montmartre, falling just next to Sacré-Cœur. Although the stained glass windows all shattered from the force of the explosions, miraculously no one died and the basilica sustained no other damage.

Discover Montmartre & Northern Paris

Getting There & Away

● **Metro** Lines 2 and 12 serve Montmartre; lines 5 and 7 serve northeastern Paris (Canal St-Martin and La Villette). Further west, the museums in Clichy are acccessed via line 2.

● **RER** RER B links the Gare du Nord with central Paris.

 Sights

Montmartre & Pigalle

Place du Tertre City Square
(Map p130; **M**Abbesses) It would be hard to miss the place du Tertre, one of the most touristy spots in all of Paris. Although today it's filled with visitors, buskers and portrait artists, it was originally the main square of the village of Montmartre before it was incorporated into the city proper.

Musée de Montmartre History Museum
(Map p130; www.museedemontmartre.fr; 12 rue Cortot, 18e; adult/18-25yr/10-17yr €8/6/4; ☉10am-6pm; **M**Lamarck–Caulaincourt) The Montmartre Museum displays paintings, lithographs and documents mostly relating to the area's rebellious and bohemian past. There's an excellent bookshop here that sells small bottles of the wine produced from grapes grown in the **Clos Montmartre** (Map p130; 18 rue des Saules, 18e).

Dalí Espace Montmartre Art Museum
(Map p130; www.daliparis.com; 11 rue Poulbot; adult/senior/8-25yr €11/7/6; ☉10am-6pm, to 8pm Jul & Aug; **M**Abbesses) More than 300 works by Salvador Dalí (1904–89), the flamboyant Catalan surrealist printmaker, painter, sculptor and self-promoter, are on display at this surrealist style basement museum located just west of place du Tertre. The collection includes Dalí's strange sculptures (most in reproduction), lithographs, many of his illustrations and furniture, including the famous Mae West lips sofa.

Cimetière de Montmartre
YVES TALENSAC/GETTY IMAGES ©

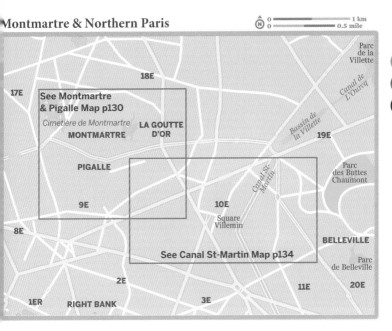

FREE **Musée de la Vie
Romantique** Museum

(Map p130; www.vie-romantique.paris.fr; 16 rue
Chaptal, 9e; permanent collections free; ⏰10am-
6pm Tue-Sun; Ⓜ Blanche or St-Georges) This
small museum is dedicated to two artists
active during the Romantic era: the writer
George Sand and the painter Ary Scheffer.
Located at the end of a film-worthy cobbled lane, the villa housing the museum
originally belonged to Scheffer and was
the setting for popular salons of the day,
attended by such notable figures as Delacroix, Liszt and Chopin (Sand's lover).

FREE **Cimetière de
Montmartre** Cemetery

(Map p130; admission free; ⏰8am-5.30pm Mon-
ri, from 8.30am Sat, from 9am Sun; Ⓜ Place de
Clichy) Established in 1798, this 11-hectare
cemetery is perhaps the most celebrated
necropolis in Paris after Père Lachaise. It
contains the graves of writers Émile Zola
(whose ashes are now in the Panthéon),
Alexandre Dumas, *fils* (son) and Stend-
hal, composers Jacques Offenbach and

Hector Berlioz, artist Edgar Degas, film
director François Truffaut and dancer
Vaslav Nijinsky, among others.

Maps showing the location of the
tombs are available free from the
conservation office (20 av Rachel) at the
cemetery's entrance.

**Musée
Jacquemart-André** Art Museum

(☎01 45 62 11 59; www.musee-jacquemart
-andre.com; 158 bd Haussmann; adult/7-17yr
€11/9.50; ⏰10am-6pm, to 9.30pm Mon & Sat
during temporary exhibits; Ⓜ Miromesnil) If you
belonged to the cream of Parisian society
in the late 19th century, the chances are
you would have been invited to one of
the dazzling soirées held at this 16-room
mansion. The home of art collectors
Nélie Jacquemart and Édouard André,
this opulent residence was designed in
the then-fashionable eclectic style, which
combined elements from different eras –
seen here in the presence of Greek and
Roman antiquities, Egyptian artefacts,
period furnishings and portraits by Dutch
masters.

127

WALTER BIBIKOW/GETTY IMAGES ©

☑ Don't Miss
Parc de la Villette

The largest park in Paris, the Parc de la Villette is a cultural centre, kids' playground and landscaped urban space all rolled into one. The French love of geometric forms defines the layout – including the colossal mirror-like sphere of the Géode cinema and the bright-red cubical pavilions known as folies – but it's intersection of two canals, the Ourcq and the St-Denis, that brings the most natural and popular element: water. Although it is a fair hike from central Paris, consider a trip here to catch for a performance or event, or if you have children.

Many of the themed gardens double as playgrounds, including the Jardin du Dragon (Dragon Garden), with an enormous dragon slide, the Jardin des Dunes (Dunes Garden) and Jardin des Miroirs (Mirror Garden). However, for young ones, the star attraction is the **Cité des Sciences** (p128) and its attached cinemas.

An information centre is at the park's southern edge; pick up a map here so you can get your bearings.

NEED TO KNOW

www.villette.com; Ⓜ Porte de la Villette or Porte de Pantin

Gare du Nord & Canal St-Martin

Cité des Sciences Science Museum
(☏ 01 40 05 12 12; www.cite-sciences.fr; Parc de la Villette; adult/under 26yr €8/6; ⏰ 10am-6pm Tue-Sat, to 7pm Sun; Ⓜ Porte de la Villette)

This is the city's top museum for kids, with three floors of hands-on exhibits for children aged two and up, plus two special-effects cinemas, a planetarium and a retired submarine. The only drawback is that each exhibit has a separate admission fee (though some combined

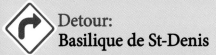

Detour:
Basilique de St-Denis

Once one of the most sacred sites in the country, the **Basilique de St-Denis** (www.monuments-nationaux.fr; 1 rue de la Légion d'Honneur; tombs adult/senior & 18-25yr €7.50/4.50, basilica free; ⏱10am-6.15pm Mon-Sat, noon-6.15pm Sun Apr-Sep, to 5.15pm Oct-Mar; Ⓜ Basilique de St-Denis (line 13)) was built atop the tomb of St Denis, the 3rd-century martyr and legendary 1st bishop of Paris who was beheaded by Roman priests. A popular pilgrimage site, by the sixth century it had become the royal necropolis: all but a handful of France's kings and queens from Dagobert I (r 629–39) to Louis XVIII (r 1814–24) were buried here (today it holds the remains of 42 kings and 32 queens).

The tombs in the crypt are the real reason to make the trip out here, however. Adorned with *gisants* (recumbent figures), those made after 1285 were carved from death masks and are thus fairly lifelike; earlier sculptures are depictions of how earlier rulers might have looked.

tickets do exist), so you'll have to do some pretrip research in order to figure out what's most appropriate.

Canal St-Martin Park
(Map p134; Ⓜ République, Jaurès, Jacques Bonsergent) The tranquil, 4.5km-long Canal St-Martin was inaugurated in 1825 to provide a shipping link between the Seine and the northeastern Parisian suburbs. Emerging from below ground near place République, its shaded towpaths take you past locks, metal bridges and ordinary Parisian neighbourhoods. It's a great place for a romantic stroll or cycle.

Companies offering 2½-hour canal cruises include **Canauxrama** (☎01 42 39 15 00; www.canauxrama.com; adult/student & senior/4-12yr €16/12/8.50), which has departures at 9.45am and 2.30pm from the Port de l'Arsenal at the Bastille and Parc de la Villette. There are also evening cruises on Fridays and Saturdays in July and August.

Eating

Montmartre & Pigalle

Le Miroir Bistro €€
(Map p130; ☎01 46 06 50 73; 94 rue des Martyrs, 18e; lunch menus €18, dinner menus €25-40;

⏱lunch Tue-Sun, dinner Tue-Sat; Ⓜ Abbesses) This unassuming modern bistro is smack in the middle of the Montmartre tourist trail, yet it remains a local favourite. There are lots of delightful pâtés and rillettes to start off with – guinea hen with dates, duck with mushrooms, haddock and lemon – followed by well-prepared standards like stuffed veal shoulder.

Le Pantruche Bistro €€
(Map p130; ☎01 48 78 55 60; www.lepantruche. com; 3 rue Victor Masse, 9e; lunch/dinner menus €17/32; ⏱Mon-Fri; Ⓜ Pigalle) Named after a nearby 19th-century theatre, classy Pantruche has been making waves in the already crowded dining hotspot of South Pigalle. It's no surprise, then, that it hits all the right notes: seasonal bistro fare, reasonable prices and an intimate setting. The menu runs from classics (steak with béarnaise sauce) to more daring creations (scallops served in a parmesan broth with cauliflower mousseline).

Cul de Poule Modern French €€
(Map p130; ☎01 53 16 13 07; 53 rue des Martyrs, 9e; 2-/3-course menus lunch €15/18, dinner €23/28; ⏱closed Sun lunch; Ⓜ Pigalle) With plastic orange cafeteria seats outside, you probably wouldn't wander into the Cul de Poule by accident. But the light-hearted spirit (yes, there is a mounted chicken's

Montmartre & Pigalle

R Etex

R Eugène Carrière

R Félix Ziem

R Steinlen

R Joseph de Maistre

R Tourlaque

R Juste Métivier

Pl Constantin Pecqueur

M Lamarck Caulaincourt

Cimetière St-Vincent

R St-Vincent

R des Saules

19

2

R Simon Dereure

Sq Suzanne Buisson

R de l'Abreuvoir

5

R Cortot

Av Junot

Giradon

R Norvins

Syndicate d'Initiative de Montmartre

1

Cimetière de Montmartre Entrance & Conservation Office

R Lepic

11

R Durantin

R Tholozé

R d'Orchampt

Pl du Calvaire

3

R Cavalotti

R Joseph de Maistre

MONTMARTRE

R Burq

Pl Émile Goudeau

R Gabrielle

R Berthe

16

R des Abbesses

10

R Constant

R Durantin

R des Trois Frères

R Cauchois

12

R Audran

R Ravignan

R Dreve?

Bd de Clichy

Cité Véron

R Lepic

R Coustou

R Véron

Pl des Abbesses

M Abbesses

17

R des Abbesses

13

21

R Puget

Villa des Platanes

8

R Germain Pilon

R d'Orse

M Place de Clichy

R Pierre Haret

R de Bruxelles

M Blanche

PIGALLE

Villa de Guelma

R André Antoine

R Houdon

R des Martyrs

R André Gill

R de Bruxelles

R de Douai

Bd de Clichy

18

R de Vintimille

R de Calais

R Blanche

R Mansart

R Pierre Fontaine

R Fromentin

R Duperré

M Pigalle

R Ballu

R Alfred Stevens

R des Martyrs

R Cardinal Mercier

R Chaptal

4

20

R Jean Baptiste Pigalle

R Frochot

R Victor Massé

14

R Escudier

R Henner

Cité Pigalle

R Henry Monnier

9

R de Liège

R la Bruyère

R Navarin

7

R de Clichy

R de la Rochefoucauld

R Clauzel

R des Martyrs

R Moncey

R Milton

R de Milan

R Laferrière

R Manuel

R d'Athènes

St-Georges M

R d'Aumale

9E

R de Londres

R de la Tour des Dames

R St-Georges

Cité de Londres

Sq d'Estienne d'Orves

M Trinité

R Taitbout

R St-Lazare

R Fléchier

R St-Lazare

Pl d'Estienne d'Orves

R de Châteaudun

Notre Dame de Lorette M

Pl Kossuth

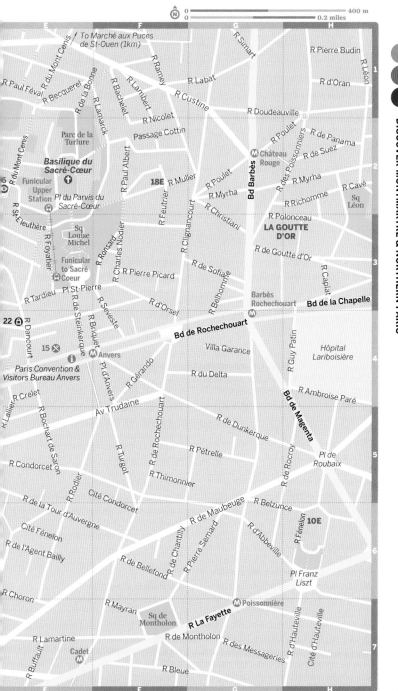

To Marché aux Puces
de St-Ouen (1km)

R Simart

R Pierre Budin

R Léon

R d'Oran

R du Mont Cenis

R Paul Féval

R Becquerel

R de la Bonne

R Bachelet

R Ramey

R Lambert

R Labat

R Custine

R Nicolet

R Doudeauville

Passage Cottin

R de Panama

R Poulet

R de Suez

R des Poissonniers

Château
Rouge

Bd Barbès

R Myrha

R Cavé

Parc de la
Turlure

R Lamarck

R du Mont Cenis

Basilique du
Sacré-Cœur

Funicular
Upper
Station

R St-Eleuthère

R Paul Albert

18E

R Muller

R Poulet

R Myrha

R Richomme

Sq
Léon

Pl du Parvis du
Sacré-Cœur

R Feutrier

R Christiani

R Polonceau

LA GOUTTE
D'OR

Sq
Louise
Michel

R Ronsard

R Charles Nodier

R Clignancourt

R de Goutte d'Or

R Caplat

Funicular
to Sacré
Cœur

R Pierre Picard

R de Sofia

R Feyatier

R Tardieu

Pl St-Pierre

R Séveste

R d'Orsel

R Belhomme

Barbès
Rochechouart

Bd de la Chapelle

22

R Dancourt

R de Steinkerque

R Briquet

Bd de Rochechouart

Villa Garance

R Guy Patin

Hôpital
Lariboisière

15

Anvers

Pl d'Anvers

Paris Convention &
Visitors Bureau Anvers

R Gérando

R du Delta

R Lallier

R Crelet

Av Trudaine

R Ambroise Paré

R Bochart de Saron

R de Rochechouart

R de Dunkerque

Bd de Magenta

Pl de
Roubaix

R Condorcet

R Turgot

R Pétrelle

R de Rocroy

R Rodier

R Thimonnier

R de la Tour d'Auvergne

Cité Condorcet

R Belzunce

10E

R Fénelon

Cité Fénelon

R de Chantilly

R de Maubeuge

R d'Abbeville

R de l'Agent Bailly

R Pierre Semard

R de Bellefond

Pl Franz
Liszt

R Choron

R Mayran

Poissonnière

R La Fayette

R Lamartine

Sq de
Montholon

R de Montholon

R des Messageries

R d'Hauteville

Cité d'Hauteville

R Buffault

Cadet

R Bleue

Montmartre & Pigalle

derrière on the wall) is deceiving; this is one of the best and most affordable kitchens in the Pigalle neighbourhood, with excellent neobistro fare that emphasises quality ingredients from the French countryside.

Le Petit Trianon   Cafe €

(Map p130; ☎ 01 44 92 78 08; www.trianoncafe. fr; 80 boulevard Rochechouart, 18e; lunch menu €13.20, mains €6.50-17.90; ⏱10am-2pm; Ⓜ Anvers) With its large windows and a few carefully chosen antiques, this recently revived belle époque cafe at the foot of Montmartre feels about as timeless as the Butte itself. Dating back to 1894 and attached to the century-old Le Trianon theatre, it's no stretch to imagine artists like Toulouse-Lautrec and crowds of show-goers once filling the place in the evening.

La Mascotte   Seafood, Cafe €€

(Map p130; ☎ 01 46 06 28 15; www.la-mascotte -montmartre.com; 52 rue des Abbesses, 18e; lunch/dinner menus €25/41; ⏱7am-midnight; Ⓜ Abbesses) Founded in 1889, this unassuming bar is about as authentic as it gets in Montmartre. It specialises in quality seafood – oysters, lobster, scallops – and regional dishes (Auvergne sausage), but you can also pull up a seat at the bar for a simple glass of wine and a plate of charcuterie.

Le Coq Rico   Poultry €€€

(Map p130; ☎ 01 42 59 82 89; www.lecoqrico. com; 98 rue Lepic, 18e; mains €20-38, whole roast chicken €95; ⏱7am-8.30pm Wed-Mon; Ⓜ Abbesses) The first *haute cuisine* restaurant to open in Montmartre in years, Le Coq Rico specialises in poultry – and not just any poultry, but red-ribbon birds that have been raised in luxurious five-star chicken coops.

A selection of eggs, gizzards, bouillons foie gras ravioli and other delicacies whet the appetite before the arrival of the pièce de résistance: an entire just-roasted chicken or guineafowl, which can be split up to four ways.

Arnaud Delmontel   Boulangerie €

(Map p130; 39 rue des Martyrs, 9e; ⏱7am-8.30pm Wed-Mon; Ⓜ Pigalle) One of several Montmartre bakeries to win Paris' 'best baguette' prize in the past decade, Delmontel specialises in gorgeous pastries, cakes and a variety of artisanal breads.

Le Relais Gascon   Southwest €€

(Map p130; ☎ 01 42 58 58 22; www.lerelaisgas con.fr; 6 rue des Abbesses, 18e; mains €12-15.50 menu €25.50; ⏱10am-2am daily; Ⓜ Abbesses) Situated just a short stroll from the place des Abbesses, the Relais Gascon has a relaxed atmosphere and authentic regional cuisine at very reasonable prices. The giant salads and *confit de* canard will satisfy big eaters, while the traditional *cassoulet* and *tartiflette* are equally delicious.

Another **branch** (Map p130; ☎ 01 42 52 41 11; 13 rue Joseph de Maistre) is just down the street. No credit cards at the main restaurant.

Chez Toinette French €€

(Map p130; ☎ 01 42 54 44 36; 20 rue Germain Pilon, 18e; mains €16-25; ☺ dinner Mon-Sat; Ⓜ Abbesses) The atmosphere of this convivial restaurant is rivalled only by its fine cuisine. In the heart of one of the capital's most touristy neighbourhoods, Chez Toinette has kept alive the tradition of old Montmartre with its simplicity and culinary expertise.

Gare du Nord & Canal St-Martin

Le Verre Volé Wine Bar €

(Map p134; ☎ 01 48 03 17 34; 67 rue de Lancry, 10e; mains €13-16; ☺ lunch & dinner; Ⓜ Jacques Bonsergent) The tiny 'Stolen Glass' – a wine shop with a few tables – is just about the most perfect wine-bar-cum-restaurant in Paris, with excellent wines and expert advice. Unpretentious and hearty *plats du jour* (dishes of the day) are excellent. Reserve well in advance for meals, or stop by just for a tasting.

L'Office Modern French €€

(Map p134; ☎ 01 47 70 67 31; 3 rue Richer, 9e; lunch menus €19-24, dinner menus €27-33; ☺ Mon-Fri; Ⓜ Poissonière or Bonne Nouvelle) Straddling the east–west Paris divide, L'Office is off the beaten track but unusual enough to merit a detour for those serious about their food. The market-inspired menu is mercifully short – as in there are only two choices for lunch – but outstanding. Don't judge this one by the menu; the simple chalkboard descriptions ('beef/polenta') belie the rich and complex flavours emerging from the kitchen.

Vivant Modern French €€€

(Map p134; ☎ 01 42 46 43 55; www.morethanorganic.com; 43 rue des Petites Écuries, 10e; mains €21-28; ☺ Mon-Fri; Ⓜ Bonne Nouvelle) Simple but elegant dishes – creamy burratta, crispy duck leg with mashed potatoes, foie gras and roasted onion, an Italian cheese

Hotel du Nord (p136), Canal St-Martin

133

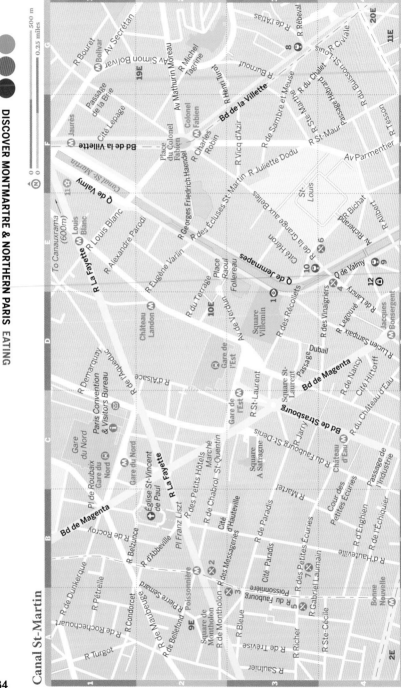

Canal St-Martin

Canal St-Martin

olate – are created to showcase the carefully sourced ingredients.

Pink Flamingo
Pizza €

(Map p134; ☎ 01 42 02 31 70; www.pinkflamingo pizza.com; 67 rue Bichat, 10e; pizzas €10.50-16; ☺ lunch Tue-Sun, dinner daily; Ⓜ Jacques Bonsergent) Not another pizza place? *Mais non, chérie!* Once the weather warms up, the Flamingo unveils its secret weapon – pink helium balloons that the delivery guy uses to locate you and your perfect canal-side picnic spot (GPS not needed). Order a Poulidor (duck, apple and chèvre) or a Basquiat (gorgonzola, figs and cured ham), pop into **Le Verre Volé** (p133) across the canal for the perfect bottle of vino and you're set.

There's also a **Marais branch** (Map p150; ☎ 01 42 71 28 20 ; www.pink flamingopizza.com; 105 rue Vieille du Temple, 3e; pizzas €10.50-16; ☺ noon-3pm & 7-11.30pm; Ⓜ St-Sébastien-Froissart).

Le Grenier à Pain
Boulangerie €

(Map p134; 91 rue Faubourg Poissonnière, 9e; ☺ 8am-8pm Thu-Tue, to 1.30pm Sun; Ⓜ Poissonnière) Michel Galloyer founded this string of artisan bakeries, which also includes an award-winning **branch** (Map p130; 38 rue

des Abbesses, 18e; ☺ 7.30am-8pm Thu-Mon; Ⓜ Abbesses) in Montmartre.

Albion
Wine Bar €€

(Map p134; ☎ 01 42 46 02 44; 80 rue du Faubourg Poissonnière, 10e; mains €17-21; ☺ lunch Tue-Fri, dinner Tue-Sat; Ⓜ Poissonnière) Albion is the ancient Greek name for England and it's no coincidence that it's a mere five-minute jaunt from the Gare du Nord, and, what's more, run by two affable English speakers. But don't read too much into the name: this sleek new place is still very Paris, with bottles of wine lining one wall, waiting to be paired with the modern cuisine.

◎ Drinking & Nightlife

Montmartre & Pigalle

La Fourmi
Bar, Cafe

(Map p130; 74 rue des Martyrs, 18e; ☺ 8am-1am Mon-Thu, to 3am Fri & Sat, 10am-1am Sun; Ⓜ Pigalle) A Pigalle institution, La Fourmi hits the mark with its high ceilings, long zinc bar and unpretentious vibe. Get up to speed on live music and club nights or sit down for a reasonably priced meal and drinks.

Gare du Nord & Canal St-Martin

Chez Prune
Bar, Cafe

(Map p134; 71 quai de Valmy, 10e; ☺ 8am-2am Mon-Sat, 10am-2am Sun; Ⓜ République) This Soho-boho cafe put Canal St-Martin on the map a decade ago and its good vibes and rough-around-the-edges look show no sign of fading in the near future.

Café Chéri(e)
Bar, Cafe

(Map p134; 44 bd de la Villette, 19e; ☺ noon-1am; Ⓜ Belleville) An imaginative, colourful bar with its signature red lighting, infamous mojitos and caipirinhas and commitment to quality tunes, Chéri(e) is everyone's darling in this part of town. Gritty art-chic crowd and electro DJs Thursday to Saturday.

Hôtel du Nord
Bar, Cafe

(Map p134; www.hoteldunord.org; 102 quai de Jemmapes, 10e; ⏰9am-2.30am; 🛜 🚹; Ⓜ Jacques Bonsergent) The setting for the eponymous 1938 film starring Louis Jouvet and Arletty, the interior of this vintage cafe feels as if it was stuck in a time warp with its zinc counter, red velvet curtains and old piano.

⭐ Entertainment

Montmartre & Pigalle

Moulin Rouge
Cabaret

(Map p130; 📞 01 53 09 82 82; www.moulinrouge.fr; 82 bd de Clichy, 18e; Ⓜ Blanche) Immortalised in the posters of Toulouse-Lautrec and later on screen by Baz Luhrmann, the Moulin Rouge twinkles beneath a 1925 replica of its original red windmill. Yes, it's rife with bus-tour crowds. But from the opening bars of music to the last high kick it's a whirl of fantastical costumes, sets, choreography and champagne. Bookings advised.

Au Lapin Agile
Cabaret

(Map p130; 📞 01 46 06 85 87; www.au-lapin-agile.com; 22 rue des Saules, 18e; adult €24, student except Sat €17; ⏰9pm-1am Tue-Sun; Ⓜ Lamarck-Caulaincourt) This rustic cabaret venue was favoured by artists and intellectuals in the early 20th century and traditional *chansons* are still performed here. The four-hour show starts at 9.30pm and includes singing and poetry.

Bus Palladium
Nightclub

(Map p130; www.lebuspalladium.com; 6 rue Pierre Fontaine, 9e; ⏰11pm-5am Tue, Fri & Sat; Ⓜ Blanche) Once the place to be back in the 1960s, the Bus is now back in business 50 years later, with funky DJs and a mixed bag of performances by indie and pop groups.

Gare du Nord & Canal St-Martin

Point Éphémère
Live Music

(Map p134; www.pointephemere.org; 200 quai de Valmy, 10e; ⏰noon-2am Mon-Sat, noon-10pm Sun; 🛜; Ⓜ Louis Blanc) This arts and music venue by the Canal St-Martin attracts an underground crowd from noon till past midnight, for drinks, meals, concerts, dance nights and even art exhibitions.

Bread and Wine by the Gare du Nord

Yes, restaurant owners and chefs go out to eat, too. Charles Compagnon, owner of **L'Office** (p133), filled us in on his staff's top dining picks in Paris' burgeoning culinary hotspot, the 10e arrondissement.

○ **Le Grenier à Pain** (p135) They bake the bread we serve at L'Office. We really like *le pain de trois*, which is a kind of country bread that's made with three different types of flour. We also recommend their *gâteau basque* (a small round pastry filled with sweet almond paste).

○ **Vivant** (p133) This is a great restaurant. The quality of the products is simply outstanding and the atmosphere is really *charmant*. It's located in an old *oisellerie* (a place where exotic birds were raised and sold); the original faience tiling is still on the walls.

○ **Albion** (p135) We really like this restaurant because of the quality of the cooking and the diverse wine selection.

Detour:
Marché aux Puces de St-Ouen

A vast flea market, the **Marché aux Puces de St-Ouen** (www.marcheauxpuces saintouen.com; rue des Rosiers, av Michelet, rue Voltaire, rue Paul Bert & rue Jean-Henri Fabre; ⏱9am-6pm Sat, 10am-6pm Sun, 11am-5pm Mon; Ⓜ Porte de Clignancourt) was founded in the late 19th century. It's said to be Europe's largest market, and has more than 2500 stalls grouped into a dozen *marchés* (market areas), each with its own speciality (eg Paul Bert for 17th-century furniture, Malik for clothing, Biron for Asian art). There are miles upon miles of 'freelance' stalls; come prepared to spend some time.

🛍 Shopping

Rue Lepic, 18e, is lined with food shops.

La Citadelle   Fashion, Accessories
(Map p130; 1 rue des Trois Frères, 18e; ⏱11am-8pm Mon-Sat, to 7pm Sun; Ⓜ Abbesses) This designer discount shop hidden away in Montmartre has some real finds from new French, Italian and Japanese designers.

Maje   Fashion, Accessories
(Map p134; 6 rue de Marseille, 10e; ⏱11am-8pm Mon-Sat, 1.30-7.30pm Sun; Ⓜ Jacques Bonsergent) A Parisian prêt-à-porter brand featured regularly on the pages of *Elle*, *Glamour* and *Marie Claire*, Maje doesn't come cheaply – that is, unless you know about this outlet store, which sells most items at a 30% discount.

Le Marais & Bastille

Hip bars, boutiques, restaurants and the city's thriving gay and Jewish communities all squeeze cheek-by-jowl into this vibrant patch.

Paris' *marais* (marsh) was cleared in the 12th century, with grand aristocratic mansions built here from the 16th century onwards. Haussmann's reformations largely bypassed the area, leaving its tangle of medieval laneways intact. After falling from grace, the Marais underwent a revitalisation in the 1960s that hasn't stopped since, and it remains a see-and-be seen spot for a *soirée* (evening out) on the town.

The adjoining Bastille was a flashpoint for the French Revolution and is still the focal point of Paris' not-infrequent political protests. This longtime grassroots district now continues to boom alongside its intertwined neighbour as a pumping party hub. Above the Bastille, the raised Promenade Plantée walkway provides a peaceful retreat from the urban action.

Village St-Paul (p171)

139

Le Marais & Bastille Highlights

Musée Carnavalet (p153)

Take an elegant walk through the history of Paris, from prehistory to modern times, at the city's atmospheric Musée Carnavalet. It is secreted inside a twinset of richly furnished 16th and 17th-century *hôtels particuliers* (private mansions): the mid-16th-century Renaissance style Hôtel Carnavalet, home to the letter-writer Madame de Sévigné from 1677 to 1696, an the Hôtel Le Peletier de St-Fargeau, which dates from the late 17th century.

Opéra Bastille (p152)

Although not as visually spectacular or palatial as the Palais Garnier, this opera house is the main opera venue in the capital. It features a 2700-seat auditorium with perfect acoustics and hosts some of the most ambitious opera productions in the city. Designed by the Uruguayan architect Carlos Ott it was inaugurated on 14 July 1989, the 200th anniversary of the storming of th Bastille.

ART ON FILE/CORBIS ©

Place des Vosges (p146)

No square thrills Paris-hungry souls more than Place des Vosges, a triumph of symmetry and understated *bon goût* (good taste). Inaugurated in 1612 as place Royale and thus the oldest square in Paris, place des Vosges is a strikingly elegant ensemble of 36 symmetrical houses with ground-floor arcades, steep slate roofs and large dormer windows arranged around a large and leafy square.

Cimetière du Père Lachaise (p144)

Pay your respects to the rich, famous and infamous at Cimetière du Père Lachaise. Gravestones in the world's most opulent cemetery read like a Who's Who of French history and the arts: some 800,000 deceased call this enormous necropolis home, including urchin sparrow Édith Piaf, rock legend Jim Morrison, writer Oscar Wilde and painter Eugene Delacroix.

Hôtel de Ville (p146)

Enjoy Paris for free with an art exhibition incorporating a Parisian theme inside the city's magnificent neo-Renaissance Hôtel de Ville. Paris' town hall rises from one of the city's busiest and best shopping thoroughfares, the rue de Rivoli. During winter, you can twirl on the ice at the open-air skating rink that sets up outside; summer often sees concerts and other events take place here. Hall of Feasts

Le Marais & Bastille Walk

Although the Marais district might be best known today for its hip shopping, dining and nightlife, this walk also takes you past many of the hôtels particuliers *(private mansions) so characteristic of this neighbourhood, which are among the most beautiful Renaissance structures in the city.*

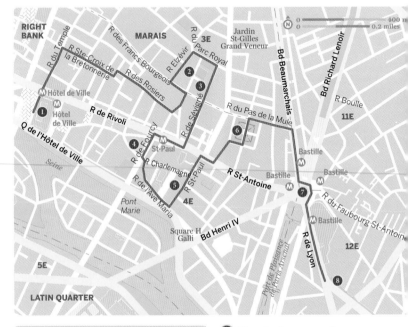

WALK FACTS

- **Start** Hôtel de Ville
- **Finish** Promenade Plantée
- **Distance** 4km
- **Duration** Two hours

① Hôtel de Ville

If Paris' statue-adorned, neo-Renaissance **Hôtel de Ville** (p146) looks familiar, it may be because photographer Robert Doisneau snapped his world-famous black-and-white portrait *Le baiser de l'hôtel de ville* (The Kiss at the Hôtel de Ville) here in 1950.

② Musée Cognacq-Jay

Cross rue de Rivoli and walk up rue du Temple. Turn right at rue Ste-Croix de la Bretonnerie into the heart of the medieval Marais. Take a left on rue Vielle du Temple and right onto rue des Roisiers, in the **Pletzl**, and join the queue at **L'As du Felafel** (p159). Continue left on rue Pavée, left on rue des Francs Bourgeois and right on rue Elzévir to reach the **Musée Cognacq-Jay** (p147) a exquisite collection of 18th-century art.

③ Musée Carnavalet

Turn right on rue du Parc Royal (**Hôtel de Vigny** at No 10 and **Hôtel Duret de Chevry** at No 8 date from around 1620). Past square Léopold Achille, turn right again on rue de

Sévigné where Paris' impressive, history museum the **Musée Carnavalet** (p153) is set back behind manicured gardens.

④ Maison Européenne de la Photographie

Continue south until turning right rue de Rivoli and left on rue de Fourcy. Despite the striking contemporary entrance to the European photography centre, the **Maison Européenne de la Photographie** (p147), the building dates from the early 18th century.

⑤ Village St-Paul

Turn left on rue Charlemagne, right into rue du Figuier and continue on to rue St-Paul. Past the quaint magic museum, the **Musée de la Magie** (p148), is the entrance to **Village St-Paul** (p171): five cobbled courtyards dotted with tiny boutiques.

⑥ Place des Vosges

The stone cloisters of this 1612-built ensemble of mansions (one of which houses the **Maison de Victor Hugo** (p146)) resonate with busking violinists and cellists, who provide an atmospheric soundtrack for browsing the arcaded galleries. In the centre of **place des Vosges** (p146)you'll see au pairs playing with their charges in the little gated park.

⑦ Place de la Bastille

Take rue du Pas de la Mule, passing the astonishing displays in the window of **Chocolaterie Joséphine Vannier** (p169) (such as chocolate shoes that look good enough to wear and far too good to eat), then turn right on bd Beaumarchais down to the historic site turned skirmishly busy roundabout at **place de la Bastille** (p149).

⑧ Promenade Plantée

Cross to rue de Lyon (the the monolithic opera house **Opéra Bastille** (p152) is on your left) and follow it to the stairs leading to the **Promenade Plantée** (p152)– a disused 19th-century railway viaduct now planted with a fragrant profusion of cherry trees, maples, rose bushes and lavender, which stretches above the **Viaduc des Arts** (p168).

⭐ The Best…

Le Pure Cafe (p161)
FERRUCCIO/ALAMY ©

Don't Miss
Cimetière du Père Lachaise

The world's most visited cemetery opened its one-way doors in 1804. Its 44 hectares entomb some 70,000 ornate, often ostentatious tombs, rendering a stroll here akin to exploring a verdant sculpture garden. Indeed Père Lachaise was intended as a park for Parisians – local neighbourhood graveyards were full and this was a ground-breaking project for Parisians to be buried outside the quartier in which they'd lived and died.

📞 01 43 70 70 33

www.pere-lachaise.com

16 rue du Repos & bd de Ménilmontant, 20e

admission free

🕐 8am-6pm Mon-Fri, from 8.30am Sat, from 9am Sun

Ⓜ Père Lachaise or Philippe Auguste

Jesuits Roots

Cimitière du Père Lachaise is named after Louis XIV's confessor, a Jesuit father known as Le Père La Chaise, who was resident on the estate where the cemetery is now located. The Jesuits bought the land in the 17th century but sold it a century later and in 1803 the land fell into city hands. Père Lachaise was built at the same time as cemeteries in Montmartre and Montparnasse, but Parisians, wary of entombing their dead so far from home, proved reluctant to purchase grave space here. It was only in 1817, after the remains of immortal 12th-century lovers Abélard and Héloïse were disinterred and reburied here beneath a neo-Gothic tombstone, that the cemetery really took off.

Famous Occupants

The only criteria to become a permanent resident of Cimitière du Père Lachaise was Paris residency; nationality did not matter, hence the cosmopolitan population of the city's most extravagant cemetery.

Among the 800,000 or so buried here include: the composer Chopin; the playwright Molière; the poet Apollinaire; writers Balzac, Proust, Gertrude Stein and Colette; the actors Simone Signoret, Sarah Bernhardt and Yves Montand; the painters Pissarro, Seurat, Modigliani and Delacroix; the *chanteuse* Édith Piaf alongside her two-year-old daughter; and the dancer Isadora Duncan.

Oscar Wilde

One of the most visited graves is that of Oscar Wilde (1854–1900), interred in division 89 in 1900. The flamboyant Irish playwright and humorist proclaimed on his deathbed in what is now L'Hôtel (p281): 'My wallpaper and I are fighting a duel to the death – one of us has *got* to go.'

Jim Morrison

The cemetery's other big hitter is 1960s rock star Jim Morrison (1943–71), who died in a flat in the Marais at **17-19 rue Beautreillis**, 4e, in 1971 and is now buried in division 6. His tomb is something of a grave concern for the cemetery these days, however: a security guard had to be posted near the grave of the rock singer not long ago after fans began taking drugs and having sex on his tomb.

Mur des Fédérés

On 27 May 1871, the last of the Communard insurgents, cornered by government forces, fought a hopeless, all-night battle among the tombstones. In the morning, the 147 survivors were lined up against the **Mur des Fédérés** (Wall of the Federalists), shot and buried where they fell in a mass grave.

A Perfect City Stroll

For those visiting in Paris for its exceptional art and architecture, this vast cemetery – the city's largest – is not a bad starting point. It's one of central Paris' biggest green spaces, laced with 5300 trees and a treasure trove of magnificent 19th-century sculptures by artists such as David d'Angers, Hector Guimard, Visconti and Chapu. Many graves are crumbling, overgrown and in need of a good scrub and polish, but such is the nature of the cemetery's exquisite faded-grandeur charm. Consider the walking tour detailed in the photographic book *Meet Me At Père Lachaise* by Anna Erikssön and Masson Bendewald, or simply start with architect Étienne-Hippolyte Godde's neoclassical chapel and portal at the main entrance and get beautifully lost.

The cemetery has five entrances, two of which are on bd de Ménilmontant. Maps indicating the location of noteworthy graves are available free from the **Conservation Office** (16 rue du Repos) in the southwestern corner of the cemetery. Organised tours (in French) also depart from here.

Discover Le Marais & Bastille

Getting There & Away

Metro Stops for the lower Marais include St-Paul (line 1), Rambuteau (line 11); for the Haut Marais, Temple (line 3) or Filles du Calvaire and St-Sébastien–Froissart (line 8); for Ménilmontant, Belleville (lines 2 and 11) Ménilmontant (line 2) or Oberkampf (line 5). Bastille metro station is a central hub.

Bus Bus 29 runs from rue des Francs Bourgeois to Bastille and Gare de Lyon; and bus 76 from rue de Rivoli to the 20e and Porte de Bagnolet.

Bicycle Handy Vélib' stations: 7 place de l'Hôtel de Ville; in Ménilmontant 81bis rue Jean-Pierre Timbaud or 137 bd Ménilmontant.

Boat Batobus stop Hôtel de Ville.

Musée des Arts et Métiers
SONNET SYLVAIN/HEMIS/CORBIS ©

Sights

FREE **Place des Vosges** City Square
(Map p150; place des Vosges, 4e; MSt-Paul or Bastille) Inaugurated in 1612 as place Royale and thus the oldest square in Paris, place des Vosges is a strikingly elegant ensemble of 36 symmetrical houses with ground-floor arcades, steep slate roofs and large dormer windows arranged around a large and leafy square with four symmetrical fountains and an 1829 copy of a mounted statue of Louis XIII, originally placed here in 1639.

Between 1832 and 1848 writer Victor Hugo lived in an apartment on the 3rd floor of the square's Hôtel de Rohan-Guéménée, moving to the mansion a year after the publication of *Notre Dame de Paris* (The Hunchback of Notre Dame) and completing *Ruy Blas* while living here. The **Maison de Victor Hugo** (Map p150; www.musee-hugo.paris. fr; admission free; ☉10am-6pm Tue-Sun; MSt-Paul or Bastille) is now a small museum devoted to the life and times of the celebrated novelist and poet, with an impressive collection of his personal drawings and portraits. Temporary exhibitions command an admission fee.

FREE **Hôtel de Ville** City Hall
(Map p150; www.paris.fr; place de l'Hôtel de Ville, 3e; MHôtel de Ville) Paris' beautiful neo-Renaissance town hall was gutted during the Paris Commune of 1871 and rebuilt in luxurious neo-Renaissance style between 1874 and 1882. The ornate facade is decorated with 108 statues of illustrious Parisians. Outstanding temporary exhibitions held inside in the **Salle**

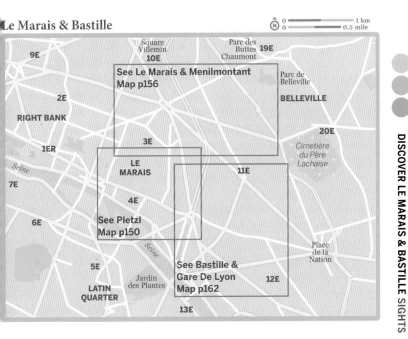

St-Jean (Map p150; 5 rue de Lobau) generally have a Parisian theme and are free.

From December to early March, an **ice-skating rink** (Patinoire de l'Hôtel de Ville; Map p150; admission free, skate rentals €5; ☺noon-10pm Mon-Fri, 9am-10pm Sat & Sun, Dec-Mar; Ⓜ Hôtel de Ville) sets up outside this beautiful building, creating something of a picture-book experience.

FREE Musée
Cognacq-Jay   Art Museum
(Map p150; www.cognacq-jay.paris.fr; 8 rue Elzévir, 3e; admission free; ☺10am-6pm Tue-Sun; Ⓜ St-Paul or Chemin Vert) This museum in Hôtel de Donon brings together oil paintings, pastels, sculpture, objets d'art, jewellery, porcelain and furniture from the 18th century assembled by Ernest Cognacq (1839–1928), founder of La Samaritaine department store, and his wife Louise Jay.

The artwork and objets d'art give a pretty good idea of upper-class tastes during the Age of Enlightenment. Temporary exhibitions command an admission fee.

Musée des Arts et Métiers   Art Museum
(Map p156; www.arts-et-metiers.net; 60 rue de Réaumur, 3e; adult/student/child €6.50/4.50/free; ☺10am-6pm Tue, Wed & Fri-Sun, to 9.30pm Thu; Ⓜ Arts et Métiers) The Arts & Crafts Museum, dating from 1794 and the oldest museum of science and technology in Europe, is a must for anyone with an interest in how things tick or work. Housed inside the sublime 18th-century priory of St-Martin des Champs, some 3000 instruments, machines and working models from the 18th to 20th centuries are displayed according to theme (from Construction and Energy to Transportation) across three floors.

Maison Européenne de la Photographie   Photography Museum
(Map p150; www.mep-fr.org; 5-7 rue de Fourcy, 4e; adult/child/under 8yr €7/4/free; ☺11am-8pm Wed-Sun; Ⓜ St-Paul or Pont Marie) The European House of Photography, housed in the overly renovated Hôtel Hénault de Cantorbe (dating – believe it or not – from the early 18th century), has cutting-edge temporary exhibits (usually

retrospectives on single photographers), as well as an enormous permanent collection on the history of photography and its connections with France.

Musée de la Magie   Magic Museum

(Map p150; www.museedelamagie.com; 11 rue St-Paul, 4e; adult/3-12yr €9/7; ⏰2-7pm Wed, Sat & Sun, daily Easter & Christmas school holidays; Ⓜ St-Paul) The ancient arts of magic, optical illusion and sleight of hand are explored in this Magic Museum, in the 16th-century *caves* (cellars) of the Marquis de Sade's former home. Admission includes a magic show and a combination ticket (€12/9) covering admission to the adjoining Musée des Automates – a collection of antique wind-up toys – is available.

Musée d'Art et d'Histoire du Judaïsme   Jewish Museum

(Map p150; www.mahj.org; 71 rue du Temple; adult/under 26yr €6.80/free; ⏰11am-6pm Mon-Fri, 10am-6pm Sun; Ⓜ Rambuteau) To delve into the historic heart of the Marais' long-established Jewish community, visit this fascinating museum, housed in the sumptuous Hôtel de St-Aignan dating from 1650. The museum traces the evolution of Jewish communities from the Middle Ages to the present, with particular emphasis on French Jewish history and the history of Jewish communities in other parts of Europe and North Africa. Highlights include documents relating to the Dreyfus Affair; and works by Chagall, Modigliani and Soutine. A creative array of music, writing and history workshops for children, adults and families complement the excellent exhibitions; see the website for details.

Musée Picasso   Art Museum

(Map p150; ☎01 42 71 25 21; www.musee-picasso.fr; 5 rue de Thorigny; Ⓜ St-Paul or Chemin Vert) One of Paris' most beloved art collections opened its doors again after massive renovation works in summer 2013. Housed in the stunning, mid-17th-century Hôtel Salé, the Musée Picasso woos art lovers with more than 3500 drawings, engravings, paintings, ceramic works and sculptures by the *grand maître* (great

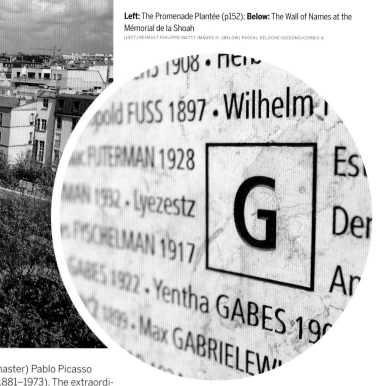

master) Pablo Picasso
1881–1973). The extraordinary collection was donated to the French government by the artist's heirs in lieu of paying inheritance tax.

FREE **Mémorial de la Shoah**   Holocaust Museum
(Map p150; www.memorialdelashoah.org; 17 rue Geoffroy l'Asnier, 4e; ⏱10am-6pm Sun-Wed & Fri, to 10pm Thu; Ⓜ St-Paul) Established in 1956, the Memorial to the Unknown Jewish Martyr has metamorphosed into the Memorial of the Holocaust and an important documentation centre. The permanent collection and temporary exhibits relate to the Holocaust and the German occupation of parts of France and Paris during WWII; the film clips of contemporary footage and interviews are heart-rending and the displays instructive and easy to follow.

The actual memorial to the victims of the Shoah, a Hebrew word meaning 'catastrophe' and synonymous in France with the Holocaust, stands at the entrance, where there is a wall (2006) inscribed with the names of 76,000 men, women and children deported from France to Nazi extermination camps.

Place de la Bastille   City Square
(Map p162; Ⓜ Bastille) The Bastille, a 14th-century fortress built to protect the city gates, is the most famous monument in Paris that no longer exists. Transformed into a dreaded state prison under Cardinal Richelieu, it was demolished shortly after a mob stormed it on 14 July 1789 and freed a total of just seven prisoners.

The *place* still resonates with the French as a symbol of revolutionary change, but first impressions of today's busy traffic circle can be a bit underwhelming. The most obvious monument is the **Colonne de Juillet** (Map p162) – the lone bronze column topped with the gilded Spirit of Liberty,

149

Pletzl

DISCOVER LE MARAIS & BASTILLE

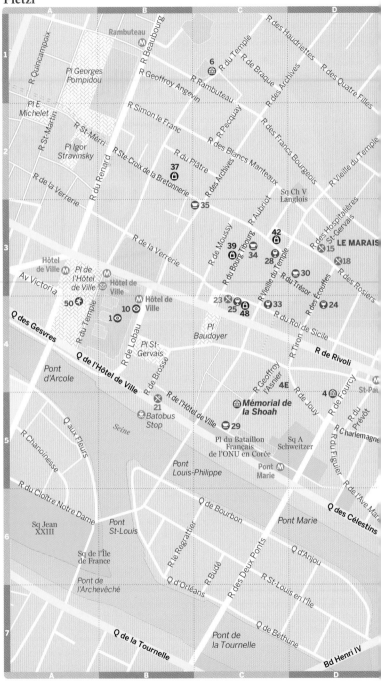

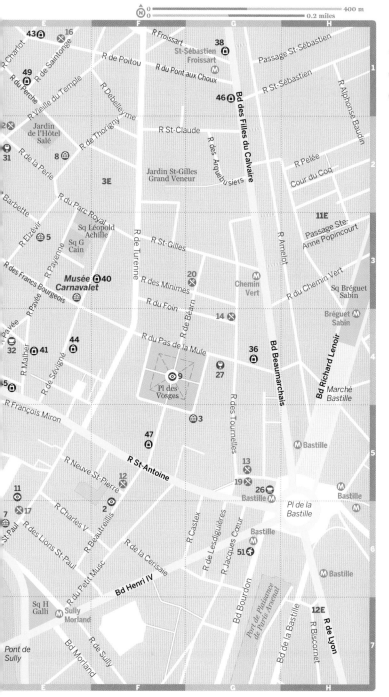

0 — 400 m
0 — 0.2 miles

R Charlot
43
16
R de Saintonge
R Froissart
38
St-Sébastien
Froissart
Passage St-Sébastien
49
R du Perche
R Vieille du Temple
R de Poitou
R du Pont aux Choux
R St-Sébastien
R Alphonse Baudin
46
Bd des Filles du Calvaire
R Debelleyme
2
Jardin
de l'Hôtel
Salé
R de Thorigny
R St-Claude
R des Arquebusiers
R Pelée
Cour du Coq
31
R de la Perle
8
3E
Jardin St-Gilles
Grand Veneur
11E
Passage Ste-
Anne Popincourt
Barbette
R du Parc Royal
R Elzévir
5
Sq Léopold
Achille
R Payenne
Sq G
Cain
R de Turenne
R St-Gilles
R Amelot
R des Francs Bourgeois
Chemin
Vert
R du Chemin Vert
Sq Bréguet
Sabin
Musée
Carnavalet
40
R des Minimes
20
R du Foin
R de Béarn
14
Bréguet
Sabin
Pavée
32
41
44
R du Pas de la Mule
36
Bd Richard Lenoir
R Malher
R de Sévigné
Pl des
Vosges
9
27
Bd Beaumarchais
Marché
Bastille
5
R François Miron
3
R des Tournelles
Bastille
47
Bastille
11
R Neuve-St-Pierre
R St-Antoine
13
Bastille
7
17
12
2
19
26
Bastille
St-Paul
R des Lions St-Paul
R Charles V
R Beautreillis
R Castex
R de Lesdiguières
R Jacques Cœur
Pl de la
Bastille
Bastille
R de la Cerisaie
Bastille
51
Bastille
Sq H
Galli
Sully
Morland
Bd Henri IV
R du Petit Musc
Bd Bourdon
Port de Plaisance
de Paris Arsenal
12E
R de Lyon
R Biscornet
Pont de
Sully
Bd Morland
R de Sully
Bd de la Bastille

Pletzl

commemoratating the victims of the later revolutions of 1830 and 1848.

Opéra Bastille
Opera House

(Map p162; www.operadeparis.fr; 2-6 place de la Bastille, 12e; guided tours adult/10-25yr/under 10yr €12/10/6; Ⓜ Bastille) In 1984, the former railway station on place de la Bastille was demolished to make way for the new opera house, the Opéra Bastille. One of former President Mitterand's pet projects, the 3400-seat venue was built with the intention of stripping opera of its elitist airs – hence the notable inauguration date of 13 July 1989, the eve of the 200th anniversary of the storming of the Bastille.

There are 1¼-hour **guided tours** of the building, which depart at wildly different times depending on the date – you'll need to check in at the **box office** (Map p162; ☎ 01 40 01 19 70; 130 rue de Lyon, 12e; ⏰ 2.30-6.30pm Mon-Sat). Tickets go on sale 10 minutes before tours begin.

Promenade Plantée
Park

(Map p162; ⏰ 8am-9.30pm May-Aug, to 5.30pm Sep-Apr; Ⓜ Bastille or Gare de Lyon) The most innovative green space in the city, the elevated Promenade Plantée was built atop the old Vincennes Railway, in operation from 1859 to 1969. Three storeys above ground level, it provides all the usual park amenities – benches, rose trellises, corridors of bamboo – but its real attraction is the unique aerial

BRUCE YUANYUE BI/GETTY IMAGES ©

✓ Don't Miss
Musée Carnavalet

Paris' history museum, secreted in a pair of remarkable *hôtels particuliers,* is one of the city's quietly wonderful surprises. Its maze of period rooms – more than 100 in all – chart the city's history from prehistory to modern times through a 600,000-piece feast of art, artefacts and historic objects. A visit here is as much about the history of interior design as city history, and a half day can be easily be spent savouring the permanent collection (free) and temporary exhibitions (admission fee).

The sublime Renaissance-style **Hôtel Carnavalet** was home to letter-writer Madame de Sévigné between 1677 and 1696. Some of her belongings are displayed on the 1st floor alongside portraits of prominent literary figures like Molière and Jean de la Fontaine, and other artworks and objects evocative of Paris in the 17th and 18th centuries. Rooms on the ground floor focus mainly on the 16th century, with a colourful collection of vintage street and shop signs. Don't miss the *chat noir* (black cat) from Montmartre and various tools depicting shop trades.

A covered gallery on the 1st floor links Hôtel Carnavalet with 17th-century **Hôtel Le Peletier de St-Fargeau**. The lovely ground-floor orangery showcases the museum's archaeological collection from prehistory and the Gallo-Roman period, and is well worth seeking out. Some of the nation's most important documents, paintings and other objects from the French Revolution (rooms 100 to 113) are on the 2nd floor. First-floor highlights include Fouquet's stunning art nouveau jewellery shop from rue Royale and Marcel Proust's cork-tiled bedroom from his apartment on bd Haussmann (room 147), where he wrote most of the 7350-page literary cycle *À la Recherche du Temps Perdu* (Remembrance of Things Past).

NEED TO KNOW

Map p150; www.carnavalet.paris.fr; 23 rue de Sévigné, 3e; ⏱10am-6pm Tue-Sun; Ⓜ St-Paul, Chemin Vert or Rambuteau

Detour:
Bois de Vincennes

Paris is flanked by two large parks, the Bois de Boulogne in the west and the Bois de Vincennes in the east. Originally royal hunting grounds, the Bois de Vincennes was annexed by the army following the Revolution and then donated to the city in 1860 by Napoleon III. Metro lines 1 (St-Mandé, Château de Vincennes) and 8 (Porte Dorée, Porte de Charenton) will get you to the eastern edges of the park.

○ **Château de Vincennes** (www.chateau-vincennes.fr; av de Paris, Vincennes; adult/18-25yr/under 18yr €8.50/5.50/free; ⊙10am-6.15pm Apr-Sep, to 5.15pm Oct-Mar; M Château de Vincennes) Originally a meagre 12th-century hunting lodge, the castle here was expanded several times throughout the centuries until it reached its present size under Louis XIV. Notable features include the beautiful 52m-high keep (1370) and the royal chapel (1552), both of which are open to visits. Note that the chapel is only open between 11am and noon, and 3pm and 4pm.

○ **Parc Floral de Paris** (Esplanade du Chateau de Vincennes; adult/7-18yr/under 7yr €5/2/free; ⊙9.30am-9pm May-Aug, shorter hours rest of year; M Château de Vincennes) This magnificent botanical park is one of the highlights of the Bois de Vincennes. Natural landscaping and a magnificent collection of plants will keep amateur gardeners happy, while Paris' largest play area (giant climbing webs and slides, jungle gyms, sandboxes, etc) will absolutely thrill families. Open-air concerts are staged throughout summer, making it a first-rate picnic destination.

○ **Lac Daumesnil** (M Porte Dorée) The largest lake in the Bois de Vincennes, this is a popular destination for walks and rowboat excursions in warmer months. A Buddhist temple is located nearby.

○ **Parc Zoologique de Paris** (M Porte Dorée) This zoo, home to some 600 animals, has been undergoing major renovations since 2008 and is expected to reopen in spring 2014.

vantage point on city life and the surrounding architecture.

The viaduct drops back to street level at the Jardin de Reuilly (1.5km), but it's possible to follow the line all the way to the Bois de Vincennes at the city's edge. This latter section, known as the Coulée Verte (3km), can also be done on a bike or in-line skates. Access to the elevated section is via staircase; there is usually at least one per city block. Beneath the park at street level is the **Viaduc des Arts** (Map p162; M Gare de Lyon or Daumesnil), which runs along av Daumesnil.

 Eating

Septime   Modern French €€€
(Map p162; ☎ 01 43 67 38 29; 80 rue de Charonne 11e; lunch/5-course menus €26/55; ⊙lunch Tue-Fri, dinner Mon-Fri; M Charonne) Reading the menu at Septime won't get you far, as it looks mostly like an obscure shopping list (hanger steak/chicory/roots, chicken's egg/foie gras/*lardo*). And that's if you even get a menu – if you order the excellent five-course meal (available for both lunch and dinner), you won't even know what's being served until it arrives.

But rest assured, the alchemists in the kitchen here, run by Bertrand Grébaut, are capable of producing some ruly beautiful creations, and the blue-mocked waitstaff go out of their way to ensure that the culinary surprises are all pleasant ones. Reserve in advance.

Au Passage
Bistro €€

(Map p156; 📞 01 43 55 07 52; www.facebook.com/aupassage; 1bis passage de St-Sébastien, 11e; 2-/3-course lunch menus €13.50/19.50, dinner €20-35; 🕙 lunch & dinner Mon-Fri, dinner Sat; M St-Sébastien-Froissart) Have faith in talented Australian chef James Henry at this raved-about *petit bar de quartier* (neighbourhood bar) with vegetable crates piled scruffily in the window and a fridge filling one corner of the old-fashioned dining room.

The lunch menu – a good-value, uncomplicated choice of two starters and two mains – is chalked on the blackboard, while dinner sees waiting staff in jeans swirl in and out of the pocket-sized kitchen with tapas-style starters to share, followed by a feisty shoulder of lamb, side of beef or other meaty cut for the entire table. Bookings are essential.

Le Dauphin
Bistro €€

(Map p156; 📞 01 55 28 78 88; 131 av Parmentier, 11e; 2-/3-course lunch menus €23/27; 🕙 lunch & dinner Tue-Fri, dinner Sat; M Goncourt) Advance reservations are essential at this buzzing wine bar. Run by the same team as **Le Chateaubriand** (p157) a few doors down, the stark white space with marble floor, marble bar, marble ceiling and marble walls (and the odd mirror) is a temple to taste. Lunch is a choice of two starters and two mains (one fish, one meat), presented like a work of art on (predictably) white china.

But the pièce de résistance is evening dining when foodies pick and choose their way through an exquisite succession of *petites assiettes comme tapas* (small tapas-style dishes).

Le Siffleur de Ballons
Wine Bar €

(Map p162; www.lesiffleurdeballons.com; 34 rue de Citeaux, 12e; lunch menus €14, mains €7-15; 🕙 10.30am-3pm & 5.30-10pm Tue-Sat; M Faidherbe Chaligny) With Tom Waits on the stereo and a few cactuses atop the register, this contemporary wine bar clearly has a dash of California in its soul. The wines, though, are all French – and all natural – and paired with a quality selection of simple but delicious offerings: tartines, soups, lentil salad with truffle oil, cheeses and Iberian charcuterie plates.

Marché Bastille
Market €

(Map p162; bd Richard Lenoir, 11e; 🕙 7am-2.30pm Thu & Sun; M Bastille or Richard Lenoir) If you only get to one open-air market in Paris, this one – stretching between the Bastille and Richard Lenoir metro stations – is among the very best.

Market stall, Bastille
STUART DEE/GETTY IMAGES ©

Le Marais & Menilmontant

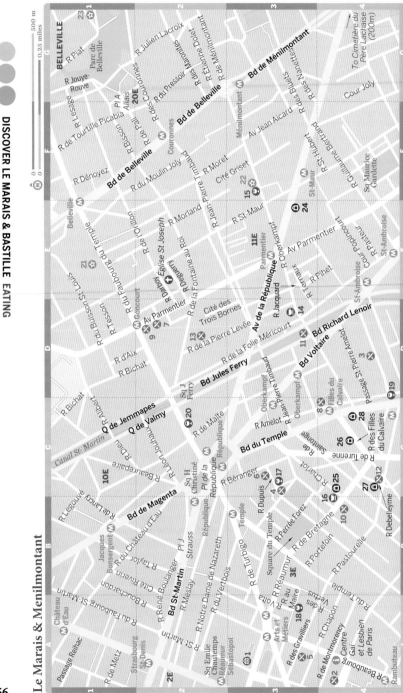

Marais & Menilmontant

Le Chateaubriand
Modern French €€€

(Map p156; ☎ 01 43 57 45 95; www.lechateau riand.fr; 129 av Parmentier, 11e; mains €27-46; ⊙ lunch & dinner Tue-Sat; M Goncourt) The quintessential *néobistrot*, Le Chateaubriand is a simple but elegantly tiled art deco dining room with some of the most imaginative cuisine in town. Chef Iñaki Aizpitarte – a name that could only be Basque – is well travelled and his dishes show that global exposure again and again in its odd combinations (watermelon and mackerel, milk-fed veal with langoustines and truffles).

Dinner is a five-course tasting menu with no choices. Divine. Advance reservations essential.

Derrière
Modern French €€

(Map p156; ☎ 01 44 61 91 95; www.derriere-resto. com; 69 rue des Gravilliers, 3e; lunch menus €25, mains €17-24; ⊙ lunch & dinner Mon-Fri & Sun, dinner Sat; M Arts et Métiers) Play table ping pong between courses, sit on the side of the bed glass of champers in hand, lounge between book cases, or entertain a dinner party of 12 – such is the nature of this apartment restaurant with courtyard eating in summer. Its vibe might be chilled in a trendy 'shoes-off' kind of way, but Derrière (literally, 'Behind') is deadly serious in the kitchen.

Classic French bistro dishes and more inventive creations are excellent, as is the Sunday brunch. Advance reservations for dinner essential.

Le Petit Marché
Bistro €

(Map p150; ☎ 01 42 72 06 67; 9 rue de Béarn, 3e; mains €12-20; M Chemin Vert) A faintly fusion cuisine is what stands out at this cosy bistro with old cream beams, candles on the tables and mirrors on the walls. Raw tuna wrapped in sesame seeds, ginger-spiced prawns and monkfish medallions with figs give a creative Asian kick to a menu that otherwise reassures with old French bistro favourites.

L'Aller-Retour
Bistro

(Map p156; 5 rue Charles-François Dupuis, 3e; mains €10-20; ⊙ lunch & dinner Tue-Fri, dinner Sat; M Temple) One of a cluster of trendy boutique addresses in the Haut Marais, this bistro is overtly retro in its interior design and a complete carnivore in the kitchen – a *bar à viande* (meat bar) is how it describes itself. Grilled meat and fine wine is its Holy Grail, with staggering success. Its €10.90 lunch deal, including a glass of *vin,* is a steal.

Chez Janou
Provençal €€

(Map p150; 📞01 42 72 28 41; www.chezjanou. com; 2 rue Roger Verlomme, 3e; mains €15-20; 🕒lunch & dinner; Ⓜ Chemin Vert) Push your way in, order a kir from the jam-packed bar while you wait for a table, and revel in the buzz of this busy spot. Cuisine is Provençal (or as close as you get to Provençal in Paris) with all the southern classics like *brandade de morue* (salt cod purée with potatoes), ratatouille and lavender-scented *crème brulée* well covered.

There's also eighty different types of pastis, and it's not recommended for the claustrophobic (unless it is summer and you succeed in nabbing a seat on the terrace). Advance reservations essential.

Bistrot Paul Bert
Bistro €€

(Map p162; 📞01 43 72 24 01; 18 rue Paul Bert, 11e; 3-course lunch/dinner menus €18/36; 🕒lunch & dinner Tue-Sat; Ⓜ Faidherbe-Chaligny) When food writers make lists of the best Paris bistros, one of the names that almost always pops up is Paul Bert. The timeless decor and perfectly executed classic dishes guarantee that you'll need to reserve well in advance, even if the service isn't always up to snuff. Favourites here

Patisserie on Rue des Rosiers

include the *steak-frites* and the *Paris-Bres* (a cream-filled pastry).

Seafood lovers should try its annex **L'Écailler du Bistrot** (Map p162; 📞01 43 72 76 77; 22 rue Paul Bert, 11e; mains €24-40, seafood platter €36; 🕒lunch & dinner Tue-Sat; Ⓜ Faidherbe Chaligny).

Chez Paul
Bistro €€

(Map p162; 📞01 47 00 34 57; www.chezpaul.com 13 rue de Charonne, 11e; mains €16-28; 🕒lunch & dinner; Ⓜ Ledru-Rollin) As far as cinematic French bistros are concerned, Chez Paul gives nearby Paul Bert a run for its money This is Paris as your grandmother would have known it: red-and-white gingham napkins, faded photographs on the walls, old red banquettes and traditional French dishes handwritten on a yellowing menu. Stick with the simplest of dishes and make sure you've booked ahead. Open to 12.30am daily.

Bofinger
Brasserie €€

(Map p150; 📞01 42 72 87 82; www.bofingerparis com; 5-7 rue de la Bastille, 4e; mains €20-38; 🕒lunch & dinner; Ⓜ Bastille) Founded in 1864, Bofinger is reputedly the oldest brasserie in Paris, though its polished

t nouveau brass, glass and mirrors throughout flags a redecoration a few decades later. As at most Parisian brasseries, specialities include Alsatian-inspired dishes such as *choucroute* (sauerkraut with assorted meats) and seafood dishes. Ask for a seat downstairs and under the *coupole* (stained-glass dome): it's the prettiest part of the restaurant. Just opposite, **Le Petit Bofinger** (Map p150; 01 42 72 05 23; 6 rue de la Bastille, 4e; mains €15-26, menus with wine €18 & €26; lunch & dinner to midnight daily; M Bastille) is the brasserie's less brash (and cheaper) little sister.

ose Bakery Salads, Tarts €
(Map p156; 01 49 96 54 01; 30 rue Debelleyme, 3e; mains €7-18; 9am-6.30pm Tue-Sun; M Filles du Calvaire or St-Sébastien–Froissart) There are savoury tarts, salads, risotto, great breakfasts, feisty organic fruit juices and lots of different teas at this hip, English-style daytime eating address with old-stone walls and an open kitchen.

Soya Cantine BIO Vegetarian €€
(Map p156; 01 48 06 33 02; www.soya75.fr; 20 rue de la Pierre Levée, 11e; mains €15-20, 2/3-course lunch menus €16/19; lunch & dinner Tue-Sat, lunch Sun; M Goncourt) A real favourite for its hip location in an old industrial atelier (think bare cement, metal columns and big windows), Soya is a full-on vegetarian eatery in what was once a staunchly working-class district. Dishes, many tofu-based, are 95% organic and the weekend brunch buffet (€23.50) is a deliciously languid and organic affair. A glass floor floods the basement area with light.

'As du Felafel Jewish €
(Map p150; 34 rue des Rosiers, 4e; takeaway dishes €5-8; noon-midnight Sun-Thu, to 5pm Fri; M St-Paul) The lunchtime queue stretching halfway down the street from this place says it all! This Parisian favourite, 100% worth the inevitable wait, is *the* address for kosher, perfectly deep-fried chickpea balls and turkey or lamb shwarma sandwiches. Do as every Parisian does and takeaway.

Chez Marianne Jewish €€
(Map p150; 2 rue des Hospitalières St-Gervais, 4e; mains €19-24; noon-midnight; M St-Paul) Absolutely heaving at lunchtime, Chez Marianne translates as elbow-to-elbow eating beneath age-old beams on copious portions of falafel, hummus, purées of aubergine and chickpeas, and 25-odd other *zakouski* (hors d'œuvres; €12/14/16 for plate of 4/5/6). Fare is Sephardic rather than Ashkenazi (the norm at most Pletzl eateries), not Beth Din kosher, and a hole-in-the-wall window sells falafel in pita (€6) to munch on the move.

Chez Nénesse Bistro €
(Map p150; 01 42 78 46 49; 17 rue Saintonge, 3e; mains €15-18; lunch & dinner Mon-Fri; M Filles du Calvaire) Very old-world bistro is the atmosphere at this tiny spot with lace curtains and a quality kitchen that only cooks classic French dishes. Its *salade de canard au vinaigre d'hydromel* (duck salad in honey vinegar) and sweet *medallions de veau au miel* (veal medallions pan fried in honey) are not to be scoffed at.

Ambassade d'Auvergne Traditional French €€
(Map p156; 01 42 72 31 22; www.ambassade-auvergne.com; 22 rue du Grenier St-Lazare; mains €16-20, lunch menu €20; lunch & dinner; M Rambuteau) For truly hungry carnivores with a fetish for only the best products, the Auvergne embassy – an easy walk from the Centre Pompidou – is the place to head. Traditional cuisine from the Auvergne has been the restaurant's mantra for more than a century and dishes like *salade tiède de lentilles vertes du Puy* (warm green Puy lentil salad) and *saucisse de Parlan à l'aligot* (feisty pork sausage) will make you want to head straight to this tasty rural region in central France.

Le Clown Bar Traditional French €
(Map p156; 01 43 55 87 35; 114 rue Amelot, 11e; plats du jour €10.50; lunch & dinner Mon-Sat; M Filles du Calvaire) A wonderful wine-bar-cum-bistro next to the **Cirque d'Hiver** (1852), the Clown Bar is like a museum with its painted ceilings, mosaics on the

wall, lovely zinc bar and circus memorabilia that touches on one of our favourite themes of all time: the evil clown. The food is simple and unpretentious traditional French.

Le Train Bleu
Brasserie €€€

(Map p162; ☎ 01 43 43 09 06; www.le-train-bleu.com; 1st fl, Gare de Lyon, 26 place Louis Armand, 12e; starters €18-28, mains €30-45, menus lunch €56, dinner €68 & €98; ⏰ 7.30am-11pm Mon-Sat, 9am-11pm Sun; 📶; ⓂGare de Lyon) In all probability you've never – ever – seen a railway station restaurant as sumptuous as this heritage-listed belle époque showpiece. This is a top-end spot to dine on such fare as foie gras with a confiture of red onions, grapes and hazelnuts, Charolles beef steak tartare and chips, and the house-made *baba au rhum*.

Aux Vins des Pyrénées
Traditional French €€

(Map p150; ☎ 01 42 72 64 94; 25 rue Beautreillis, 4e; mains €15-20; ⏰lunch & dinner Sun-Fri, dinner Sat; ⓂSt-Paul or Bastille) Tucked in a former wine warehouse, this is a lovely place to enjoy an unpretentious French meal with much fine wine. The fish, meat and game dishes are all good, but the foi gras and *pavé de rumsteak* (thick rump steak) are both worth a special mention as is the wine list that features both celebrated and little-known estate wines.

Pozzetto
Ice Cream €

(Map p150; www.pozzetto.biz; 39 rue du Roi de Sicile, 4e; ⏰11.30am-9pm Mon-Thu, to 11.30pm Fri-Sun; ⓂSt-Paul) Urban myth says this gelato maker opened when a group of friends from northern Italy couldn't find their favourite ice cream in Paris, so they imported the ingredients to create it from scratch. Twelve flavours – spatula'd not scooped – include *gianduia torinese* (hazelnut chocolate from Turin) and *zabaione*, made from egg yolks, sugar and sweet Marsala wine, along with the more usual peach, pistachio and poire William. Great Italian coffee, too.

Le Trumilou
Bistro €

(Map p150; ☎ 01 42 77 63 98; www.letrumilou.com; 84 quai de l'Hôtel de Ville, 4e; menus €16.5 & €19.50; ⓂHôtel de Ville) This no-frills bistro just round the corner from the Hôtel de Ville and facing the posh Île de St-Louis square has been a Parisian institution for over a century. If you're looking for an authentic menu from the early 20th century and prices (well, almost) to match, you won't do better than this. Specialities of the house include *canard aux pruneaux* (duck with prunes)and *ris de veau grand-mère* (veal sweetbreads in mushroom cream sauce).

Marché aux Enfants Rouges
International

(Map p156; 39 rue de Bretagne, 3e; ⏰8.30am-1pm & 4-7.30pm Tue-Fri, 4-8pm Sat 8.30am-2pm Sun; ⓂFilles du Calvaire) Built in 1615, Paris

Delicacies at Chez Marianne (p159)

oldest covered market is secreted behind an inconspicuous green metal gate – and for good reason. A glorious maze of 20-odd food stalls selling ready-to-eat dishes from around the globe, it is a great place to come for a meander and munch with locals. Grab a Japanese bento box, Caribbean platter or a more traditional French crêpe, and consume at communal tables. End with a coffee across the street at **Café Charlot** (Map p156; www.cafecharlot paris.com; 38 rue de Bretagne, 3e; ⏰7-2am; Ⓜ Filles du Calvaire), a great neighbourhood cafe in a former bakery with retro white tiles and the perfect pavement terrace to lap up authentic Haut Marais vibe.

🍷 Drinking & Nightlife

A lively mix of gay-friendly (and gay-only) cafe society and bourgeois arty spots, with an interesting sprinkling of eclectic bars and relatively raucous pubs, the Marais is a spot par excellence when it comes to a night out. Rue Oberkampf is the essential hub of the Ménilmontant bar crawl, springing from a few cafes to being the epicentre of a vibrant, rapidly expanding bar scene. But as Oberkampf commercialises, the arty/edgy crowd is moving steadily outwards, through cosmopolitan Belleville and towards La Villette.

Bastille invariably draws a crowd, particularly to heaving rue de Lappe.

Le Baron Rouge   Wine Bar
(Map p162; 1 rue Théophile Roussel, 12e; ⏰10am-2pm & 5-10pm Mon-Fri, 10am-10pm Sat, 10am-4pm Sun; Ⓜ Ledru-Rollin) Just about the ultimate Parisian wine-bar experience, this place has a dozen barrels of the stuff stacked up against the bottle-lined walls. As unpretentious as you'll find, it's a local meeting place where everyone is welcome and is especially busy on Sundays after the **Marché d'Aligre** (Map p162; http://marchedaligre.free.fr; rue d'Aligre, 12e; ⏰8am-1pm & 4-7.30pm Tue-Sat, 8am-2pm Sun; Ⓜ Ledru-Rollin) wraps up. All the usual

suspects – cheese, charcuterie and oysters – will keep your belly full.

For a small deposit, you can even fill up one-litre bottles straight from the barrel for under €5.

Le Pure Café   Cafe
(Map p162; 14 rue Jean Macé, 11e; ⏰daily; Ⓜ Charonne) A classic Parisian haunt, this rustic, cherry-red corner cafe was featured in the art-house film *Before Sunset*, but it's still a refreshingly unpretentious spot for a drink or well-crafted fare like veal with chestnut purée.

La Fée Verte   Bar
(Map p162; 108 rue de la Roquette, 11e; dishes €10-16; ⏰daily; 🛜; Ⓜ Voltaire) You guessed it, the 'Green Fairy' specialises in absinthe (served traditionally with spoons and sugar cubes), but this fabulously old-fashioned neighbourhood cafe and bar also serves terrific food, including Green Fairy cheeseburgers.

Le Pick-Clops   Bar, Cafe
(Map p150; 16 rue Vieille du Temple, 4e; ⏰daily; 🛜; Ⓜ Hôtel de Ville or St-Paul) This buzzy bar-cafe – all shades of yellow and lit by neon – has Formica tables, ancient bar stools and plenty of mirrors. Attracting a friendly flow of locals and passers-by, it's a great place for morning or afternoon coffee, or that last drink alone or with friends. Great rum punch served with copious amounts of peanuts.

Le Loir dans La Théière   Cafe
(Map p150; 3 rue des Rosiers, 4e; ⏰daily; Ⓜ St-Paul) The Dormouse in the Teapot is a wonderful old space filled with retro toys, comfy couches and scenes of *Through the Looking Glass* on the walls. Its dozen different types of tea poured in the company of tip-top savoury tarts and crumble-type desserts ensure a constant queue on the street outside. They do breakfast (€12) and brunch (€19.50), too.

Aux Deux Amis   Cafe, Bar
(Map p156; 📞01 58 30 38 13; 45 rue Oberkampf, 11e; ⏰8am-2am Tue-Sat; Ⓜ Oberkampf) This quintessential Parisian neighbourhood

Bastille & Gare de Lyon

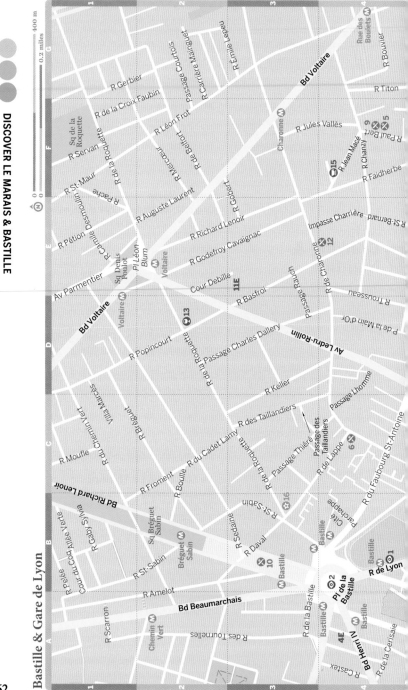

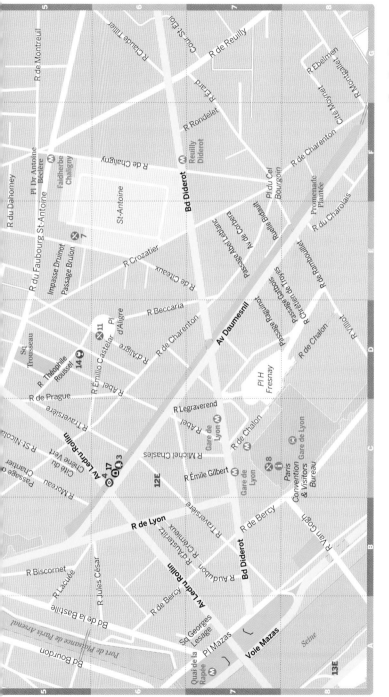

R de Montreuil

R du Dahomey

Pl Dr Antoine
Béclère

R Claude Tillier

Cour-St-Eloi

R de Reuilly

R E'belmen

Cité Moynet

R Montgallet

R Erard

R Rondelet

R de Chaligny

Faidherbe
Chaligny

Reuilly
Diderot

Bd Diderot

R de Charenton

St-Antoine

R du Faubourg St-Antoine

Impasse Druinot

Passage Brulon

7

Pl du Cel
Bourgoin

Promenade
Plantée

R du Charolais

Passage Abel Leblanc

Av de Cotéra

Ruelle Bideault

R Crozatier

R de Créteaux

R Beccaria

Passage Gatbois

R de Rambouillet

R de Chalon

R Chrétien de Troyes

Passage Raguinot

R Villiot

Av Daumesnil

11

Pl
d'Aligre

R de Charenton

R Emilio Castelar

R Abel

d'Aligre

Sq
Trousseau

R. Théophile
Roussel

14

R de Prague

R Traversière

R Legraverend

R Abel

Gare de
Lyon

R de Chalon

Pl H
Fresnay

R Michel Chasles

Gare de
Lyon

Av Ledru-Rollin

Cité du
Chêne Vert

R St-Nicolas

Passage Chantier

R Moreau

4

17

3

12E

R Emile Gilbert

8

Paris
Convention
& Visitors
Bureau

Gare de Lyon

R de Lyon

R Traversière

R de Bercy

R Van Gogh

R d'Austerlitz

R Crémieux

R de Bercy

Bd Diderot

R Biscornet

R Lacuée

R Jules César

Av Ledru Rollin

Audubon

Bd de la Bastille

Bd Bourdon

Port de Plaisance de Paris Arsenal

Quai de la
Rapée

Sq Georges
Lesage

Pl Mazas

Voie Mazas

Seine

13E

163

Bastille & Gare de Lyon

bar is steps from the noisy fruit, veg and cheese stalls of the Tuesday and Friday morning market, **Marché Popincourt** (Map p156; bd Richard Lenoir; MOberkampf). It's perfect for a coffee any time from dawn to dark, and it serves a great choice of tapas-style nibbles and wine in the evening.

But to get the full flavour of Aux Deux Amis, you have to come after the market on Friday when the house speciality – *tartare de cheval* (finely cut horsemeat seasoned with a secret mix of herbs and seasonings) – is cooked up (or rather not cooked) as a *plat du jour* (dish of the day) at lunchtime and as tapas in the evening.

Andy Walhoo　　　　Cocktail Bar
(Map p156; 69 rue des Gravilliers, 3e; ⊙Tue-Sat; MArts et Métiers) Casablanca meets pop-artist Andy Warhol in this cool, multicoloured cocktail lounge hidden away just north of the Centre Georges Pompidou. Its clever name means 'I have nothing' in Arabic and is a major misnomer: its acid-yellow colour, sweet cocktails, pushy staff and loud house music may be too much for some palates. Happy hour, 5pm to 8pm, ushers in a great-value €5 *cocktail du jour* and the courtyard behind is paradise for smokers and pullers.

Panic Room　　　　　　　　　Bar
(Map p156; www.panicroomparis.com; 101 rue Amelot, 11e; ⊙Mon-Sat; MSt-Sébastien–Froissart) This brazenly wild bar just east of

the Haut Marais is not quite as terrifying or forbidding as its name suggests. A wildly flavoured cocktail – such as gin shaken with strawberries and basil, or a cognac-based creation mixing cucumber coriander and ginger – is the thing to sip here, especially during happy hour (6.30pm to 8.30pm). Check its website for DJ sets, gigs and happenings.

Le Barav　　　　　　　　　Wine Bar
(Map p156; ☎ 01 48 04 57 59; www.lebarav.fr; 6 rue Charles-François Dupuis, 3e; ⊙Tue-Sat; MTemple) This hipster *bar à vin*, on one of the trendiest streets in the Haut Marais, oozes atmosphere – and has one of the city's loveliest pavement terraces. Its extensive wine list is complemented by tasty food (lunch *plat du jour* €10.50), seating is at vintage bistro tables or on bar stools, and its wine shop a few doors down hosts great *dégustations à thème* (themed wine tastings; reserve in advance).

Café Charbon　　　　　　Bar, Cafe
(Map p156; www.lecafecharbon.com; 109 rue Oberkampf, 11e; ⊙daily; 🛜; MParmentier) With its post-industrial belle époque ambience, the Charbon was the first of the hip cafes and bars to catch on in Ménilmontant. It's always crowded and worth heading to for the distressed decor with high ceilings, chandeliers and perched DJ booth. Food (mains €12.50 to €15) and evening tapas (€6) are both good.

La Belle Hortense
Literary Bar

(Map p150; www.cafeine.com; 31 rue Vieille du Temple, 4e; ⊙daily; MHôtel de Ville or St-Paul) This literary wine bar named after a Jacques Roubaud novel fuses shelf after shelf of good books to read with an equally good wine list and enriching weekly agenda of book readings, signings and art events. A zinc bar and original 19th-century ceiling set the mood perfectly.

La Chaise au Plafond
Cafe

(Map p150; 10 rue du Trésor, 4e; ⊙daily; MHôtel de Ville or St-Paul) The 'Chair on the Ceiling' is a peaceful, warm place, with wooden tables outside on a terrace giving onto tranquil passage du Trésor. It's a real oasis from the frenzy of the Marais and worth knowing about in summer.

La Perle
Bar

(Map p150; 78 rue Vieille du Temple, 3e; ⊙daily; MSt-Paul or Chemin Vert) Notorious for being the bar next door where shamed fashion designer John Galliano hung out (and, indeed, was arrested in February 2011), this party bar is where *bobos* (bohemian bourgeois) come to slum it over *un rouge* (glass of red wine) in the Marais until

the DJ arrives to liven things up. Unique trademarks: the (for real) distressed look of the place and the model locomotive over the bar.

Café Baroc
Bar, Cafe

(Map p150; 37 rue du Roi de Sicile, 4e; ⊙Tue-Sun; MSt-Paul) The old cinema seats here are ideal for sipping flavoured beer (a big deal here). Normally a chilled, almost classy little place, things get hyper when bar staff play fabulously camp 1980s tunes.

Café des Phares
Cafe

(Map p150; 7 place de la Bastille, 4e; ⊙daily; MBastille) There is no better spot to bask in the morning sun and watch Parisian traffic twirl around the Colonne de Juillet than the Beacons Café, the city's original *bistrot philo* (philosophers' bistro) where pensive Parisians meet on Sunday morning to debate the meaning of life and all that. Posy Paris at its best!

Café Martini
Bar

(Map p150; www.cafemartini.fr; 9 rue du Pas de la Mule, 4e; ⊙daily; MChemin Vert) Skip the twinset of unmemorable cafe-bars on place des Vosges and nip around

DISCOVER LE MARAIS & BASTILLE DRINKING & NIGHTLIFE

Bar at Bofinger (p158)

the corner instead to this cosy den with wood-panelled entrance, beamed ceiling and buzzing after-work crowd – the saggy sofa is the hot spot! Spoil yourself with smoothies and thick-enough-to-spoon *chocolat chaud à l'ancienne* by day, copious cheese and cold meat platters (€6) at dusk, and €5 cocktails during happy hour from 5pm to 9pm.

Open Café
Cafe, Gay

(Map p150; www.opencafe.fr; 17 rue des Archives, 4e; ⏰daily; Ⓜ Hôtel de Ville) A gay venue for all types at all hours, this spacious bar-cafe with twinkling disco balls strung from the starry ceiling has bags of appeal – not least a big buzzing pavement terrace, a kitchen serving breakfast (€8.70) and all-day *tartines* (€6.70), and four-hour happy hour kicking in daily at 6pm.

Scream Club
Club, Gay

(Map p156; www.scream-paris.com; 18 rue du Faubourg du Temple, 11e; ⏰daily; Ⓜ Belleville or Goncourt) What started out as a summer party is now a permanent fixture on the city's gay scene (marketed as Paris's biggest gay party).

3w Kafé
Bar, Gay

(Map p150; 8 rue des Écouffes, 4e; ⏰Tue-Sat; Ⓜ St-Paul) The name of this flagship cocktail bar-pub on a street with several lesbian bars means 'Women with Women so it can't be any clearer. It's relaxed and there's no ban on men (but they must be accompanied by a girl). On weekends there's dancing downstairs with a DJ and themed evenings take place regularly.

Le Tango
Club, Gay

(Map p156; www.boite-a-frissons.fr; 13 rue au Maire, 3e; ⏰Fri-Sun; Ⓜ Arts et Métiers) Le Tango hosts a mixed and cosmopolitan, gay and lesbian crowd in a historic 1930s dancehall. Its atmosphere and style is retro and festive, with waltzing, salsa and tango getting going from the moment it opens. From about 12.30am onwards DJs play. Sunday's gay tea dance is legendary.

Mariage Frères
Tea

(Map p150; www.mariagefreres.com; 30, 32 & 35 rue du Bourg Tibourg, 4e; ⏰daily; Ⓜ Hôtel de Ville) Founded in 1854, this is Paris' first and arguably finest tearoom with a shop where you can also buy more than 500 varieties of tea sourced from some 35 countries.

La Caféthèque
Cafe

(Map p150; www.lacafeotheque. com; 52 rue de l'Hôtel de Ville, 4e; ⏰daily; 🛜; Ⓜ St-Paul or Hôtel de Ville) From the industrial grinder by the door to the elaborate tasting notes in the menu, this coffee house is serious. Grab a pew (next to the piano perhaps or, if you're lucky, in the corner leather armchair), pick your bean (Guatemala, Panama, Brazil,

Teapots at Mariage Frères

Gay & Lesbian Paris

Le Marais, especially around the intersection of rue Ste-Croix de la Bretonnerie and rue des Archives, and eastwards to rue Vieille du Temple, has been Paris' main centre of gay nightlife for decades. The lesbian scene centres on a few cafes and bars, especially along rue des Écouffes. The **Centre Gai et Lesbien de Paris** (CGL; ☎ 01 43 57 21 47; www.centrelgbtparis.org; 61-63 rue Beaubourg, 3e; ⏰ 6-8pm Mon, 3.30-8pm Tue-Thu, 1-8pm Fri & Sat; **M** Rambuteau or Arts et Métiers) is gay and lesbian travellers' single best source of information in Paris, and has a sociable bar.

onduras, Peru etc) and get it served st the way you like it (such as espresso, stretto or latte).

⭐ Entertainment

e Nouveau Casino   Live Music
lap p156; www.nouveaucasino.net; 109 rue berkampf, 11e; ⏰ Tue-Sun; **M** Parmentier) This lub-concert annexe of **Café Charbon** 164) has made a name for itself amid e bars of Oberkampf with its live music oncerts (usually Tuesday, Thursday and riday) and lively club nights on week-nds. Electro, pop, deep house, rock – the rogram is eclectic, underground and al-ays up to the minute. Check the website r up-to-date listings.

a Java   World Music
lap p156; www.la-java.fr; 105 rue du Faubourg u Temple, 11e; **M** Goncourt) Built in 1922, this the dance hall where Édith Piaf got her rst break, and it now reverberates to the ound of live salsa, rock and world music. ve concerts usually take place during e week at 8pm or 9pm. Afterwards a stive crowd gets dancing to electro, ouse, disco and Latino DJs.

Le Balajo   Nightclub
(Map p162; www.balajo.fr; 9 rue de Lappe, 11e; ⏰ daily; **M** Bastille) A mainstay of Parisian nightlife since 1936, this ancient ballroom is devoted to salsa classes and Latino music during the week, with an R&B slant on weekends. At times it can be some-what tacky, but it scores a mention for its historical value and its old-fashioned *musette* (accordion music) gigs on Monday afternoons.

Le Vieux Belleville   Chansons
(Map p156; www.le-vieux-belleville.com; 12 rue des Envierges, 20e; **M** Pyrénées) This old-fashioned bistro and *musette* at the top of Parc de Belleville is an atmospheric venue for performances of *chansons* featuring accordions and an organ grinder three times a week. It's a lively favourite with lo-cals, though, so booking ahead is advised. The 'Old Belleville' serves classic bistro food (open for lunch Monday to Friday, dinner Tuesday to Saturday).

🔒 Shopping

The lower Marais has long been fashion-able, but the haut Marais (upper, ie northern Marais, sometimes referred to as NoMa) is rapidly becoming a hub for up-and-coming fashion designers, art galleries, and vintage, accessories and homewares boutiques, alongside long-established enterprises enjoying a renais-sance. Keep tabs via http://hautmarais. blogspot.com, listing new openings, exhibitions, events and pop-up shops.

Merci   Concept Store
(Map p150; www.merci-merci.com; 111 bd Beau-marchais, 3e; **M** St-Sébastien–Froissart) The landmark Fiat Cinquecento in the court-yard marks the entrance to this unique multistorey concept store whose rallying cry is one-stop shopping: fashion, acces-sories, linens, lamps and various other nifty designs for the home (a kitchen brush made from recycled egg shells and coffee grounds anyone?).

And a trio of inspired eating-drinking spaces complete Paris' hippest shopping

167

experience. All proceeds go to a children's charity in Madagascar.

Maison Georges Larnicol   Chocolate

(Map p150; www.chocolaterielarnicol.fr; 9 rue du Roi de Sicile & 14 rue de Rivoli, 4e; ⏱9.30am-10pm; Ⓜ Chemin Vert) Syrupy, chewy *koui-gnettes,* traditional Breton butter cakes unusually made in mini dimensions and 16 different flavours (€2.50 per 100g) are the main reason to visit this master chocolate maker and pastry chef from Brittany. Oh, and the glass jars of *caramel au beurre salé* (butter caramel) that come complete with a small spoon...

Lieu Commun   Concept Store

(Map p156; www.lieucommun.fr; 5 rue des Filles du Calvaire, 3e; Ⓜ Filles du Calvaire) Music, fashion, jeans, household items, furniture and gadgets are the essential pillars of this alternative design space on one of the Marais' most shop-interesting streets.

Viaduc des Arts   Arts, Crafts

(Map p162; www.viaducdesarts.fr; av Daumesnil, 12e; ⏱hours vary; Ⓜ Bastille or Gare de Lyon) Located beneath the red-brick arches of the **Promenade Plantée** (p152) is the Viaduc des Arts, where traditional artisans and contemporary designers carry out antique renovations and create new items using traditional methods. Artisans include furniture and tapestry restorers, interior designers, cabinetmakers, violin- and flute-makers, embroiderers and jewellers.

Violette et Léonie   Fashion

(Map p150; www.violetteleonie.com; 1 rue de Saintonge, 3e; Ⓜ Filles du Calvaire) So chic and of such high quality that it really doesn't seem like second-hand, Violette et Léonie is a first-class *depôt-vente* boutique specialising in vintage.

Grand Bonton   Kids

(Map p150; www.bonton.fr; 5 bd des Filles du Calvaire, 3e; Ⓜ Filles du Calvaire) Chic and

stylish, this concept store designed squarely with kids in mind stocks vintage-inspired fashion, furnishings and knick-knacks for babies, toddlers and children.

My E-Case _Accessories_

(Map p150; http://myecase.com; 3 rue de Birague & 27 rue des Écouffes, 4e; Ⓜ Chemin Vert or St-Paul) Studded in sparkling diamante, shaped like an old tape cassette, covered in 'sugar' like a doughnut, or encrusted with miniature cupcakes (from wild and wacky to Cath Kidston flowers and plain grey) this boutique sells protective coverings for Smartphones in every imaginable design. Gloves with touch-screen tips, too.

Rougier & Plé _Fine Arts_

(Map p156; www.rougier-ple.fr; 13 bd des Filles du Calvaire, 3e; ⊘ 11am-7pm Tue-Sat, 2.30-7pm Sun & Mon; Ⓜ Filles du Calvaire) The city's oldest _beaux arts_ (fine arts), in business since 1854, sells paper, pens, arts and crafts materials – everything imaginable

in fact for _le plaisir de crée_ (the pleasure of creation).

Chocolaterie Joséphine Vannier _Chocolate_

(Map p150; www.chocolats-vannier.com; 4 rue du Pas de la Mule, 3e; ⊘ 11am-7pm Tue-Sat, 2.30-7pm Sun & Mon; Ⓜ Chemin Vert) Miniature piano keyboards, violins, smiley-face boxes or a pair of jogging shoes...you name it, _chocolatier_ Joséphine Vannier can create it out of chocolate.

Popelini _Cakes_

(Map p156; 29 rue Debelleyme, 3e; ⊘ 11am-7pm Tue-Sat, 10am-3pm Sun; Ⓜ St-Sébastien–Frossart) Forget cupcakes and macarons! The hottest thing to buy at this bijou, bright pink cube of a shop is bite-sized _choux_ (éclairs), flavoured in a dozen and more different ways: jasmine, pistachio and cherry jam, strawberry and lychee, Grand Marnier, Baileys...the list is endless. The _chou du jour_ (éclair of the day; €2.80) promises to thrill.

Marais à la Mode

No surprise that New Yorker Kasia Dietz, when she moved to Europe, intuitively plumped for a part of Paris that subsequently morphed into the city's trendiest neighbourhood: Le Marais. The reversible totes, clutches and other bags this handbag designer creates are 100% home-grown – cut and stitched near République, hand painted in her Haut Marais studio, and more often than not dreamt up over *un café* or three in one of her favourite local hang-outs.

PERFECT SATURDAY

Wandering around Village St-Paul (p171), a hidden enclave with tiny boutiques, galleries, cafes and restaurants. Sometimes there is a farmers market or fair. Lunch at **La Petite Maison dans La Cour** (Map p150; 9 rue St-Paul, 4e; ☺lunch Wed-Sun; Ⓜ St-Paul), a tiny place with tasty home-cooking and gorgeous summer terrace.

BEST VINTAGE

I pass Violette et Léonie (p168) almost every day and usually end up popping in to try something on. The window seems to change daily and it stocks a real mix of fashions and labels, everything from H&M to Chanel.

FORGET THE BUZZ! HYPELESS DINING

Le Petit Marché (p157), nicely understated, is the best address around place des Vosges. Then there's L'Aller-Retour (p157), quite meat-heavy. Rather than ordering wine by the glass they simply bring the bottle to your table and you pay for what you drink (really unusual for Paris). It's on my favourite street in the Marais.

EVENING APÉRO

Café Crème (Map p156; 4 rue Dupetit Thouars, 3e; Ⓜ Temple) is a quintessential Parisian bistro, a really local, unpretentious place with good burgers and a great terrace – perfect for an easy *apéro* (predinner drink). Café Charbon (p164) is more 'the scene', very hip, an address I love. Then there is La Perle (p165), a lively spot on any given night, where locals mix with expats.

Fleux · Design, Household

(Map p150; www.fleux.com; 39 & 52 rue Sainte Croix de la Bretonnerie, 4e; ☺11am-7.30pm Mon-Fri, 10.30am-8pm Sat, 2-7.30pm Sun; Ⓜ Hôtel de Ville) Innovative designs by European designers fill this big white space. Think products for the home that range from kitsch to clever to plain crazy.

Le Studio des Parfums · Perfume

(Map p150; ☎01 40 29 90 84; www.artisan parfumeur.com; 23 rue du Bourg Tibourg, 4e; Ⓜ St-Paul) Learn how to use a perfume maker's organ with more than 150 different scents and create your own fragrance (€95/175 for one/three hours) at this charming perfume studio. Little girls will love the scent workshops for children (45 minutes, €30).

Losco · Accessories

(Map p150; www.losco.fr; 20 rue de Sévigné, 4e; ☺2-7pm Sun-Tue, 11am-1pm & 2-7pm Wed-Sat; Ⓜ St-Paul) This artisan *ceinturier* epitomises the main draw of shopping in Paris – stumbling upon tiny boutique-workshops selling 101 quality variations of one single item, in this case *ceintures* (belts). Pick leather, length and buckle to suit just you.

L'Éclaireur
Fashion

(Map p150; www.leclaireur.com; 40 rue de Sévigné, 4e; M St-Paul) Part art space, part lounge and part deconstructionist fashion statement, this shop for women is known for having the next big thing first. The nearby **menswear store** (Map p150; www.leclaireur.com; 12 rue Malher, 4e; M St-Paul) fills an equally stunning, old warehouse-turned-art space.

L'Habilleur
Fashion, Accessories

(Map p150; 44 rue de Poitou, 4e; M St-Sébastien–Froissart) For 15 years this shop has been known for its discount designer wear – offering 50% to 70% off original prices. It generally stocks last season's collections including such lines as Paul & Joe, Giorgio Brato and Belle Rose.

Un Chien dans le Marais
Pets

(Map p150; www.unchiendanslemarais.com; 35bis rue du Roi de Sicile, 4e; M St-Paul) Only in Paris: this pocket-sized boutique has to be seen to be believed: Ballerina tutus, fur coats, woolly jumpers, black tailed coats, hoodies, frilly blouses and sweaters with 101 different logos – all for your dog.

Julien Caviste
Wine

(Map p156; 50 rue Charlot, 3e; M Filles du Calvaire) This independent wine shop focuses on small, independent producers and organic wines. The enthusiastic merchant Julien will locate and explain (and wax lyrical about) the wine for you, whatever your budget.

Boutique Obut
Games, Hobbies

(Map p156; www.labouleobut.com; 60 av de la République, 11e; M Parmentier) This is the Parisian mecca for fans of *pétanque* or the similar (though more formal) game of boules, a form of bowls played with heavy steel balls wherever a bit of flat and shady ground can be found. It will kit you out with all the equipment necessary to get a game going and even has team uniforms.

Secret Shopping in Le Marais

Some of the Marais' sweetest boutique shopping is secreted down peaceful alleyways and courtyards, free of cars, as they were centuries ago.

Don't miss **Village St-Paul** (Map p150; rue St-Paul, des rue Jardins St-Paul & rue Charlemagne, 4e; M St-Paul), a designer set of five vintage courtyards, refashioned in the 1970s from the 14th-century walled gardens of King Charles V, with tiny artisan boutiques, galleries and antique shops.

Les Mots à la Bouche
Books

(Map p150; www.motsbouche.com; 6 rue Ste-Croix de la Bretonnerie, 4e; ⊙11am-11pm Mon-Sat, 1-9pm Sun; M Hôtel de Ville) 'On the Tip of the Tongue' is Paris' premier gay and lesbian bookshop with some English-language books, too.

🜚 Sports & Activities

FREE Rollers & Coquillages
Inline Skating

(Map p150; www.rollers-coquillages.org; 37 bd Bourdon, 4e; ⊙2.30-5.30pm Sun, arrive 2pm) Suitable for all levels of ability, Rollers & Coquillages sets off on 21km-or-so routes from **Nomades** (Map p150; www.nomadeshop.com; 37 bd Bourdon, 4e; skate rental half-/full day from €5/8, weekend/week €15/30; M Bastille), where you can buy or rent inline skates and protective equipment.

The Islands

Paris' geographic and historic heart is situated here in the Seine. The city's watery beginnings took place on the Île de la Cité, the larger of the two inner-city islands. Today, all distances in France are measured from Point Zéro, marked by a bronze star outside Notre Dame. The island is also home to the beautiful Ste-Chapelle; the Conciergerie, where Marie Antoinette was imprisoned; a colourful flower market; and some picturesque parks such as place Dauphine and square du Vert Galant.

To the east, the tranquil Île St-Louis is graced with elegant mansions that are among the city's most exclusive residential addresses, along with a handful of intimate hotels and exquisite boutiques.

Connecting the two islands, the Pont St-Louis is an impossibly romantic spot at sunset. After nightfall, the Seine dances with the watery reflections of streetlights, headlamps, stop signals and the dim glow of curtained windows.

GARDEL BERTRAND/GETTY IMAGES ©

The Islands Highlights

Notre Dame (p178)

Revel in the crowning glory of medieval Gothic architecture at the Cathédrale de Notre Dar de Paris and its brilliantly bestial rooftop walk where you'll find yourself face-to-face with t most frightening of the cathedral's fantastic gargoyles, as well as the 13-tonne bell Emmar in the South Tower and a spectacular view of Paris from the Galerie des Chimères (Gargoy Gallery).

Pont Neuf (p183)

Pont Neuf, the oldest 'New Bridge' in town and an architectural delight, offe some of the most fantastic views of t Seine, day and night, especially from romantic recessed stone benches. T bridge is a prime example of the Ital Renaissance period – its style was meant to reflect Paris as the capital a powerful centralised state.

Conciergerie (p182)

Learn how Marie Antoinette and thousands of others lived out their final days before being beheaded at the Conciergerie. Here you can also admire the city's best example of the Rayonnant Gothic style in the 14th-century Cavalrymen's Hall, the largest surviving medieval hall in Europe, and the adjacent Tour de l'Horloge (Clock Tower). Built in 1353, it's held a public clock aloft since 1370.

BRUCE YUANYUE BI/GETTY IMAGES ©

GREG ELMS/GETTY IMAGES ©

Ste-Chapelle (p188)

Tucked away within the walls of the Palais de Justice (Law Courts), Ste-Chapelle is Paris' most exceptional Gothic building. Try to time your visit for a bright day, when sunlight streams through the glass. A *billet jumelé* combination ticket with the nearby Conciergerie is the best way to skip the long ticket queues. To experience the setting at its most ethereal, take in a classical concert here.

Berthillon (p183)

It's largely undisputed that Paris' best ice cream comes from Île St-Louis-based *glacier* (ice-cream maker) Berthillon. Buy a scoop of fresh-fruit sorbet, creamy coffee, *nougat au miel* (honey nougat) or luscious *noisette* (hazelnut) and wander, cone in hand, along the Seine or rue St-Louis en l'Île – or linger on Pont St-Louis and watch the buskers and street entertainers perform.

The Islands Walk

The Île de la Cité and the Île St-Louis might be tiny but there's plenty to take in on this walk, from Roman remains to the twin Gothic splendours Notre Dame cathedral and Ste-Chapelle, as well as Paris' oldest market – and its best ice cream.

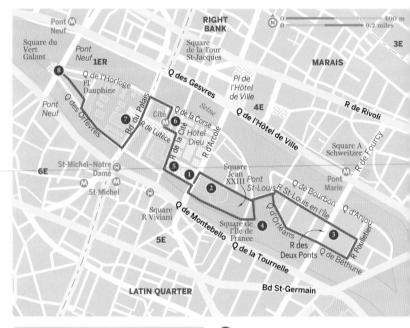

WALK FACTS
- **Start** Point Zéro
- **Finish** Pont Neuf
- **Distance** 3km
- **Duration** 1½ hours

❶ Point Zéro

Where better to start your exploration of the islands than **Point Zéro** – the point from which all distances in France are measured, marked by a bronze star on the place du Parvis Notre Dame.

❷ Notre Dame

Unthinkably, the glorious **Notre Dame** (p178), was slated for demolition following damage during the French Revolution. Salvation came with the popularity of Victor Hugo's 1831 novel, *The Hunchback of Notre Dame*, which sparked a petition to save it.

❸ Berthillon

Turn left (north) then right on rue du Cloître Notre Dame. Cross Pont St-Louis to the Île St-Louis and walk along rue St-Louis en l'Île past charming shops to **Berthillon** (p183). Although shops and cafes all over the islands and beyond sell these exquisite sorbets and ice creams, you can't beat buying it here from the company's own premises.

④ Mémorial des Martyrs de la Déportation

Pass the baroque church **Église St-Louis en l'Île** and turn right on rue Poulletier then right again and follow the river back to Pont St-Louis. Back on the Île de la Cité, the **Mémorial des Martyrs de la Déportation** (p183) sits on the island's eastern tip. Up ahead, one of the best views of Notre Dame is from **square Jean XXIII**, the little park behind the cathedral, where you can appreciate the forest of ornate flying buttresses.

⑤ Crypte Archéologique

Continue west along Notre Dame's southern side past the **statue of Charlemagne**, emperor of the Franks. Beneath your feet, the **Crypte Archéologique** (p179) reveals, layer by layer, the Île de la Cité's history from the Gallo-Roman town of Lutetia to the 20th century.

⑥ Marché aux Fleurs

Head north on rue de la Cité and turn right opposite the **Préfecture de Police de Paris**, the city's imposing police headquarters, then cut through the fragrant flower market, the **Marché aux Fleurs** (p187), alive with birdsong on Sunday from the bird market.

⑦ Ste-Chapelle

Follow the river around to turn left into bd du Palais; on your right is the **Conciergerie** (p182), a 14th-century royal palace used as a prison during the French Revolution before inmates were tried next door in the **Palais de Justice** (Law Courts). Within the Palais de Justice is the Gothic jewel **Ste-Chapelle** (p188); you can see the chapel's exterior by the law courts' magnificently gilded 18th-century gate facing rue de Lutèce.

⑧ Pont Neuf

Walk west around the island's southern side to rue de Harlay and cut across **place Dauphine** to **Pont Neuf** (p183). Steps lead from the bridge down to the pretty **square du Vert Gallant** (p183), perched at the Île de la Cité's western tip, which is an idyllic spot to rest your feet.

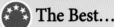
The Best…

PLACES TO EAT

Berthillon Premium all-natural ice cream and sorbets in some 70 flavours. (p183)

Le Tastevin Traditional lace-curtained decor and timeless French cuisine such as *escargots* (snails). (p184)

Mon Vieil Ami Vegetables are the star at neobistro 'My Old Friend'. (p184)

PLACES TO DRINK

Café St-Régis A deliciously Parisian hangout any time of day. (p186)

Taverne IV Authentic wine bar serving cheese and charcuterie platters. (p186)

La Charlotte de l'Isle Tiny, delightful *salon de thé* (tearoom). (p187)

PLACES TO ROMANCE

Tours de Notre Dame Hidden corners, stairwells and the rooftop. (p179)

Pont St-Louis Buskers by day and beautiful sunset views.

Pont Neuf Semicircular stone benches perfect for watching the riverboats pass beneath. (p183)

Square du Vert Galant Romantically situated on the tip of the Île de la Cité. (p183)

Mon Vieil Ami restaurant (p184)

Don't Miss
Notre Dame

Cathédrale de Notre Dame de Paris, the most visited unticketed site in Paris with upwards of 14 million people crossing its threshold a year, is not just a masterpiece of French Gothic architecture but was also the focus of Catholic Paris for seven centuries. Its stained-glass lit interior has wow factor aplenty, but it is the sky-high meander around its gargoyle-guarded rooftop that most visitors swoon over.

Map p184

www.cathedrale
deparis.com

6 place du Parvis
Notre Dame, 4e

admission free

⏱ 7.45am-7pm

M Cité

Architecture

Built on a site occupied by earlier churches and, a millennium before that, a Gallo-Roman temple, Notre Dame was begun in 1163 and largely completed by the early 14th century. The cathedral was badly damaged during the Revolution, prompting architect Eugène Emmanuel Viollet-le-Duc to oversee extensive renovations between 1845 and 1864. Enter the magnificent forest of ornate **flying buttresses** that encircle the cathedral chancel and support its walls and roof.

Notre Dame is known for its sublime balance, though if you look closely you'll see all sorts of minor asymmetrical elements introduced to avoid monotony, in accordance with standard Gothic practice. These include the slightly different shapes of each of the three main **portals**, whose statues were once brightly coloured to make them more effective as a *Biblia pauperum* – a 'Bible of the poor' to help the illiterate faithful understand Old Testament stories, the Passion of the Christ and the lives of the saints.

Rose Windows

Entering the cathedral, its grand dimensions are immediately evident: the interior alone is 130m long, 48m wide and 35m high and can accommodate more than 6000 worshippers.

The most spectacular interior features are three rose windows. The most renowned is the 10m-wide window over the western façade above the 7800-pipe organ, and the window on the northern side of the transept (virtually unchanged since the 13th century).

Treasury

In the southeastern transept, the **trésor** (adult/child €4/1; ⊙9.30am-6pm) contains artwork, liturgical objects and first-class relics. Among these is the **Ste-Couronne** (Holy Crown), purportedly the wreath of thorns placed on Jesus' head before he was crucified. It is exhibited between 3pm and 4pm on the first Friday of each month, 3pm to 4pm every Friday during Lent, and 10am to 5pm on Good Friday.

Towers

A constant queue marks the entrance to the **Tours de Notre Dame** (adult/child €8.50/ free; ⊙10am-6pm). Climb the 422 spiralling steps to the top of the western façade of the **North Tower** where you'll find yourself face-to-face with the cathedral's most frightening gargoyles, as well as the 13-tonne bell **Emmanuel** in the **South Tower**, and a spectacular view of Paris from the **Galerie des Chimères** (Gargoyles Gallery).

Crypt

Under the square in front of Notre Dame lies the **Crypte Archéologique** (adult/child €4/2; ⊙10am-6pm), a 117m-long and 28m-wide area displaying *in situ* the remains of structures built on this site during the Gallo-Roman period.

The Heart of Paris

Notre Dame really is the heart of the city, so much so that distances from Paris to every part of metropolitan France are measured from the square in front, the **place du Parvis Notre Dame**, across which Charlemagne (AD 742–814), emperor of the Franks, rides his steed. A bronze star across the street from the cathedral's main entrance marks the exact location of **Point Zéro des Routes de France**.

Music at Notre Dame

Music has been a sacred part of Notre Dame's soul since birth and there's no better day to revel in the cathedral's rousing musical heritage than on Sunday at a Gregorian or polyphonic Mass (10am and 6.30pm, respectively) or a free organ recital (4.30pm). From October to June, the cathedral stages evening sound-and-image 'operas' (admission free) and a wonderful repertoire of evening concerts; buy tickets (€18) from the welcome desk at the main entrance and find the program online at www. musique-sacree-notredamedeparis.fr.

Notre Dame Timeline

1160 Maurice de Sully becomes bishop of Paris. Mission: to grace growing Paris with a lofty new cathedral.

1182–90 The **choir with double ambulatory** ❶ is finished and work starts on the nave and side chapels.

1200–50 The **west facade** ❷, with rose window, three portals and two soaring towers, goes up. Everyone is stunned.

1345 Some 180 years after the foundation stone was laid, the Cathédrale de Notre Dame is complete. It is dedicated to *Notre Dame* (Our Lady), the Virgin Mary.

1789 Revolutionaries smash the original **Gallery of Kings** ❸, pillage the cathedral and melt all its bells except the great bell Emmanuel. The cathedral becomes a Temple of Reason, then a warehouse.

1831 Victor Hugo's novel *The Hunchback of Notre Dame* inspires new interest in the half-ruined Gothic cathedral.

1845–50 Architect Viollet-le-Duc undertakes its restoration. Twenty-eight new kings are sculpted for the west facade. The heavily decorated **portals** ❹ and **spire** ❺ are reconstructed. The neo-Gothic **treasury** ❻ is built.

1860 The area in front of Notre Dame is cleared to create the *parvis*, an alfresco classroom where Parisians can learn a catechism illustrated on sculpted stone portals.

1935 A rooster bearing part of the relics of the Crown of Thorns, St Denis and St Geneviève is put on top of the cathedral spire to protect those who pray inside.

1991 The architectural masterpiece of Notre Dame and its Seine-side riverbanks become a Unesco World Heritage Site.

2013 Notre Dame celebrates 850 years since construction began with a bevy of new bells and restoration works.

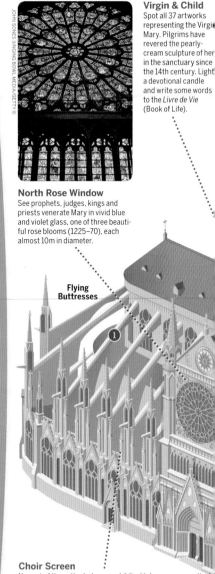

Virgin & Child
Spot all 37 artworks representing the Virgin Mary. Pilgrims have revered the pearly-cream sculpture of her in the sanctuary since the 14th century. Light a devotional candle and write some words to the *Livre de Vie* (Book of Life).

North Rose Window
See prophets, judges, kings and priests venerate Mary in vivid blue and violet glass, one of three beautiful rose blooms (1225–70), each almost 10m in diameter.

Flying Buttresses

Choir Screen
No part of the cathedral weaves biblical tales more evocatively than these ornate wooden panels, carved in the 14th century after the Black Death killed half the country's population. The faintly gaudy colours were restored in the 1960s.

Spire

⑤

Treasury

This was the cash reserve of French kings, who ordered chalices, crucifixes, baptism fonts and other sacred gems to be melted down in the Mint during times of financial strife – war, famine and so on.

⑥

Great Bell

Navigate an elf-sized door and 22 wooden steps to reach the bell Emmanuel: its peal is so pure thanks to the precious gems and jewels Parisian women threw into the pot when it was recast from copper and bronze in 1631.

Chimera Gallery

Scale the north tower for a Paris panorama admired by birds, dragons, grimacing gargoyles and grotesque chimera. Nod to celebrity chimera Stryga, who has wings, horns, a human body and sticking-out tongue. This bestial lot warns off demons.

North Tower

South Tower

Great Gallery

West Rose Window

②

Transept

③

North Tower Staircase

④

Portal of St-Anne

Entrance

Portal of the Last Judgement

The 'Mays'

On 1 May 1630, city goldsmiths offered a ?m-high painting to the cathedral – a tradition they continued every 1 May until 1707 when their bankrupt guild folded. View 13 of these huge artworks in the side chapels.

Three Portals

Play I spy (Greed, Cowardice et al) beneath these sculpted doorways, which illustrate the seasons, life and the 12 vices and virtues alongside the Bible.

Portal of the Virgin

Exit

Parvis Notre Dame

The Islands

🔀 Getting There & Away

○ **Metro** The closest stations are Cité (line 4) and Pont Marie (line 7).

○ **Bus** Bus 47 links Île de la Cité with the Marais and Gare de l'Est; bus 21 with Opéra and Gare St-Lazare. On Île St Louis it's bus 67 to Jardin des Plantes and Place d'Italie, and bus 87 through the Latin Quarter to École Militaire and Champ de Mars.

○ **Bicycle** Île de la Cité has a trio of handy Vélib' stations: one at place Louis Lépine by the Cité metro station; others at 1 quai aux Fleurs and 5 rue d'Arcole, both by Cathédrale de Notre Dame.

◎ Sights

Île de la Cité was the site of the first settlement in Paris (c 3rd century BC) and later the centre of Roman Lutetia. The island remained the hub of royal and ecclesiastical power, even after the city spread to both banks of the Seine in the Middle Ages. Smaller Île St-Louis was actually two uninhabited islets called Île Notre Dame (Our Lady Isle) and Île aux Vaches (Cows Island) in the early 17th century – until a building contractor and two financiers worked out a deal with Louis XIII to create one island and build two stone bridges to the mainland.

Conciergerie   Monument
(Map p184; www.monuments-nationaux. fr; 2 bd du Palais, 1er; adult/under 18yr €8.50/free, 1st Sun of month Nov-Mar free; 🕤9.30am-6pm; Ⓜ Cité) The Conciergerie was built as a royal palace in the 14th century, but later lost favour with the kings of France and became a prison and torture chamber. During the Reign of Terror (1793–94) it was used to incarcerate alleged enemies of the Revolution before they were brought before the Revolutionary Tribunal, next door in the Palais de Justice.

Among the almost 2800 prisoners held in the dungeons here (in various 'classes' of cells, no less) before being sent in tumbrels (carts) to the guillotine were Queen Marie Antoinette (see a reproduction of her cell) and, as the Revolution began to turn on its own, the radicals Danton, Robespierre and, finally, the judges of the Tribunal themselves. The 14th-century **Salle des**

Square at Pont Neuf, Île de la Cité

Gens d'Armes (Cavalrymen's Hall), a fine example of Rayonnant Gothic style, is Europe's largest surviving medieval hall.

A joint ticket with Sainte Chapelle costs €12.50.

Pont Neuf   Bridge

Map p184; M Pont Neuf) Paris' oldest bridge has linked the western end of Île de la Cité with both river banks since 1607 when the king inaugurated it by crossing the bridge on a white stallion. The occasion is commemorated by an equestrian **statue of Henri IV** (Map p184), known to his subjects as the Vert Galant (the 'jolly rogue' or 'dirty old man', depending on your perspective).

View the bridge's seven arches, decorated with humorous and grotesque figures of barbers, dentists, pickpockets, loiterers etc, from a spot along the river or a boat.

Pont Neuf and nearby place Dauphine were used for public exhibitions in the 18th century. In the last century the bridge became an objet d'art in 1963, when School of Paris artist Nonda built, exhibited and lived in a huge Trojan horse of steel and wood on the bridge; in 1984 when Japanese designer Kenzo covered it with flowers; and in 1985 when Bulgarian-born 'environmental sculptor' Christo famously wrapped the bridge in beige fabric.

Mémorial des Martyrs de la Déportation   Monument

Map p184; Square de l'Île de France, 4e; ⏰10am-noon & 2-7pm Apr-Sep, to 5pm Oct-Mar; M St-Michel–Notre Dame) The Memorial to the Victims of the Deportation, erected in 1962, remembers the 160,000 residents of France (including 76,000 Jews, of whom 11,000 were children) deported to and murdered in Nazi concentration camps during WWII. A single barred 'window' separates the bleak, rough concrete courtyard from the waters of the Seine. Inside lies the **Tomb of the Unknown Deportee**.

🍴 Eating

The Île St-Louis' most famous foodstuff is Berthillon ice cream, which is sold at outlets around the island including Berthillon's own premises. But it's not the only *glacier* here. Some places sell other ice cream brands that people mistake for Berthillon – check the sign. And gelato maker Amorino opened its inaugural shop at 47 rue St-Louis en l'Île on the Île St-Louis and now has outlets as far afield as the South Pacific.

Berthillon   Ice Cream €

(Map p184; 31 rue St-Louis en l'Île, 4e; ice cream from €2; ⏰10am-8pm Wed-Sun; M Pont Marie) Berthillon is to ice cream what Château Lafite Rothschild is to wine and Valhrona is to chocolate. And with nigh on 70 flavours to choose from, you'll be spoiled for choice.

While the fruit-flavoured sorbets (cassis, blackberry etc) produced by this celebrated *glacier* (ice-cream maker) are renowned, the chocolate, coffee, *marrons glacés* (candied chestnuts), Agenaise (Armagnac and prunes),

The Islands

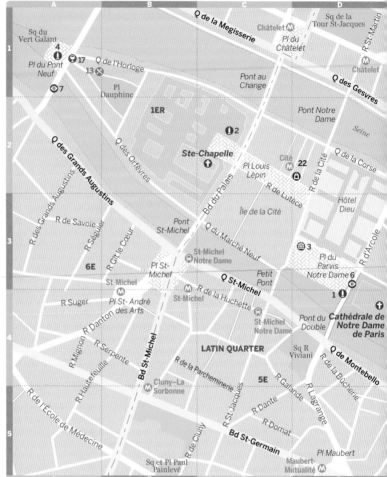

noisette (hazelnut) and nougat au miel (honey nougat) are richer. Eat in or grab a cone with one/two/three/four small scoops (€2.30/3.60/4.90/6.20) to takeaway.

Le Tastevin   Traditional French €€€

(Map p184; ☎ 01 43 54 17 31; www.letastevin -paris.com; 46 rue St-Louis en l'Île, 4e; starters €16-24.50, mains €23-31, menus €28-67; ⊙lunch Wed-Sun, dinner to 11pm Tue-Sun; Ⓜ Pont Marie) With its old-fashioned lace curtains, wood panelling and beamed ceiling, this lovely old-style address in a 17th-century building smacks of charm. Its excellent cuisine is equally traditional: think escargots (snails), foie gras, sole or ris de veau (calf sweetbreads) with morels and tagliatelli.

Mon Vieil Ami   Traditional French €€€

(Map p184; ☎ 01 40 46 01 35; www.mon-vieil-ami. com; 69 rue St-Louis en l'Île, 4e; plats du jour €13, menus €41; ⊙lunch & dinner Wed-Sun;

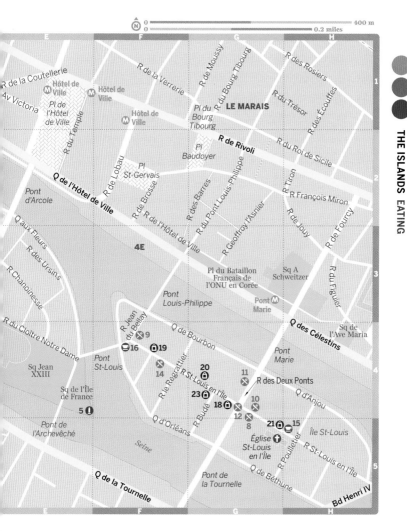

M Pont Marie) Alsatian chef Antoine West-
rmann is the creative talent behind this
sleek black neobistro where guests are
treated like old friends (hence the name)
and vegetables get royal treatment. The
lunchtime *plat du jour* (dish of the day) is
especially good value and a perfect reflection of the season.

For dinner try artichokes and potatoes
cooked with lemon confit and pan-fried
skate-fish. Unusually for Paris, Mon Veil
Ami opens for dinner at 6.30pm – handy
for those seeking an early dine.

Les Fous de l'Île Brasserie **€€**
(Map p184; www.lesfousdelile.com; 33 rue des
Deux Ponts, 4e; lunch 2-/3-course menu €18/24,
dinner €22/27; ⊙10am-2am; **M** Pont Marie)
This typical brasserie is a somewhat gen-
teel address with a lovely open kitchen
and cockerel theme throughout. Hearty
fare like *cassoulet* (traditional Languedoc
stew with beans and meat) and lighter
Spanish-inspired tapas dishes are served
continuously from noon to 11pm.

The Islands

Ma Salle à Manger   Bistro €€
(Map p184; ☎ 01 43 29 52 34; 26 place Dauphine, 1er; mains €15-25; ☯ lunch & dinner Mon-Fri; Ⓜ Cité) Spilling onto a terrace on tucked-away Place Dauphine, this cute little pink-and-red-decorated bistro and wine bar chalks its changing menu on the blackboard. Its name means 'my dining room'; with simple yet inspired dishes like foie gras with mango chutney, you'll wish it was yours.

L'îlot Vache   Traditional French €€
(Map p184; ☎ 01 46 33 55 16; http://restaurant -ilotvache.com; 35 rue St-Louis en l'Île, 4e; menu €37; ☯ dinner; Ⓜ Pont Marie) This traditional French restaurant is named for one of the Île St-Louis' two previous islands and decorated with cow statuettes. Its candles give exposed stone and wooden beams a romantic glow.

🍷 Drinking

Drinking venues on the islands are as scarce as hens' teeth. They do exist but use them as a starting point as very few places stay open after the witching hour of midnight.

Taverne Henri IV   Wine Bar
(Map p184; 13 place du Pont Neuf, 1er; ☯ Mon-Fri; Ⓜ Pont Neuf) One of the very few places to drink on Île de la Cité, this is a serious wine bar dating back to 1885. A tasty choice of inexpensive *tartines* (open sandwiches), charcuterie (cold cooked

Café St-Regis

Hip and historical with an effortless dose of retro vintage thrown in, **Le Saint Regis** (Map p184; http://cafesaintregisparis.com; 6 rue du Jean de Bellay, 4e; ☯ daily; 🛜; Ⓜ Pont Marie) – as those in the know call this cafe – is a deliciously Parisian hang-out any time of day, with free wi-fi, magazines and newspapers to read, and a lovely white ceramic-tiled interior. From boiled eggs with *bio* bread for breakfast to a midmorning crêpe, brasserie lunch or early-evening oyster platter, the food hits the spot. Weekend brunch jostles with happy hour (7pm to 9pm daily) for the best crowd-packed moment.

meats) and cheese platters complement ts extensive wine list, making it a lovely iverside place to drink with friends.

Predictably, it lures a fair few legal ypes from the nearby Palais de Justice.

a Charlotte de l'Isle   Tearoom
(Map p184; www.lacharlottedelisle.fr; 24 rue t-Louis en l'Île, 4e; ⏰11am-7pm Wed-Sun; Ⓜ Pont Marie) This tiny place is a particularly lovely *salon de thé* (tearoom) with a quaint fairy-tale theme, old-fashioned glass sweets jars on the shelf and a fine collection of tea to taste in situ or buy to sip at home. Hot chocolate, chocolate sculptures, cakes and pastries are other sweet reasons to come here.

e Flore en l'Île   Cafe
(Map p184; www.lefloreenlile.com; 42 quai 'Orléans, 4e; ⏰8am-1am; Ⓜ Pont Marie) A ourist crowd piles into this excellent eople-watching spot with prime views of he buskers on Pont St-Louis.

🔒 Shopping

Île de St-Louis is a shopper's delight for crafty boutiques and tiny specialist stores; Île de la Cité for souvenirs and tourist kitsch.

Marché aux Fleurs   Market
(Map p184; place Louis Lépin, 4e; ⏰8am-7.30pm Mon-Sat; Ⓜ Cité) Blooms have been sold at this flower market since 1808, making it the oldest market of any kind in Paris. On Sunday it transforms into a twittering bird market, **Marché aux Oiseaux** (Map p184; ⏰9am-7pm).

Il Campiello   Crafts
(Map p184; www.ilcampiello.com; 88 rue St-Louis en l'Île, 4e; ⏰11am-7pm; Ⓜ Pont Marie) Venetian carnival masks – intricately crafted from papier mâché, ceramics and leather – are the speciality of this exquisite shop, which also sells jewellery made from Murano glass beads. It was established by a native of Venice, to which the Île St-Louis bears more than a passing resemblance.

isplay at Marché aux Fleurs, Île de la Cité

COLSTRAVEL/ALAMY ©

✔ Don't Miss
Ste-Chapelle

Try to save Ste-Chapelle for a sunny day when Paris' oldest, finest stained glass is at its dazzling, sunlit best. Enshrined within the **Palais de Justice** (Law Courts), this gemlike Holy Chapel is Paris' most exquisite Gothic monument.

Ste-Chapelle was built in just six years (compared with nearly 200 years for Notre Dame) and was consecrated in 1248. The chapel was conceived by Louis IX to house his personal collection of holy relics, including the famous Holy Crown (now in Notre Dame) – acquired by the French king in 1239 from the emperors of Constantinople for a sum of money easily exceeding the amount it cost to build the chapel!

The bijou chapel is sumptuously decorated with statues, foliage-decorated capitals, angels and so on. But it is the 1113 scenes depicted in its 15 floor-to-ceiling stained- glass windows – 15.5m high in the nave, 13.5m in the apse – that stun. From the bookshop in the former ground-floor chapel reserved for palace staff, spiral up the staircase to the upper chapel where only the king and his close friends were allowed. Grab a storyboard in English to 'read' the 15-window biblical story – from Genesis through to the resurrection of Christ.

NEED TO KNOW

Map p184; 4 bd du Palais, 1er; adult/under 18yr €8.50/free; ⊙9.30am-5pm Nov-Feb, to 6pm Mar-Oct; Ⓜ Cité

La Petite Scierie
Food
(Map p184; www.lapetitescierie.fr; 60 rue St-Louis en l'Île, 4e; ⊙11am-7pm Thu-Mon; Ⓜ Pont Marie)

The Little Sawmill sells every permutation of duck edibles imaginable, with an emphasis on foie gras.

Bouquinistes

Lining both banks of the Seine through the centre of Paris (not on the islands themselves), the open-air *bouquiniste* stalls selling secondhand, often out-of-print, books, rare magazines, postcards and old advertising posters are a definitive Parisian sight. The name comes from *bouquiner*, meaning 'to read with appreciation'. At night, *bouquinistes*' dark-green metal stalls are folded down and locked like suitcases. Many open only from spring to autumn (and many shut in August), but even in the depths of winter you'll still find somewhere to barter for antiquarian treasures.

Librairie Ulysse Books
(Map p184; www.ulysse.fr; 26 rue St-Louis en l'Île, 4e; ⊙2-8pm Tue-Fri; Ⓜ Pont Marie) You can barely move in between this shop's antiquarian and new travel guides, *National Geographic* back editions and maps. Opened in 1971 by the intrepid Catherine Domaine, this was the world's first travel bookshop. Hours vary, but ring the bell and Catherine will open up if she's around.

Clair de Rêve Toys
(Map p184; www.clairdereve.com; 35 rue St-Louis en l'Île, 4e; Ⓜ Pont Marie) This shop is all about wind-up toys, music boxes and puppets – mostly marionettes, which sway and bob suspended from the ceiling.

Première Pression Provence Olive Oil
(Map p184; 51 rue St-Louis en l'Île, 4e; Ⓜ Pont Marie) Its name evokes the first pressing of olives to make oil in the south of France and that is precisely what this gourmet boutique sells – be it as oil or in any number of spreads and sauces (pesto, tapenade etc). The gigantic mill stone in the window makes the small shopfront impossible to miss.

Latin Quarter

So named because university students here used Latin until the French Revolution, the Latin Quarter is renowned worldwide as an intellectual incubator and remains the centre of academic life in Paris.

The quarter centres on the Sorbonne's main university campus, which is graced by fountains and lime trees. In the surrounding area you'll encounter students and professors lingering at late-night bookshops and secondhand record shops on and around the 'boul Mich' (bd St-Michel). You'll also encounter them researching in its museums like the Musée National du Moyen Âge (aka Cluny); at the library within its exquisite art deco–Moorish mosque; in its botanic gardens, the Jardin des Plantes; or simply relaxing in its pigeon-filled squares and gardens.

To really take the area's pulse, head to its liveliest commercial street, rue Mouffetard, a colourful jumble of student bars, cheap eateries, market stalls and inexpensive clothing and homewares shops.

The Pantheon (p205)

Latin Quarter Highlights

Institut du Monde Arabe (p202)

Inspired by traditional latticed-wood windows, this stunning building blends modern and traditional Arab and Western elements, including thousands of *mushrabiyah* (or *mouche-arabies*): photo-electrically sensitive apertures built into the glass walls that allow you to s[ee] out without being seen. The apertures are opened and closed by electric motors in order [to] regulate the amount of light and heat that reaches the building's interior.

1

Jardin des Plantes (p196)

2

Paris' sprawling botanical gardens inc[or]porate a winter garden, tropical green[-]houses and an alpine garden with 20[00] plants, as well as the École de Botar[iy] (School of Botany) gardens, used by students and green-fingered Parisia[ns.] It also encompasses a zoo – the Ménagerie du Jardin des Plantes – a[nd] the Musée National d'Histoire Natur[elle,] France's natural-history museum wi[th a] trio of museums including the kid-frie[ndly] Grande Galerie de l'Évolution.

Musée National du Moyen Âge (p201)

3

France's fascinating medieval history museum, the Musée National du Moyen Âge, doesn't attract the same volume of tourists as other major sights, so any time is generally good to visit. Audioguides are typically included in the admission price; for medieval history buffs wanting to delve even deeper, the museum's document centre (open by appointment) has thousands of references.

4

Shakespeare & Company (p208)

Not merely a bookshop but the stuff of legends, the original shop at 12 rue l'Odéon (closed by the Nazis in 1941) was run by Sylvia Beach and became the meeting point for Hemingway's 'Lost Generation'. George Whitman opened the present incarnation in 1951, and today Whitman's daughter, Sylvia Beach Whitman, maintains Shakespeare & Company's serendipitous magic.

5

Panthéon (p205)

Let your soul soar inside the Panthéon. Built as a church and completed the year the Revolution broke out, this sublime neoclassical structure now serves as a mausoleum for 'les grands hommes de l'époque de la liberté francaise' (great men of the era of French liberty), though in 1995 it welcomed its first woman, Nobel Prize-winner Marie Curie, who was reburied here along with her husband, Pierre.

Latin Quarter Walk

This walk through Paris' academic heartland contains lessons in Arab arts, horticulture and natural history at the city's botanic gardens, literary history at the haunts of writers including Hemingway and George Orwell, French medieval history and more.

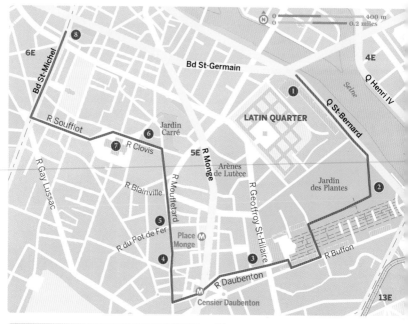

WALK FACTS
- **Start** Institute du Monde Arabe
- **Finish** Musée National du Moyen Age
- **Distance** 3km
- **Duration** Two hours

① Institut du Monde Arabe
Even from the outside, the **Institut du Monde Arabe** (p202) is extraordinary. The building confirmed French architect Jean Nouvel's reputation is a masterpiece of 1980s architecture, melding contemporary and traditional Arab and Western elements to reflect the Arabic arts displayed inside.

② Jardin des Plantes
Turn right from the Institut du Monde Arabe, follow the river for 400m before entering the green oasis of Paris' botanic gardens, the **Jardin des Plantes** (p196). In the southwest corner is the **Musée National d'Histoire Naturelle** (p196).

③ Mosquée de Paris
Across rue Geoffroy St-Hilaire from the Musée National d'Histoire Naturelle, you'll see the 26m-high minaret topping Paris' magnificently tiled art deco Moorish mosque, the **Mosquée de Paris** (p197). (Take an idyllic break with a sweet mint tea and North African pastry in its tearoom).

④ Rue Mouffetard

Head west from the Mosquée de Paris along rue Daubenton. Cross rue Monge and continue to the end, then turn right up **rue Mouffetard** (p209) This old Roman road is thronged with market stalls (except Mondays) as well as food shops and bars (look up: several have murals above).

⑤ Rue du Pot de Fer

In 1928 George Orwell stayed in a cheap boarding house above **6 rue du Pot de Fer** while working as a dishwasher. Read about it and the street, which he called 'rue du Coq d'Or' (Street of the Golden Rooster), in *Down and Out in Paris and London*. Rue du Pot de Fer's concentration of good-value restaurants includes the 1539-built **Le Pot de Terre** (p204) which d'Artagnan and the musketeers reputedly frequented.

⑥ Église St-Étienne du Mont

Beyond **place de la Contrescarpe** rue Mouffetard's northern continuation is rue Descartes. Follow it north before turning left on rue Clovis. On your right, **Église St-Étienne du Mont** contains Paris' only surviving rood screen (1535), separating the chancel from the nave (the other rood screens were removed during the late Renaissance because they prevented the faithful in the nave from seeing the priest celebrate Mass).

⑦ Panthéon

Still on rue Clovis, the domed, neoclassical **Panthéon** (p205) rises on your left. Originally built as a church, it's now a mausoleum for France's finest intellectuals.

⑧ Musée National du Moyen Age

West of the Panthéon, turn right on bd St-Michel. To your right, place de la Sorbonne links bd St-Michel and the Chapelle de la Sorbonne, the prestigious **Sorbonne** (p197) university's domed church, built in the early 7th century. Just a few metres ahead on your right is the Middle Ages museum the **Musée National du Moyen Age** (p201).

✸ The Best...

PLACES TO EAT

L'AOC Nothing but the finest ingredients and wines. (p200)

L'Agrume Watch chefs turn seasonal produce into sensational meals. (p200)

La Tour d'Argent Centuries-old establishment overlooking Notre Dame (p202)

Le Coupe-Chou Seductive French fare in a romantic candelit setting. (p203)

Bistrot Les Papilles Rustic bistro with wonderful wines. (p203)

PLACES TO DRINK

Café de la Nouvelle Mairie Local wine bar hidden away on a small square round the corner from the Panthéon. (p206)

Le Verre à Pied Classic cafe that's scacely changed since 1870. (p206)

Le Pub St-Hilaire Fun-loving student pub. (p206)

JAZZ CLUBS

Café Universel Adventurous program that includes jam sessions. (p207)

Le Caveau des Oubliettes Jazz in a 12th-century dungeon. (p207)

Le Petit Journal St-Michel Sophisticated jazz venue across from the Jardin du Luxembourg. (p207)

Restaurants in the Latin Quarter

Discover Latin Quarter

⟷ Getting There & Away

○ **Metro** The most central metro stations are St-Michel by the Seine; Cluny–La Sorbonne or Maubert-Mutualité on bd St-Germain; and Censier Daubenton or Gare d'Austerlitz by the Jardin des Plantes.

○ **Bus** Convenient bus stops include the Panthéon for bus 89 to Jardin des Plantes and 13e; bd St-Michel for bus 38 to Centre Pompidou, Gare de l'Est and Gare du Nord; and rue Gay Lussac for bus 27 to Île de la Cité and Opéra.

○ **Bicycle** Handy Vélib' stations include 42 rue St-Severin, 5e, by bd St-Michel; 40 rue Boulangers, 5e, near Cardinal Lemoine metro station; and 27 rue Lacépède, 5e, near Place Monge.

○ **Boat** Batobus stops Notre Dame (on quai de Montebello) and Jardin des Plantes (on quai St-Bernard).

Padlocks on the Pont de l'Archevêché
AFP/GETTY IMAGES ©

◉ Sights

Jardin des Plantes   Botanic Garden
(Map p198; www.jardindesplantes.net; 57 rue Cuvier, 5e; adult/child €6/4; ⏱7.30am-7.45pm Apr–mid-Oct, 8.30am-5.30pm mid-Oct–Mar; Ⓜ Gare d'Austerlitz, Censier Daubenton or Jussieu) Founded in 1626 as a medicinal herb garden for Louis XIII, Paris' 24-hectare botanical gardens are a serious institute rather than a leisure destination, but fascinating all the same, and idyllic to stroll or jog around.

A two-day pass covering access to all areas of the Jardin des Plantes costs €25/20 per adult/child.

Ménagerie du Jardin des Plantes   Zoo
(Map p198; www.mnhn.fr; 57 rue Cuvier & 3 quai St-Bernard, 5e; adult/child €9/7; ⏱9am-5pm; Ⓜ Gare d'Austerlitz, Censier Daubenton or Jussieu) Like the Jardin des Plantes in which it's located, this 1000-animal zoo is more than a tourist attraction, also doubling as a research centre for the reproduction of rare and endangered species. During the Prussian siege of 1870, the animals of the day were themselves endangered, when almost all were eaten by starving Parisians.

Musée National d'Histoire Naturelle   History Museum
(Map p198; www.mnhn.fr; 57 rue Cuvier, 5e; Ⓜ Censier Daubenton or Gare d'Austerlitz) France's National Museum of Natural History incorporates the **Galerie de Minéralogie et de Géologie** (Mineralogy & Geology Gallery; 36 rue Geoffroy St-Hilaire; adult/child €8/6; ⏱10am-6pm Wed-Mon)

(closed for renovation at the time of writing); the **Galerie d'Anatomie Comparée et de Paléontologie** (2 rue Buffon; adult/child €7/5; ⊙10am-5 or 6pm Wed-Mon), covering anatomy and fossils; and the topical **Grande Galerie de l'Évolution** (Great Gallery of Evolution; 36 rue Geoffroy St-Hilaire; adult/child €7/5; ⊙10am-6pm Wed-Mon), highlighting humanity's effect on the planet's ecosystems.

The National Museum of Natural History was created in 1793 and became a site of significant scientific research in the 19th century. Of its three museums, the Grande Galerie de l'Évolution is a particular winner if you're travelling with kids: life-sized elephants, tigers and rhinos play safari and imaginative exhibits on evolution and global warming fill 6000 sq metres.

FREE Musée de la Sculpture en Plein Air   Sculpture Museum

(Map p198; quai St-Bernard, 5e; admission free; ⊙24hr; M Gare d'Austerlitz) Along quai St-Bernard, this open-air sculpture museum (also known as the Jardin Tino Rossi) features over 50 unfenced sculptures from the late 20th century, and makes a great picnic spot.

Mosquée de Paris   Mosque

(Map p198; ☎01 45 35 97 33; www.la-mosquee. com; 2bis place du Puits de l'Ermite, 5e; adult/child €3/2; ⊙mosque 9am-noon & 2-6pm Sat-Thu, souk 11am-7pm daily; M Censier Daubenton or Place Monge) Paris' central mosque with its striking 26m-high minaret was built in 1926 in an ornate art deco Moorish style. The complex includes a wonderful North African–style *salon de thé* (tearoom) and restaurant and a *hammam* (traditional Turkish-style bathhouse), as well as a vibrant Moroccan-style *souk* (market). Visitors must be modestly dressed.

Sorbonne   University

(Map p198; 12 rue de la Sorbonne, 5e; M Cluny–La Sorbonne or RER Luxembourg) The crème de la crème of academia flock to this distinguished university, one of the world's most famous. Founded in 1253 by Robert de Sorbon, confessor to Louis IX, as a college for 16 impoverished theology students, the

Sorbonne soon grew into a powerful body with its own government and laws.

Place de la Sorbonne links bd St-Michel and the **Chapelle de la Sorbonne**, the university's distinctive domed church, built between 1635 and 1642.

FREE Arènes de Lutèce   Roman Ruins

(Map p198; www.arenesdelutece.com; 49 rue Monge, 5e; ⊙9am-9.30pm Apr-Oct, 8am-5.30pm Nov-Mar; M Place Monge) The 2nd-century Roman amphitheatre Lutetia Arena once accommodated around 10,000 people for gladiatorial combats and other events. Discovered by accident in 1869 when rue Monge was under construction, it's now used by locals playing football and, especially, boules and *pétanque*.

🍴 Eating

First-time visitors often think the touristy, restaurant-filled maze of tiny streets between the Seine and bd St-Germain in the 5e constitutes the Latin Quarter. But this neighbourhood encompasses so much more: there are wonderful bistros,

Latin Quarter

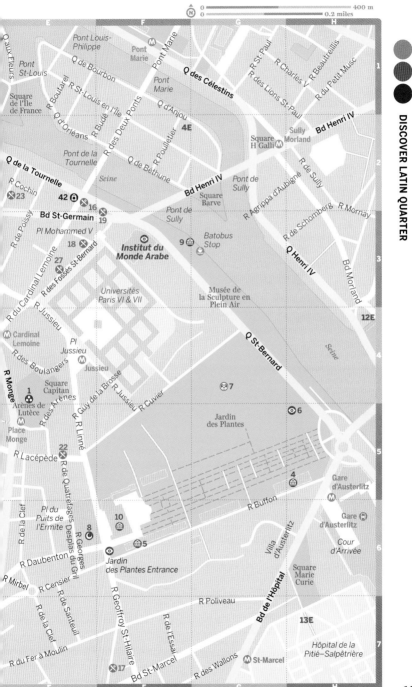

Pont Louis-Philippe
Q aux Fleurs
Pont St-Louis
Square de l'Île de France
Q de Bourbon
R Boutarel
R St-Louis en l'Île
R Budé
R des Deux Ponts
Q d'Orléans
Pont Marie
Pont Marie
Pont Marie
Q des Célestins
R St-Paul
R des Lions St-Paul
R Charles V
R Beautreillis
R du Petit Musc
Q d'Anjou
Q Poulletier
4E
Square H Galli
Sully Morland
Bd Henri IV
Pont de la Tournelle
Q de Béthune
Bd Henri IV
R de Sully
Q de la Tournelle
Seine
R Cochin
23
42
16
19
Bd St-Germain
Pl Mohammed V
18
R de Poissy
R du Cardinal Lemoine
27
R des Fossés St-Bernard
R Jussieu
Pont de Sully
Square Barve
Pont de Sully
Pont de Sully
R Agrippa d'Aubigné
R de Schomberg
R Mornay
Q Henri IV
Bd Morland
Institut du Monde Arabe
9
Batobus Stop
Universités Paris VI & VII
Musée de la Sculpture en Plein Air
12E
Cardinal Lemoine
R des Boulangers
Pl Jussieu
Jussieu
Q St-Bernard
R Monge
1
Square Capitan
R des Arènes
R Guy de la Brosse
R Jussieu
R Cuvier
Seine
Arènes de Lutèce
Place Monge
R Linné
7
6
R Lacépède
22
R de Quatrefages
Jardin des Plantes
R de la Clef
Pl du Puits de l'Ermite
Desplas
du Gril
10
8
5
4
Gare d'Austerlitz
R Buffon
R Daubenton
R Georges
R Censier
Jardin des Plantes Entrance
Gare d'Austerlitz
Cour d'Arrivée
R Mirbel
R de la Clef
R de Santeuil
R Geoffroy St-Hilaire
R de l'Essai
R Poliveau
Villa d'Austerlitz
Square Marie Curie
R du Fer à Moulin
17
Bd St-Marcel
R des Wallons
St-Marcel
Bd de l'Hôpital
13E
Hôpital de la Pitié−Salpêtrière

0   400 m
0   0.2 miles

Latin Quarter

restaurants, pubs, cafes, wine bars and squares tucked throughout the entire *arrondissement*.

L'AOC
Regional Cuisine €€

(Map p198; ☎ 01 43 54 22 52; www.restoaoc.com; 14 rue des Fossés St-Bernard, 5e; 2-/3-course lunch menus €21/29, mains €18-32; ☉lunch & dinner Tue-Sat; Ⓜ Cardinal Lemoine) *'Bistrot carnivore'* is the strapline of this ingenious restaurant concocted around France's most respected culinary products. The concept here is Appellation d'Origine Contrôlée (AOC), meaning everything has been reared or made according to strict guidelines designed to protect a product unique to a particular village, town or area. The result? Only the best!

L'Agrume
Neobistro €€

(Map p198; ☎ 01 43 31 86 48; 15 rue des Fossés St-Marcel, 5e; 2-/3-course lunch menus €19/24, mains €26-39; ☉lunch & dinner Tue-Sat; Ⓜ Censier Daubenton) Snagging a table at L'Agrume (meaning 'Citrus Fruit') is tough; reserve several days ahead. The reward is watching chefs work with seasonal products in the open kitchen while you dine – at a table, bar stool or *comptoir* (counter) – in this pocket-sized contemporary bistro on a little-known street on the Latin Quarter's southern fringe.

Lunching is magnificent value and a real gourmet experience. Evening dining is an exquisite, no-choice *dégustation* (tasting) melody of five courses that are different every day.

GLENN BEANLAND/GETTY IMAGES ©

✓ Don't Miss
Musée National du Moyen Âge

Medieval history comes to life at France's Musée National du Moyen Âge. This National Museum of the Middle Ages is often referred to as the Musée de Cluny (or just Cluny), due to the fact that it's partly – and atmospherically – housed in the 15th-century Hôtel de Cluny, Paris' finest civil medieval building. Spectacular displays include illuminated manuscripts, weapons, suits of armour, and objets d'art made of gold, ivory and enamel.

Long before construction began on the Hôtel de Cluny, the Gallo-Romans built *thermes* (baths) here around AD 200. The Musée National du Moyen Âge also occupies the *frigidarium* (cooling room), which holds remains of the **baths**. Look for the display of the fragment of mosaic, *Love Riding a Dolphin*.

Initially the residential quarters of the Cluny Abbots, the **Hôtel de Cluny** was later occupied by Alexandre du Sommerard, who moved in in 1833 with his collection of medieval and Renaissance objects. Bought by the state after his death, the museum opened a decade later, retaining the Hôtel de Cluny's original layout and features.

The museum's circular Room 13 on the 1st floor displays *La Dame à la Licorne* (The Lady with the Unicorn), a sublime series of late-15th-century **tapestries** from the southern Netherlands (pictured above). Five are devoted to the senses; the sixth is the enigmatic *À Mon Seul Désir* (To My Sole Desire), a reflection on vanity.

Small **gardens** to the museum's northeast, including the Jardin Céleste (Heavenly Garden) and the Jardin d'Amour (Garden of Love), are planted with flowers, herbs and shrubs that appear in masterpieces hanging throughout the museum. To the west, the **Forêt de la Licorne** (Unicorn Forest) is based on the illustrations in the tapestries.

NEED TO KNOW

Map p198; www.musee-moyenage.fr; 6 place Paul Painlevé; adult/18-25yr/under 18yr €8.50/6.50/free; ⏰9.15am-5.45pm Wed-Mon; Ⓜ Cluny–La Sorbonne

ARCAID/CORBIS © ARCHITECT JEAN NOUVEL

✓ Don't Miss
Institut du Monde Arabe

The Institute of the Arab World, set up by France and 20 Arab countries to promote cultural contacts between the Arab world and the West, is housed in a highly praised building blending modern and traditional Arab and Western elements, designed by Jean Nouvel and opened in 1987. Its new-look museum, showcasing Arab art, artisanship and science, was unveiled in 2012.

Allow time to savour the exterior of this visionary example of 1980s architecture.

Inside, the overhauled museum paints a global vision of the Arab world through 9th- to 19th-century art and artisanship, instruments from astronomy and other fields of scientific endeavour in which Arab technology once led the world, contemporary Arab art and so forth.

From the top (9th) floor **observation terrace**, incredible views stretch across the Seine as far as Sacré-Cœur. In addition to a panoramic restaurant here, the building also contains a cafe and a cafeteria, as well as a cinema and library.

NEED TO KNOW

Map p198; Institute of the Arab World; www.imarabe.org; 1 place Mohammed V; adult/under 26yr €8/free; ⊙10am-6pm Tue-Fri, to 7pm Sat & Sun; Ⓜ Jussieu

La Tour d'Argent Gastronomic €€€ (Map p198; ☏ 01 43 54 23 31; www.latourdargent. com; 15 quai de la Tournelle, 5e; lunch menus €65, dinner menus €170-190; ⊙lunch & dinner Tue-Sat; Ⓜ Cardinal Lemoine or Pont Marie) The venerable 'Silver Tower' is famous for its *caneton* (duckling), rooftop garden with glimmering Notre Dame views and a fabulous history harking back to 1582 – from Henry III's inauguration of the first fork in France to inspiration for the winsome animated film *Ratatouille*. Its wine cellar s one of Paris' best; dining is dressy and exceedingly fine.

Buy fine food and accessories in its **boutique** directly across the street.

Le Coupe-Chou
Traditional French €€

(Map p198; ☎ 01 46 33 68 69; www.lecoupechou.com; 9 & 11 rue de Lanneau, 5e; 2-/3-course lunch menus €27, mains €18-25; ⏱ Mon-Sat; Ⓜ Maubert-Mutualité) This maze of candlelit rooms inside a vine-clad 17th-century townhouse is overwhelmingly romantic. Ceilings are beamed, furnishings are antique, and background classical music mingles with the intimate chatter of diners. As in the days when Marlene Dietrich dined here, advance reservations are essential.

Timeless French dishes include Burgundy snails, steak tartare and bœuf bourguignon, finished off with fabulous cheeses sourced from *fromagerie* (cheese shop) Quatrehomme and a silken crème brûlée.

Bistrot Les Papilles
Bistro €€

(Map p198; ☎ 01 43 25 20 79; www.lespapillesparis.com; 30 rue Gay Lussac, 5e; lunch/dinner menus from €22/31; ⏱ 10.30am-midnight Mon-Sat; Ⓜ Raspail or RER Luxembourg) This hybrid bistro, wine cellar and *épicerie* (specialist grocer) with sunflower-yellow façade is one of those fabulous dining experiences that packs out the place. Dining is at simply dressed tables wedged beneath bottle-lined walls, and fare is market-driven: each weekday there's a different *marmite du marché* (market casserole). But what really sets it apart is its exceptional wine list.

Boulangerie Bruno Solques
Boulangerie, Patisserie €

(Map p198; 243 rue St-Jacques, 5e; ⏱ 6.30am-3pm Mon-Fri; 👬; Ⓜ Place Monge or RER Luxembourg) Inventive *pâtissier* Bruno Solques crafts oddly shaped flat tarts with mashed fruit, fruit-filled brioches and subtly spiced gingerbread. This small, bare-boards shop is also filled with wonderfully rustic breads. It's on the pricey side, but worth it – kids from the school across the way can't get enough.

Les Pipos
Wine Bar €€

(Map p198; ☎ 01 43 54 11 40; www.les-pipos.com; 2 rue de l'École Polytechnique, 5e; mains €13.50-25; ⏱ 8am-2am Mon-Sat; Ⓜ Maubert-Mutualité) A feast for the eyes and the senses, this *bar à vins* is above all worth a visit for its food. Its *charcuteries de terroir* (regional cold meats and sausages) is mouth-watering, as is its cheese board, which includes all the gourmet names (bleu d'Auvergne, St-Félicien, St-Marcellin etc). No credit cards.

Chez Nicos
Crêperie €

(Map p198; 44 rue Mouffetard, 5e; crêpes €3.50-6; ⏱ 10am-2am; 👬; Ⓜ Place Monge) The signboard outside crêpe artist Nicos' unassuming little shop chalks up dozens of fillings, but ask by name for his masterpiece, 'La Crêpe du Chef', stuffed with aubergines, feta, mozzarella, lettuce, tomatoes and onions. There's a handful of tables inside; otherwise get it wrapped up in foil and head to a nearby park.

Le Petit Pontoise
Bistro €€

(Map p198; ☎ 01 43 29 25 20; 9 rue de Pontoise, 5e; mains €19.50-28; ⏱ lunch & dinner; Ⓜ Maubert-Mutualité) Sit down at a wooden table behind the lace curtains hiding you from the world and indulge in fantastic old-fashioned classics like *rognons de veau à l'ancienne* (calf kidneys), *boudin campagnard* (black pudding) and sweet apple purée or roast quail with dates. Dishes – like the decor – might seem simple, but you'll leave pledging to return.

Moissonnier
Lyonnais €€€

(Map p198; ☎ 01 43 29 87 65; 28 rue des Fossés St-Bernard, 5e; 4-/6-course dinner menus €75/115, mains €35-49; ⏱ lunch & dinner Tue-Sat; Ⓜ Cardinal Lemoine) It's Lyon, not Paris, that French gourmets venerate as the French food capital. Take one bite of a big, fat *andouillette* (pig-intestine sausage), *tablier de sapeur* (breaded, fried stomach), traditional *quenelles* (dumplings) or *boudin noir aux pommes* (black pudding with apples) and you'll realise why. A perfect reflection of one of France's most unforgettable regional cuisines.

🌱 Le Jardin des Pâtes
Organic, Pasta €

(Map p198; 📞 01 43 31 50 71; 4 rue Lacépède, 5e; pasta €10-16.50; 🕐 lunch & dinner; 🚻; Ⓜ Place Monge) A crisp white-and-green façade handily placed next to a Vélib' station flags the Pasta Garden, a simple, smart 100% *bio* (organic) place where pasta comes in every guise imaginable – barley, buckwheat, rye, wheat, rice, chestnut and so on. Try the *pâtes de chataignes* (chestnut pasta) with duck breast, nutmeg, crème fraiche and mushrooms.

Le Pot de Terre
Traditional French €

(Map p198; 📞 01 43 31 15 51; www.lepotdeterre.com; 22 rue du Pot de Fer, 5e; lunch/dinner menus from €9/18; 🕐 lunch & dinner; 🚻; Ⓜ Place Monge) This place was built in 1539, and legend has it that d'Artagnan and the musketeers slaked their thirst here between sword duels. The great-value fare – *tartatouille* (puff pastry–encased ratatouille), *magret de canard aux framboises* (duck breast in raspberry sauce) and old-fashioned desserts like chocolate mousse – make it worth hunting down on this restaurant-clad street.

Le Pot O'Lait
Crêperie €

(Map p198; www.lepotolait.com; 41 rue Censier, 5e; lunch menus €12, crêpes €2.80-11.50; 🕐 lunch & dinner Tue-Sat; 🚻; Ⓜ Censier Daubenton) It might not have the lace-and-china atmosphere of a traditional Breton crêperie, but this bright, contemporary crêperie is the business when it comes to *galettes* (savoury buckwheat crêpes) like *andouille* (Breton sausage), onions and creamy mustard sauce, and sweet crêpes such as pistachio ice cream, zesty orange, hot chocolate and whipped cream.

Le Comptoir du Panthéon
Cafe, Brasserie €€

(Map p198; 📞 01 43 54 75 56; 5 rue Soufflot, 5e; salads €10-15, mains €12-26; 🕐 cafe 7am-2am Mon-Sat, to 11pm Sun, brasserie 11am-11pm Mon-Sat, to 7pm Sun; Ⓜ Cardinal Lemoine or RER Luxembourg) Enormous, creative meal-sized salads are the reason to pick this as a dining spot. Magnificently placed across from the domed Panthéon on the shady side of the street, its pavement terrace is big, busy and oh so Parisian – turn your head away from Voltaire's burial place and the Eiffel Tower pops into view. Service is superspeedy and food is handily served all day.

La Salle à Manger
Traditional French €

(Map p198; 📞 01 55 43 91 99; 138 rue Mouffetard, 5e; mains €11.50-15; 🕐 8am-4pm Mon-Fri, to 7pm Sat & Sun; Ⓜ Censier Daubenton) With a sunny pavement terrace beneath trees enviably placed at the foot of foodie street rue Mouffetard, the 'Dining Room' is prime real estate. Its 360-degree outlook – market stalls, fountain, church and garden with playground for

Cellar at Tour d'Argent (p202)

HUW JONES/GETTY IMAGES ©

✓ Don't Miss
Panthéon

The Panthéon is a superb example of 18th-century neoclassicism. The domed landmark was commissioned by Louis XV around 1750 as an abbey, but due to financial and structural problems it wasn't completed until 1789 – not a good year for church openings in Paris. Two years later the Constituent Assembly turned it into a secular mausoleum.

Louis XV originally dedicated the church to Ste Geneviève in thanksgiving for his recovery from an illness. It reverted to its religious duties twice more after the Revolution but has played a secular role ever since 1885, and now is the resting place of some of France's greatest thinkers.

Beneath the dome is **Foucault's pendulum**, which he used to demonstrate the earth's rotation on its axis.

Narrow stairs lead from behind the pendulum down to the labyrinthine **crypt**. Among its 80 or so permanent residents are Voltaire, Jean-Jacques Rousseau, Louis Braille, Émile Zola and Jean Moulin. The first woman to be interred in the Panthéon was the two-time Nobel Prize–winner Marie Curie (1867–1934), reburied here (along with her husband, Pierre) in 1995.

NEED TO KNOW

Map p198; www.monum.fr; place du Panthéon; adult/under 18yr €8.50/free; ☺10am-6.30pm Apr-Sep, to 6pm Oct-Mar; Ⓜ Maubert-Mutualité, Cardinal Lemoine or RER Luxembourg

tots – couldn't be prettier, and its salads, tartines (open-faced sandwiches), tarts and pastries ensure packed tables at breakfast, lunch and weekend brunch.

Le Baba Bourgeois   Modern French €€
(Map p198; ☎ 01 44 07 46 75; http://lebababour geois.com; 5 quai de la Tournelle, 5e; 2-/3-course

lunch menus €17/20, 2-/3-course dinner menus €25/36; ⏱11am-11.30pm Tue-Sat, to 5pm Sun; Ⓜ Cardinal Lemoine or Pont Marie) In a former architect's studio with a 1970s Italian designer interior, 'le BB' opens to a superb Seine-side pavement terrace facing Notre Dame. The menu – *tartes salées* (savoury tarts) and salads – makes for a simple stylish bite any time; Sunday ushers in a splendid all-day buffet brunch, à *volonté* (all you can eat; €27).

🍷 Drinking & Nightlife

Café de la Nouvelle Mairie   Wine Bar

(Map p198; 19 rue des Fossés St-Jacques, 5e; ⏱9am-8pm Mon-Fri; Ⓜ Cardinal-Lemoine) Shhhh...just around the corner from the Panthéon but hidden away on a small, fountained square, the narrow wine bar Café de la Nouvelle is a neighbourhood secret, serving blackboard-chalked wines by the glass as well as bottles. Accompanying tapas-style food is simple and delicious.

Le Verre à Pied   Cafe

(Map p198; http://leverreapied.fr; 118bis rue Mouffetard, 5e; ⏱9am-9pm Tue-Sat, 9.30am-4pm Sun; Ⓜ Censier Daubenton) Little has changed at this *café-tabac* since 1870. Its nicotine-hued mirrored wall, moulded cornices and original bar make it part of a dying breed, but the place oozes the charm, glamour and romance of an old Paris everyone loves, including stall holders from the rue Mouffetard market who yo-yo in and out.

Contemporary photography and art adorns one wall. Lunch is a busy, bustling affair, and live music quickens the pulse a couple of evenings a week.

Le Pub St-Hilaire   Pub

(Map p198; www.pubsainthilaire.com; 2 rue Valette, 5e; ⏱3pm-2am Mon-Thu, 3pm-4am Fri, 4pm-4am Sat, 4pm-midnight Sun; Ⓜ Maubert-Mutualité) 'Buzzing' fails to do justice to the pulsating vibe inside this student-loved pub. Generous happy hours last several hours and the place is kept packed with pool tables, board games, music on two floors, hearty bar food and various gimmicks to rev up the party crowd.

Curio Parlor Cocktail Club
Cocktail Bar

(Map p198; www.curioparlor.com; 16 rue des Bernardins, 5e; ⏰7pm-2am Mon-Thu, to 4am Fri-Sun; Ⓜ Maubert-Mutualité) Run by the same switched-on, chilled-out team as the Experimental Cocktail Club et al, this hybrid bar-club looks to the interwar *années folles* (crazy years) of 1920s Paris, London and New York for inspiration. Its racing-green façade with a simple brass plaque on the door is the height of discretion.

Go to its Facebook page to find out which party is happening when.

Café Delmas
Cafe

(Map p198; www.cafedelmasparis.com; 2 place de la Contrescarpe, 5e; ⏰8am-2am Sun-Thu, to 4am Fri & Sat; Ⓜ Place Monge) Enviably situated on tree-studded place de la Contrescarpe, the Delmas is a hot spot for chilling over *un café*/cappuccino or all-day breakfast. Cosy up beneath overhead heaters outside to soak up the street atmosphere or snuggle up between books in the library-style interior – awash with students from the nearby universities.

If you're looking for the bathrooms, Jacqueline is for women, Jacques for men.

Le Vieux Chêne
Bar

(Map p198; 69 rue Mouffetard, 5e; ⏰9am-2am Sun-Thu, to 5am Fri & Sat; Ⓜ Place Monge) This rue Mouffetard institution is reckoned to be Paris' oldest bar. Indeed, a revolutionary circle met here in 1848 and it was a popular *bal musette* (dancing club) in the late 19th and early 20th centuries. These days it's a student favourite, especially during happy 'hour' (4pm to 9pm Tuesday to Sunday, and from 4pm until closing on Monday).

Resident DJs mix it up on Friday and Saturday nights.

⭐ Entertainment

Café Universel
Jazz, Blues

(Map p198; 📞01 43 25 74 20; http://cafeuniversel.com; 267 rue St-Jacques, 5e; admission free; ⏰from 9pm Tue-Sat; 📶; Ⓜ Censier Daubenton or RER Port Royal) Café Universel hosts a brilliant array of live concerts with everything from bebop and Latin sounds to vocal jazz sessions. Plenty of freedom is given to young producers and artists, and its convivial relaxed atmosphere attracts a mix of students and jazz lovers. *La Confiture des Mardis* (Tuesday jam sessions) are particularly lively, with vocal jams until just after midnight.

Le Champo
Cinema

(Map p198; www.lechampo.com; 51 rue des Écoles, 5e; Ⓜ St-Michel or Cluny–La Sorbonne) This is one of the most popular of the many Latin Quarter cinemas, featuring classics and retrospectives looking at the films of such actors and directors as Alfred Hitchcock, Jacques Tati, Alain Resnais, Frank Capra, Tim Burton and Woody Allen. One of the two *salles* (cinemas) has wheelchair access.

A couple of times a month Le Champo screens films all night for night owls, kicking off at midnight (three films plus breakfast €15).

Le Caveau des Oubliettes
Jazz, Blues

(Map p198; 📞01 46 34 24 09; www.caveaudesoubliettes.fr; 52 rue Galande, 5e; ⏰5pm-4am; Ⓜ St-Michel) From the 16th-century ground-floor pub, descend to the 12th-century dungeon for cutting-edge jazz, blues and funk concerts and jam sessions (from 10pm).

Le Petit Journal St-Michel
Jazz, Blues

(Map p198; 📞01 43 26 28 59; www.petitjournalsaintmichel.com; 71 bd St-Michel, 5e; admission incl 1 drink €17-20, incl dinner €46-50; ⏰Mon-Sat; Ⓜ Cluny–La Sorbonne or RER Luxembourg) Classic jazz concerts kick off at 9.15pm in the atmospheric downstairs cellar of this sophisticated jazz venue across from the Jardin du Luxembourg. Everything ranging from Dixieland and vocals to big band and swing gets patrons' toes tapping. Dinner is served at 8pm.

Caveau de la Huchette
Jazz, Blues

(Map p198; 01 43 26 65 05; www.caveaudela huchette.fr; 5 rue de la Huchette, 5e; admission Sun-Thu €12, Fri & Sat €14, under 25yr €10; 9.30pm-2.30am Sun-Wed, to 4am Thu-Sat; St-Michel) Housed in a medieval *caveau* (cellar) used as a courtroom and torture chamber during the Revolution, this club is where virtually all the jazz greats have played since the end of WWII. It attracts its fair share of tourists, but the atmosphere can be more electric than at the more serious jazz clubs. Sessions start at 10pm.

🔒 Shopping

Shakespeare & Company
Books

(Map p198; www.shakespeareandcompany.com; 37 rue de la Bûcherie, 5e; 10am-11pm Mon-Fri, from 11am Sat & Sun; St-Michel) A kind of spell descends as you enter this enchanting bookshop, where nooks and crannies overflow with new and secondhand English-language books. Fabled for nurturing writers, at night its couches turn into beds where writers stay in exchange for stacking shelves. Readings by emerging to illustrious authors take place at 7pm most Mondays; it also hosts workshops and literary festivals.

Magie
Games, Hobbies

(Map p198; 01 43 54 13 63; www.mayette. com; 8 rue des Carmes, 5e; 1-8pm Mon-Sat; Maubert-Mutualité) One of a kind, this magic shop established in 1808 is said to be the world's oldest. Since 1991 it's been in the hands of world-famous magic pro Dominique Duvivier. Professional and hobbyist magicians flock here to discuss king sandwiches, reverse assemblies, false cuts and other card tricks with him and his daughter, Alexandra.

Should you want to learn the tricks of the trade, Duvivier has magic courses up his sleeve.

Fromagerie Laurent Dubois
Food, Drink

(Map p198; www.fromageslaurentdubois.fr; 47ter bd St-Germain, 5e; 8.30am-7.30pm Tue-Sat, to 1pm Sun; Maubert-Mutualité) One of the best *fromageries* in Paris, this cheese-lover's nirvana is filled with to-die-for delicacies such as St-Félicien with Périgord truffles. Rare, limited-production cheeses include blue Termignon and Tarentaise goats cheese. All are appropriately cellared in warm, humid or cold environments. There's also a 15e **branch** (www.fromageslau rentdubois.fr; 2 rue de Lourmel, 15e; 9am-1pm & 4-7.45pm Tue-Fri, 8.30am-7.45pm Sat, 9am-1pm Sun; Dupleix).

Abbey Bookshop
Books

(Map p198; 01 46 33 16 24; rue de la Parcheminerie, 5e; 10am-7pm Mon-Sat; St-Michel or Cluny–La Sorbonne) In a heritage-listed townhouse, this welcoming Canadian-run

Market stalls on rue Mouffetard
GREG ELMS/GETTY IMAGES ©

Rue Mouffetard

Originally a Roman road, the sloping, cobbled rue Mouffetard acquired its name in the 18th century, when the now-underground River Bievre became the communal waste-disposal for local tanners and wood-pulpers. The odours gave rise to the name Moffettes (literally 'skunk'), which evolved into Mouffetard.

Today the aromas on 'La Mouffe', as it's called by locals, are infinitely more enticing. Grocers, butchers, fishmongers and other food purveyors set their goods out on street stalls during the **Marché Mouffetard** (Map p198; ☺8am-7.30pm Tue-Sat, to noon Sun; MCensier Daubenton).

bookshop serves free coffee (sweetened with maple syrup) to sip while you browse tens of thousands of new and used books; it also organises literary events and countryside hikes.

Au Vieux Campeur   Outdoor Equipment
(Map p198; www.auvieuxcampeur.fr; 48 rue des Écoles, 5e; ☺11am-8pm Mon-Wed & Fri-Sat, to 9pm Thu; MMaubert-Mutualité or Cluny–La Sorbonne) This sporting-gear chain runs 29 shops in the Latin Quarter, each selling equipment for a specific outdoor activity.

Marché Maubert   Market
(Map p198; place Maubert, 5e; ☺7am-2.30pm Tue, Thu & Sat; MMaubert-Mutualité) The Left Bank's bohemian soul lives on at this colourful street market. Expect regular market fare: fresh food and veggies.

Marché Monge   Market
(Map p198; place Monge, 5e; ☺7am-2pm Wed, Fri & Sun; MPlace Monge) The open-air Marché Monge is laden with wonderful cheeses, baked goods and a host of other temptations.

St-Germain, Les Invalides & Montparnasse

Despite gentrification since its early 20th century bohemian days, there remains a startling cinematic quality to this soulful part of the Left Bank where artists, writers, actors and musicians cross paths and where *la vie germanopratine* (St-Germain life) is *belle*.

West towards the Eiffel Tower the Invalides area is an elegant if staid *quartier* (quarter) bordered by the smooth lawns of Esplanade des Invalides.

To the south, the Tour Montparnasse is an unavoidable sight, but its observation deck is an unrivalled spot to get to grips with the lie of the land. At its feet are the cafes, brasseries and backstreets where some of the early 20th century's most seminal artists and writers hung out – albeit now swathed by urban grit. The area's tree-filled cemetery is a peaceful spot to escape – and to visit famous graves of many of those same visionaries.

St-Germain de Prés

St-Germain, Les Invalides & Montparnasse Highlights

Musée d'Orsay (p216)

Revel in a wealth of impressionist masterpieces and art nouveau architecture in resplendently renovated surrounds at the glorious Musée d'Orsay, the home of France's national collection from the impressionist, postimpressionist and art nouveau movements, with world-famous works on display. Entry to the Musée d'Orsay is cheaper in the late afternoon so it's an ideal time to check out its breathtaking collections.

Les Catacombes (p226)

Venture into the spine-prickling, subterranean tunnels of Paris' creepy ossuary Les Catacombes, to ogle the freakishly large number of bones and skulls surrounding you. Millions of Parisians' remains are neatly packed along each and every wall of the 1.7km of underground corridors. During WWII these tunnels were used as a headquarters for the Resistance, and today they're the city's most macabre tourist attraction.

ROETTING/POLLEX/GETTY IMAGES ©

Hôtel des Invalides (p229)

The monumental Hôtel des Invalides was built in the 17th century to house infirm war veterans. At the southern end of the esplanade, laid out between 1704 and 1720, is the final resting place of Napoleon. Also here is France's largest military museum, as well as the Musée des Plans-Reliefs, with scale models of towns, fortresses and châteaux across France.

CHEOH WEE KEAT/GETTY IMAGES ©

Musée Rodin (p225)

Indulge in an exquisitely Parisian moment in the sculpture-filled gardens of the Musée Rodin. The collection of the master sculptor's works are displayed not only in his former workshop and showroom, the *hôtel particulier* Hôtel Biron (1730), but also beyond the doors of the mansion in its rose-covered garden – one of the most peaceful places in central Paris.

Les Deux Magots (p234)

If ever there were a cafe that summed up St-Germain des Prés' early-20th-century literary scene, it's this former hang-out of anyone who was anyone. You will spend *beaucoup* to sip a coffee in a wicker chair on the terrace shaded by dark-green awnings and geraniums spilling from window boxes, but it's an undeniable piece of Parisian history.

St-Germain, Les Invalides & Montparnasse Walk

Graceful gardens, monumental museums and centuries-old churches all feature on this walk, as well as time to linger along the neighbourhood's elegant streets.

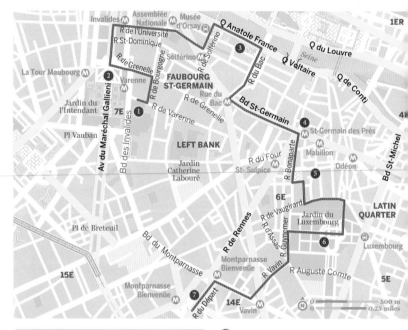

WALK FACTS

- **Start** Musée Rodin
- **Finish** Tour Montparnasse
- **Distance** 6.5km
- **Duration** Three hours

❶ Musée Rodin

Sculptor Rodin's former workshop and showroom is the 18th-century Hôtel Biron. Even if you don't have time to visit the mansion itself, at least stop to see the **Musée Rodin's** (p225) sculpture-filled gardens (reduced garden-only entry is available).

❷ Hôtel des Invalides

Head east on rue de Varenne and take your first left on rue de Bourgogne – on your left, you can see baguettes being baked through the viewing window of *boulangerie* **Besnier** (p232). Turn left onto rue de Grenelle and continue to place des Invalides. The **Hôtel des Invalides** (p229) complex, with the **Musée de l'Armée** military museum, and **Napoleon's tomb** are to your left. Turn right and stroll along av du Maréchal Gallieni through the grand lawns of the Esplanade des Invalides.

❸ Musée d'Orsay

From the Esplanade des Invalides, turn right on rue de l'Université, passing the **Assemblée Nationale** – the French Parliament's

ower house – on your left. Turn left on rue
e Solférino, and right around the **Musée
l'Orsay** (p216) on the riverfront. Not only
oes the d'Orsay contain breathtaking art-
vorks and artefacts from the art nouveau
ra, but the former railway station in which
t's housed, the Gare d'Orsay, is also an art
ouveau architectural wonder.

④ Église St-Germain des Prés

t the Gare d'Orsay's eastern end, turn
ight on rue du Bac. On your right at No 46,
uck into the 1831-established taxidermist
Deyrolle, which is overrun with stuffed
reatures including lions, tigers, zebras and
torks. Continue south to bd St-Germain
ind turn right until you reach Paris' oldest
hurch, **Église St-Germain des Prés**
p220), dating from the 11th century. Op-
osite the church is fêted literary cafe **Les
Deux Magots** (p234).

⑤ Église St-Sulpice

ollow rue Bonaparte south of the Église
St-Germain des Prés to another landmark
hurch, the **Église St-Sulpice** (p220).
ronted by dramatic Italianate columns,
nighlights inside include frescoes by Eugène
Delacroix in the Chapelle des Stes-Agnes,
ind the Rose Line (to the right of the middle
of the nave), featured in a pivotal scene of
The Da Vinci Code.

⑥ Jardin du Luxembourg

rom Église St-Sulpice, head south on to
ue Férou. Cross rue de Vaugirard and enter
he enchanting **Jardin du Luxembourg**
p218) near the early 17th-century **Palais
lu Luxembourg** (p219), which now houses
he French Sénat (upper house).

⑦ Tour Montparnasse

Stroll through the gardens to the octago-
al pond. Turn right at the pond and exit
he gardens at rue Guynemer, turning left.
Cross rue d'Assas and take rue Vavin until
urning right on bd du Montparnasse – up
head you can't miss the towering **Tour
Montparnasse** skyscraper, which has sen-
ational views from its observation terrace.

⭐ The Best…

PLACES TO EAT

Bouillon Racine An art nouveau jewel with
traditional French fare. (p224)

Huîterie Regis Small but supremely
stylish oyster bar. (p227)

Ze Kitchen Galerie Not just a Michelin-
starred restaurant but a smart art gallery
too. (p226)

L'Arpège Triple Michelin-starred
masterpiece helmed by vegetable maestro
Alain Passard. (p228)

PLACES TO DRINK

Les Deux Magots A literary stalwart, whose
former regulars included Hemingway. Their
hot chocolate is a must. (p234)

Au Sauvignon Authentic *bar à vin* (wine
bar) with an original zinc bar. (p234)

Brasserie O'Neil Paris' original
microbrewery, serving thin-crusted
flammekueches (Alsatian pizzas). (p235)

CHURCHES

Église St-Germain des Prés Built in the
11th century, this is Paris' oldest church.
(p220)

Église St-Sulpice Frescoes by Eugène
Delacroix and a starring role in *The Da
Vinci Code*. (p220)

Interior of Bouillon Racine (p224)
LONELY PLANET/GETTY IMAGES ©

Don't Miss
Musée d'Orsay

The home of France's national collection from the impressionist, postimpressionist and art nouveau movements is, appropriately, the glorious former Gare d'Orsay, itself an art nouveau showpiece. The museum opened in 1986 with a roll call of instantly recognisable works from French and international masters. Today, the Musée d'Orsay is fresh from a renovation program, incorporating a re-energised layout and increased exhibition space. Rather than being lost in a sea of white, prized paintings now gleam from richly coloured walls creating a much more intimate atmosphere, with high-tech illumination literally casting the works in a new light.

Map p230

www.musee
-orsay.fr

62 rue de Lille, 7e

adult/18-25yr/
under 18yr
€9/6.50/free

⊙9.30am-6pm Tue
Wed & Fri-Sun, to
9.45pm Thu

M Assemblée
Nationale or RER
Musée d'Orsay

The Building

...ven on its completion, just in time for the 1900 Exposition Universelle, painter ...douard Detaille declared that the new ...tation looked like a Palais des Beaux ...rts. But although it had all the mod-cons ...f the day – including luggage lifts and ...assenger elevators – by 1939 the in...reasing electrification of the rail network ...eant the Gare d'Orsay's platforms were ...oo short for mainline trains, and within a ...ew years all rail services ceased.

The station was used as a mailing ...entre during WWII, and in 1962 Orson ...elles filmed Kafka's *The Trial* in the ...en-abandoned building. Fortunately, ...was saved from being demolished ...nd replaced with a hotel complex ...y a Historical Monument listing in ...973, before the government set about ...stablishing the palatial museum.

The Paintings

...op of every visitor's must-see list is the ...orld's largest collection of impression...t and postimpressionist art. Just some ...f its highlights include Manet's *On The ...each* and *Woman With Fans*; Monet's ...ardens at Giverny and *Rue Montorgueil, ...aris, Festival of June 30, 1878*; Cézanne's ...ard players, *Green Apples* and *Blue Vase*; ...enoir's *Ball at the Moulin de la Galette* ...nd *Young Girls at the Piano*; Degas' ...allerinas; Toulouse-Lautrec's cabaret ...ancers; Pissarro's *The Harvest*; Sisley's ...iew of the Canal St-Martin*; and Van ...ogh's self-portraits, *Bedroom in Arles* ...nd *Starry Night over the Rhône*. One of ...e newest acquisitions is James Tissot's ...868 painting *The Circle of the Rue Roy...e*, classified as a national treasure.

Decorative Arts

...ousehold items such as hat and coat ...tands, candlesticks, desks, chairs, ...ookcases, vases, pot-plant holders, ...ee-standing screens, wall mirrors, water ...tchers, plates, goblets, bowls and even ...oup terrines become works of art in ...e hands of their creators from the era, ...corporating exquisite design elements ...nd motifs.

Sculptures

The cavernous former station is a magnificent setting for sculptures, including works by Degas, Gauguin, Claudel, Renoir and Rodin.

Graphic Arts

Drawings, pastels and sketches from major artists are another highlight. Look for Seurat's *The Black Bow* (c 1882), which uses crayon on paper to define forms by contrasting between black and white, and Gauguin's poignant self-portrait (c 1902), drawn near the end of his life.

Guided Tours

'Masterpieces of the Musée d'Orsay' **guided tours** (⏱1½ hrs; €6) in English generally run at least once a day from Tuesday to Saturday – check the website for seasonal departure times. Kids under 13 aren't permitted on tours.

Practicalities

Save money by purchasing a combined ticket with the Musée de l'Orangerie, (€14). Musée d'Orsay admission drops to €6.50 for entry after 4.30pm (after 6pm on Thursday). Under new rules, photography of all kinds (including from mobile phones) is now forbidden in the museum.

Dining

The new **Café Campana** (dishes €9-18; ⏱10am-5pm Tue, Wed & Fri-Sun, to 9pm Thu), adjacent to the impressionist gallery, serves a stylish menu of internationally inspired hot dishes such as PPP (penne rigate, Parma ham and parmesan – plus pesto) and wok-fried beef with Chinese noodles. Time has scarcely changed the museum's chandeliered **Restaurant Musée d'Orsay** (☎01 45 49 47 03; lunch/dinner menus €16.50/55; ⏱lunch Tue-Sun, dinner Thu, afternoon tea 2.45-5.45pm Tue-Sun).

✅ Don't Miss
Jardin du Luxembourg

The merest ray of sunshine is enough to draw apartment-dwelling Parisians outdoors, but this inner-city oasis of formal terraces, chestnut groves and lush lawns has a special place in their hearts. Napoleon dedicated the 23 gracefully laid-out hectares of the Luxembourg Gardens to the children of Paris, and many residents spent their childhood prodding little wooden sailboats with long sticks on the octagonal pond, watching puppets perform Punch & Judy–type shows, and riding the carousel or ponies. All those activities are still here today, as well as modern play equipment, tennis courts and other sporting and games venues.

Map p222

numerous entrances

admission free

🕑 hours vary

Ⓜ St-Sulpice, Rennes or Notre Dame des Champs, or RER Luxembourg

Grand Bassin

[A]ll ages love the octagonal **Grand Bassin**, [a] serene ornamental pond where adults [c]an lounge and kids can prod 1920s **toy [s]ailboats** (⊙Apr-Oct; per 30/60 minutes €2/3.20) with long sticks. Nearby, littlies [c]an take **pony rides** (€4.70) or romp [a]round the **playgrounds** – the green half [i]s for kids aged seven to 12 years, the blue [h]alf for under-sevens.

Puppet Shows

[Y]ou don't have to be a kid or speak French [t]o be delighted by marionette shows, [w]hich have entertained audiences in [F]rance since the Middle Ages. The lively [p]uppets perform in the Jardin du Luxem-[b]ourg's little **Théâtre du Luxembourg** ([h]ttp://guignolduluxembourg.monsite-orange.fr; [t]ickets €4.70; ⊙3.15pm Wed, 11am & 3.15pm [S]at & Sun, daily during school holidays). Show [t]imes can vary; check the program online [a]nd arrive half an hour ahead.

Orchards

[D]ozens of apple varieties grow in the **or-[c]hards** in the gardens' south. Bees have [p]roduced honey in the nearby apiary, the **[R]ucher du Luxembourg**, since the 19th [c]entury. The annual Fête du Miel (Honey [F]estival) offers two days of tasting and [b]uying its sweet harvest in late Septem-[b]er in the ornate **Pavillon Davioud**.

Palais du Luxembourg

[T]he gardens are the backdrop to the the **[P]alais du Luxembourg**, built in the 1620s [f]or Marie de Médici, Henri IV's consort, to [a]ssuage her longing for the Pitti Palace [i]n Florence.

Since 1958 the palace has housed [t]he French **Sénat** (☏01 44 54 19 49; www.[s]enat.fr; rue de Vaugirard, 6e; adult/18-25yr [€]8/6). It's occasionally visitable by [g]uided tour.

East of the palace is the Italianate **[F]ontaine des Médici**, an ornate [f]ountain built in 1630. During Baron [H]aussmann's 19th-century reshaping [o]f the roads, it was moved 30m and [t]he pond and dramatic statues of the [g]iant bronze Polyphemus discovering

the white-marble lovers Acis and Galatea were added.

Musée du Luxembourg

Prestigious temporary art exhibitions, such as 'Cézanne et Paris', take place in the **Musée du Luxembourg** (www. museeduluxembourg.fr; 19 rue de Vaugirard, 6e; most exhibitions adult/child around €13.50/9; ⊙10am-8pm Sun-Thu, to 10pm Fri & Sat). It was the first French museum to be opened to the public, in 1750, before re-locating here in 1886; following closures, it's mounted exhibitions regularly here since 1979.

Around the back of the museum, lemon and orange trees, palms, grenadiers and oleanders shelter from the cold in the palace's **orangery**. Nearby, the heavily guarded **Hôtel du Petit Luxembourg** was where Marie de Médici lived while Palais du Luxembourg was being built. The president of the Senate has called it home since 1825.

Picnicking

Kiosks and cafes are dotted throughout the park. If you're planning on picnicking, forget bringing a blanket – the elegantly manicured lawns are off-limits apart from a small wedge on the southern boundary. Instead, do as Parisians do, and corral one of the iconic 1923-designed green metal chairs and find your own favourite part of the park.

Discover St-Germain, Les Invalides & Montparnasse

Getting There & Away

○ **Metro** Get off at metro stations St-Germain des Prés, Mabillon or Odéon for its busy bd St-Germain heart. Montparnasse Bienvenüe is the transport hub for Montparnasse and the 15e. Bibliothèque and Place d'Italie are the main stops in Place d'Italie and Chinatown.

○ **Bus** Bus 86 stops on bd St-Germain for Odéon and Bastille; bus 96 on rue de Rennes for place Châtelet, Hôtel de Ville, St-Paul (Marais) and Ménilmontant; and bus 73 by the Musée d'Orsay for place de la Concorde, av des Champs-Élysées and La Défense.

○ **Bicycle** Handy Vélib' stations include 141 bd St-Germain, 6e; opposite 2 bd Raspail, 6e; and 62 rue de Lille, 7e.

○ **Boat** Batobus stops St-Germain des Prés and Musée d'Orsay.

◉ Sights

Église St-Germain des Prés
Church

(Map p222; www.eglise-sgp.org; 3 place St-Germain des Prés, 6e; ◔8am-7pm Mon-Sat, 9am-8pm Sun; Ⓜ St-Germain des Prés) Paris' oldest standing church, the Romanesque St Germanus of the Fields was built in the 11th century on the site of a 6th-century abbey and was the dominant place of worship in Paris until the arrival of Notre Dame. Despite numerous alterations since, the **Chapelle de St-Symphorien** (to the right as you enter) was part of the original abbey.

The Chapelle de St-Symphorien is believed to be the resting place of St Germanus (AD 496–576), the first bishop of Paris. Over the western entrance, the **bell tower** has changed little since 990, although the spire dates only from the 19th century.

Église St-Sulpice
Church

(Map p222; www.paroisse-saint-sulpice-paris.org; place St-Sulpice 6e; ◔7.30am-7.30pm; Ⓜ St-Sulpice) In 1646 work started on the twin-towered Church of St Sulpicius and took six architects 150 years to finish. What draws most people is not its striking Italianate façade with two rows of superimposed columns, Counter-Reformation-influenced neoclassical decor or even the frescoes by Delacroix, but its setting for a murderous scene in Dan Brown's *The Da Vinci Code*.

Musée de la Monnaie de Paris
Mint Museum

(Map p222; ☎ 01 40 46 56 66; www.monnaiedeparis.fr; 11 quai de Conti, 6e; Ⓜ Pont Neuf)

Candles at the Église St-Sulpice
LYDIA EVANS/GETTY IMAGES ©

St Germain, Les Invalides & Montparnasse

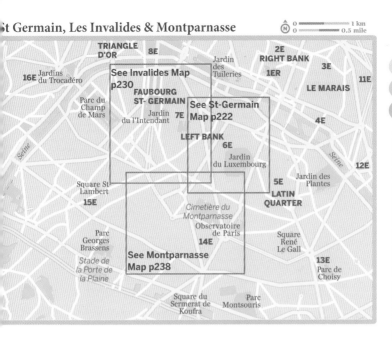

Closed for renovations at the time of writing, the Parisian Mint Museum traces the history of French coinage from antiquity onwards, with displays that help to bring to life this otherwise niche subject. It's housed in the 18th-century royal mint, the Hôtel de la Monnaie, which is still used by the Ministry of Finance to produce commemorative medals and coins.

The overhaul of this sumptuous neoclassical building with one of the longest façades on the Seine is slated to incorporate triple Michelin-starred chef Guy Savoy's new cafe and restaurant.

Bibliothèque Nationale de France
National Library

🖉 01 53 79 40 41, 01 53 79 53 79; www.bnf.fr; 11 quai François Mauriac, 13e; temporary exhibitions adult/18-26yr from €7/5; ⊙ 10am-7pm Tue-Sat, 7pm Sun; M Bibliothèque) With four sunlit towers shaped like open books, the National Library of France is well worth visiting for its excellent temporary exhibitions (use entrance E) that revolve around 'the word' – from storytelling to bookbinding and French heroes.

Docks en Seine
Cultural Centre

(Cité de la Mode et du Design; www.paris-docks -en-seine.fr; 36 quai d'Austerlitz, 13e; M Gare d'Austerlitz) Framed by a lurid-lime wave-like glass façade, this transformed Seine-side warehouse hosts the French fashion institute, the **Institut Français de la Mode** (hence the docks' alternative name, Cité de la Mode et du Design), with a growing program of fashion and design exhibitions and events throughout the year.

Its hottest new drawcard is the 2012-opened 'creative space' **Wanderlust** (32 Quai d'Austerlitz, 13e; ⊙ noon-6am, Wed-Sun; M Gare d'Austerlitz), with the city's largest terrace – a whopping 1600 sq m – as well as an open-air cinema, bar, club, restaurant, markets and more.

Cimetière du Montparnasse
Cemetery

(Map p238; www.paris.fr; bd Edgar Quinet & rue Froidevaux, 14e; ⊙ 8am-6pm Mon-Fri, 8.30am-6pm Sat, 9am-6pm Sun; M Edgar Quinet or Raspail) Opened in 1824, Montparnasse Cemetery, Paris' second-largest after Père Lachaise, sprawls over 19 hectares

St-Germain

DISCOVER ST-GERMAIN, LES INVALIDES & MONTPARNASSE

LATIN QUARTER

5E

14E

Jardin du Luxembourg

Bd St-Michel

Bd Raspail

R de Rennes

R du Depart

R du Regard

R Monsieur le Prince

R de Médicis

Pl Edmond Rostand

R Soufflot

R Toullier

R Victor Cousin

Sorbonne (Universités - Paris III & IV)

Pl de la Sorbonne

R Champollion

R Malebranche

R St-Jacques

R Gay Lussac

R des Ursulines

R Royer-Collard

R le Goff

R de l'Abbé de l'Epée

R Henri Barbusse

R Herschel

Luxembourg

Jardin R Cavelier-de-la-Salle

Jardin du Marco Polo

Av de l'Observatoire

R Auguste Comte

Université Paris V

R Michelet

R des Chartreux

R Joseph Baea

Pl Paul Claudel

R Rotro

R Servandoni

R Férou

R Bonaparte

R Madame

R Cassette

R de Vaugirard

R de Fleurus

R Jean Bart

R d'Assas

R Guynemer

Av Vavin

R Vavin

R Notre Dame des Champs

Notre Dame des Champs

Pl P Lafue

R Stanislas

R Ste-Beuve

R Bréa

R de Cicé

Pl et Sq Ozanam

Bd du Montparnasse

R du Montparnasse

R Huysmans

Vavin

St-Placide

Bd du Montparnasse

R de l'Abbé Grégoire

R du Cherche Midi

R de Vaugirard

R Jean Ferrandi

R Littré

Montparnasse Bienvenüe

Montparnasse Bienvenüe

Rennes

223

St-Germain

shaded by 1200 trees including maples, ash, lime trees and conifers.

Some of the illustrious 'residents' at Cimetière du Montparnasse include poet Charles Baudelaire, writer Guy de Maupassant, playwright Samuel Beckett, sculptor Constantin Brancusi, painter Chaim Soutine, photographer Man Ray, industrialist André Citroën, Captain Alfred Dreyfus of the infamous affair, actress Jean Seberg, and philosopher Jean-Paul Sartre and his partner, writer Simone de Beauvoir, as well as crooner Serge Gainsbourg. Free maps are available from the conservation office.

📷 Le Ballon Air de Paris
Scenic Balloon

(📞 01 44 26 20 00; www.ballondeparis.com; Parc André Citroën, 2 rue de la Montagne de la Fage, 15e; admission Mon-Fri €10/9, Sat & Sun €12/10; ⏰ 9am-30min prior to park closure; Ⓜ Balard or Lourmel) Drift up and up but no away – this helium-filled balloon remains tethered to the ground as it lifts you 150m into the air for spectacular panoramas over Paris. Confirm ahead as the balloon doesn't ascend in windy conditions.

🍴 Eating

St-Germain

Bouillon Racine Brasserie €€
(Map p222; 📞 01 44 32 15 60; www.bouillonracine. com; 3 rue Racine, 6e; lunch menu €14.50, menus €30-41; ⏰ noon-11pm; Ⓜ Cluny–La Sorbonne) Inconspicuously situated in a quiet street this heritage-listed art nouveau 'soup kitchen', with mirrored walls, floral motifs and ceramic tiling, was built in 1906 to

MUNTZ/GETTY IMAGES ©

Don't Miss

Musée Rodin

Sculptor, painter, sketcher, engraver and collector Auguste Rodin donated his entire collection to the French state in 1908 on the proviso they dedicate his former workshop and showroom, the beautiful Hôtel Biron (1730), to displaying his works. The collection includes Rodin's prized collection of works by artists including Van Gogh and Renoir as well as fifteen sculptures by Camille Claudel, Rodin's muse, protégé and mistress.

The first large-scale cast of Rodin's famous sculpture *The Thinker* (*Le Penseur*), made in 1902, resides in the garden – which is the perfect place to contemplate this heroic naked figure conceived by Rodin to represent intellect and poetry (it was originally titled *The Poet*).

Another masterpiece, *The Gates of Hell* (La Porte de l'Enfer), was commissioned in 1880 as the entrance for a never-built museum, and Rodin worked on his sculptural masterwork up until his death in 1917. Standing 6m high by 4m wide, its 180 figures comprise an intricate scene from Dante's *Inferno*.

The quintessential marble monument to love, *The Kiss* (Le Baiser), was originally part of *The Gates of Hell*. The sculpture's entwined lovers caused controversy on its completion due to Rodin's then-radical approach of depicting women as equal partners in ardour.

NEED TO KNOW

Map p230; www.musee-rodin.fr; 79 rue de Varenne, 7e; permanent exhibition adult/under 25yr €7/5, garden €1/free; ☺10am-5.45pm Tue-Sun; Ⓜ Varenne

feed market workers. Despite the magnificent interior, the food – inspired by age-old recipes – is by no means an afterthought.

Superbly executed dishes include stuffed, spit-roasted suckling pig, pork shank in Rodenbach red beer, and

RUNE JOHANSEN/GETTY IMAGES ©

✓ Les Catacombes

In 1785 it was decided to solve the hygiene and aesthetic problems posed by Paris' overflowing cemeteries by exhuming the bones and storing them in the tunnels of three disused quarries.

The Catacombes is one such ossuary, created in 1810. The route through the Catacombes begins at a small, dark-green belle époque building in the centre of a grassy area of av Colonel Henri Roi-Tanguy, adjacent to Place Denfert Rochereau. After descending 20m (130 steps) from street level, you follow 2km of subterranean passages with a mind-boggling amount of bones and skulls of millions of Parisians neatly packed along each and every wall. During WWII these tunnels were used as a headquarters by the Resistance; thrill-seeking cataphiles are often caught (and fined) roaming the tunnels at night.

Renting an audioguide greatly enhances the experience. In the tunnels the temperature is a cool 14° Celsius – bring a jacket, even in summer. The exit is back up 83 steps on rue Remy Dumoncel (Mouton-Duvernet), 700m southwest of av Colonel Henri Roi-Tanguy.

Map p238; www.catacombes.paris.fr; 1 av Colonel Henri Roi-Tanguy, 14e; adult/13-26yr/under 13yr €8/4/free; ⊙10am-5pm Tue-Sun; Ⓜ Denfert Rochereau

scallops and shrimps with lobster coulis. Finish off your foray in gastronomic history with an old-fashioned sherbet.

Ze Kitchen Galerie
Gastronomic €€€

(Map p222; ☎01 44 32 00 32; www.zekit chengalerie.fr; 4 rue des Grands Augustins, 6e; lunch/dinner menus €26.50/65; ⊙lunch & dinner

on-Fri, dinner Sat; **M** St-Michel) William
edeuil's passion for Southeast Asian travel
hows in the feisty dishes he creates in his
Michelin-starred glass-box kitchen. Hosting
hree to five art exhibitions a year, the res-
aurant/gallery's menu is a vibrant feast.

uîterie Regis   Oyster Bar €€
Map p222; **J** 01 44 41 10 07; 3 rue de Montfau-
on, 6e; dozen oysters, glass wine & coffee from
26; ⏱11am-midnight Tue-Sun; **M** Mabillon)
lip, trendy, tiny and white, this is *the* spot
or slurping oysters on crisp winter days.
hey come only by the dozen, along with
resh bread and butter, but wash them
own with a glass of chilled Muscadet
nd *voilà*, one perfect lunch. A twinset of
ables loiter on the pavement outside;
therwise it's all inside.

uisine de Bar   Sandwich Bar €
Map p222; 8 rue du Cherche Midi, 6e; dishes
7.50-13; ⏱8.30am-7pm Tue-Sat; **M** Sèvres-
abylone) As next-door neighbour to one
f Paris' most famous bakers, this is not
ny old sandwich bar. Rather, it is an
ltrachic spot to lunch between designer
outiques on open sandwiches cut from
hat celebrated **Poilâne** (p228) bread and
abulously topped with gourmet goodies
uch as foie gras, smoked duck, gooey St-
Marcellin cheese and Bayonne ham.

rasserie Lipp   Brasserie €€
Map p222; **J** 01 45 48 53 91; 151 bd St-Germain,
e; mains €17-24; ⏱11.45am-12.45am; **M** St-
ermain des Prés) Waiters in black waist-
oats, bow ties and long white aprons
erve brasserie favourites like *jarret de
orc aux lentilles* (pork knuckle with lentils)
t this celebrated wood-panelled estab-
shment. Opened by Léonard Lipp in 1880,
 achieved immortality when Hemingway
ang its praises in *A Moveable Feast*.

a Jacobine   Tearoom €€
Map p222; **J** 01 46 34 15 95; www.lajacobine.
om; 59-61 rue St-André des Arts, 6e; mains €16-
1; ⏱5-11.30pm Mon, noon-11.30pm Tue-Sun;
M Odéon) Olde-worlde tearoom/busy lunch
pot La Jacobine is packed to the rafters by
oon for its homemade tarts, giant-sized
alads and crêpes. Its lovely location inside

Paris' Oldest Restaurant & Cafe

With classical decor and cuisine, **À la
Petite Chaise** (Map p222; **J** 01 42 22 13
35; www.alapetitechaise.fr; 36 rue de Grenelle,
6e; lunch/dinner menus from €27/33;
⏱lunch & dinner Mon-Sat; **M** Sèvres-
Babylone) hides behind an iron gate
that's been here since it opened in
1680, when wine merchant Georges
Rameau served food to the public to
go with his wares.

Hot on the heels of À la Petite
Chaise's opening, **Le Procope**
(Map p222; www.procope.com; 13 rue de
l'Ancienne Comédie, 6e; 2-/3-course menus
from €21/28; ⏱11.30am-midnight; 🚹;
M Odéon) welcomed its first patrons
in 1686. Enduring house specialities
include calf's head casserole.

Cour du Commerce St-André, a glass-
covered passageway built in 1735 to link
two Jeu de Paume (old-style tennis) courts,
makes it all the more romantic.

Polidor   Traditional French €€
(Map p222; **J** 01 43 26 95 34; www.polidor.
com; 41 rue Monsieur le Prince, 6e; menus
from €22; ⏱lunch & dinner; **M** Odéon) A
meal at this quintessentially Parisian
crèmerie-restaurant is like a trip to Victor
Hugo's Paris: the restaurant and its decor
date from 1845. *Menus* of tasty, family-
style French cuisine ensure a never-
ending stream of diners eager to sample
bœuf bourguignon, *blanquette de veau à
l'ancienne* (veal in white sauce) and Po-
lidor's famous *tarte tatin*. Expect to wait.

Roger la
Grenouille   Traditional French €€
(Map p222; **J** 01 56 24 24 34; 26-28 rue des
Grands Augustins, 6e; lunch/dinner menus from
€19/24; ⏱lunch Tue-Sat, dinner Mon-Sat;
M St-Michel) Nine varieties of frogs' legs are
served at the time-worn institution 'Roger
the Frog', but if you're squeamish about

devouring Roger and his mates, dishes like roast pheasant with dried figs are also on the menu. Frog sculptures are scattered throughout the restaurant, along with B&W pictures of 1920s Paris on the white-washed walls and an array of old lamps illuminating the low sepia-coloured ceiling.

Le Petit Zinc
Brasserie €€

(Map p222; ☎01 42 86 61 00; www.petit-zinc.com; 11 rue St-Benoît, 6e; 2-/3-course menus €21/28.50, seafood platters from €24; ☻noon-midnight; Ⓜ St-Germain des Prés) This is not a 'little bar' as its name would suggest, but a large, wonderful brasserie serving mountains of fresh seafood, traditional French cuisine and regional specialities from the south-west in art nouveau splendour. The term 'brasserie' is used loosely here; you'll feel more like you're in a starred restaurant, so book ahead and dress accordingly.

Chez Allard
Bistro €€

(Map p222; ☎01 43 26 48 23; 41 rue St-André des Arts, 6e; lunch menus €27.90, mains €21-40; ☻lunch & dinner; Ⓜ St-Michel) Staff couldn't be kinder or more professional at this Left Bank favourite, even during its enormously busy lunchtime. The food is superb: try a dozen snails, some *cuisses de grenouilles* (frogs' legs) or *un poulet de Bresse* (France's most fêted chicken, from Burgundy) for two. Reservations are essential. Enter from 1 rue de l'Éperon.

Poilâne
Boulangerie €

(Map p222; www.poilane.fr; 8 rue du Cherche Midi, 6e; ☻7.15am-8.15pm Mon-Sat; Ⓜ Sèvres-Babylone) Pierre Poilâne opened his *boulangerie* on arriving from Normandy in 1932. Today his granddaughter runs the company, which still turns out wood-fired, rounded sourdough loaves made with stone-milled flour and Guérande sea salt.

Gérard Mulot
Patisserie €

(Map p222; www.gerard-mulot.com; 76 rue de Seine, 6e; ☻6.45am-8pm; Ⓜ Odéon or Mabillon) Fruit tarts (peach, lemon, apple), *tarte normande* (apple cake) and *clafoutis* (cherry flan) are among this celebrated patisserie's specialities.

Le Salon d'Hélène
Contemporary €€€

(Map p222; ☎01 42 22 00 11; www.helene darroze.com; 4 rue d'Assas, 6e; lunch/dinner menus from €28/85; ☻lunch & dinner Tue-Sat; Ⓜ Sèvres-Babylone) Female star chefs are a rarity in Paris, but Hélène Darroze is a major exception. These premises house both her elegant Michelin-starred restaurant upstairs and this relaxed downstairs salon renowned for its multicourse tasting menus, where dishes reflect Darroze's native southwestern France, such as wood-grilled foie gras.

Au Pied de Fouet
Bistro €

(Map p222; ☎01 43 54 87 83; www.aupiede fouet.com; 50 rue St-Benoît, 6e; mains €9-12.50; ☻Mon-Sat; Ⓜ St-Germain des Prés) Wholly classic bistro dishes such as *entrecôte* (steak), *confit de canard* (duck cooked slowly its own fat) and *foie de volailles sauté* (pan-fried chicken livers) at this busy bistro are astonishingly good value. Round off your meal with a *tarte tatin*, wine-soaked prunes or bowl of *fromage blanc* (a cross between yoghurt, sour cream and cream cheese).

Les Invalides

L'Arpège
Gastronomic €€€

(Map p230; ☎01 47 05 09 06; www.alain -passard.com; 84 rue de Varenne, 7e; menus from €120; ☻lunch & dinner Mon-Fri; Ⓜ Varenne) Triple Michelin-starred chef Alain Passard specialises in vegetables and inspired desserts like his signature tomatoes stuffed with a veritable orchard of a dozen dried and fresh fruits and served with aniseed ice cream. Book at least two weeks ahead.

Les Cocottes
Contemporary €€

(Map p230; www.leviolondingres.com; 135 rue Ste-Dominique, 7e; 2-/3-course lunch menus €9/15, mains €14-28; ☻lunch & dinner Mon-Sat; Ⓜ École Militaire or RER Port de l'Alma) Christian Constant's chic concept space is devoted to *cocottes* (casseroles), with a buoyant crowd feasting on inventive seasonal creations cooked to perfection in little black enamel, oven-to-table *cocottes* (casserole dishes). Seating is on bar

GEORG HANF/GETTY IMAGES ©

Don't Miss
Hôtel des Invalides

The Hôtel des Invalides was built in the 1670s by Louis XIV to provide housing for 4000 *invalides* (disabled war veterans). On 14 July 1789, a mob forced its way into the building and, after fierce fighting, seized 32,000 rifles before heading on to storm the prison at Bastille and start the French Revolution.

North of the main courtyard is the **Musée de l'Armée** (Army Museum; Map p230; www.invalides.org; 129 rue de Grenelle, 7e; ⊙10am-6pm Mon & Wed-Sat, to 9pm Tue), the nation's largest collection on French military history. Sobering wartime footage screens at this army museum, which also has weaponry, flag and medal displays as well as a multimedia area dedicated to Charles de Gaulle.

South of the main courtyard is the **Église du Dôme**, which, with its sparkling golden dome (1677–1735), is one of the finest religious edifices erected under Louis XIV, and was the inspiration for the United States Capitol building. The very extravagant Tombeau de Napoléon 1er (Napoleon's Tomb), in the centre of the Église du Dôme, comprises six coffins fitting into one another like a Russian doll. Also south of the main courtyard is the **Église St-Louis des Invalides**, once used by soldiers.

Within the Hôtel des Invalides, the esoteric **Musée des Plans-Reliefs** is full of scale models of towns, fortresses and châteaux across France.

NEED TO KNOW

Map p230; www.invalides.org; 129 rue de Grenelle, 7e; adult/child €9/free; ⊙10am-6pm Mon & Wed-Sun, 10am-9pm Tue, to 5pm Oct-Mar, closed 1st Mon of month; Ⓜ Invalides

stools around high tables and it doesn't take reservations: get here at noon sharp or by 7.15pm.

Le Square Regional Cuisine €€
(Map p230; ☏01 45 51 09 03; www.restaurant lesquare.com; 31 rue St-Dominique, 7e;

Les Invalides

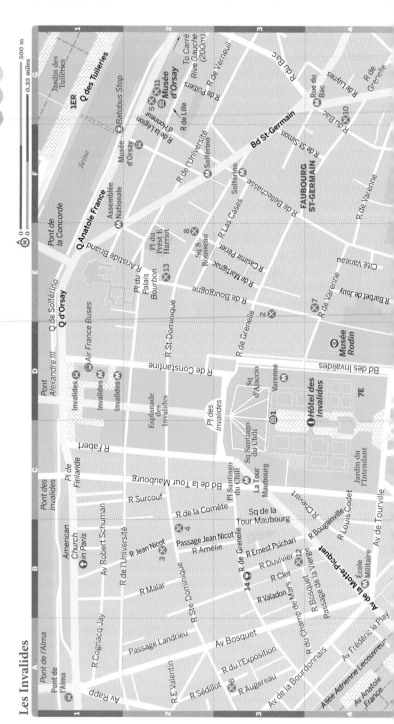

500 m
0.25 miles

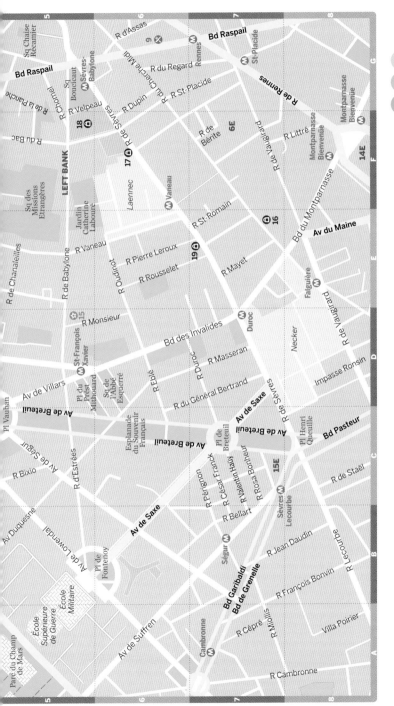

Les Invalides

lunch/dinner menus from €19.50/26; ⊙lunch & dinner Mon-Sat; Ⓜ Solférino) The terrace tables along rue Casimir-Périer are the best seats in the house for views of the neighbouring twin-spired Basilique Ste Clotilde, which resembles a mini-Notre Dame. Inside, autumnal hued banquettes and wood panelling are an elegant spot to dine on classical dishes with a southwestern accent, such as beef with béarnaise sauce and potato gratin.

To drink in the views, the bar opens from 8am to 11pm.

Besnier
Boulangerie €

(Map p230; 40 rue de Bourgogne, 7e; ⊙7am-8pm Mon-Fri Sep-Jul; Ⓜ Varenne) You can watch baguettes being made through the viewing window of this award-winning *boulangerie/patisserie*.

Tante Marguerite
Regional Cuisine €€€

(Map p230; 📞 01 45 51 79 42; www.bernard -loiseau.com; 5 rue de Bourgogne, 7e; lunch/dinner menus €38/52; ⊙lunch & dinner Mon-Fri; Ⓜ Assemblée Nationale) Opened by one of France's most decorated chefs, the late Bernard Loiseau, and helmed by chef Pedro Gomes, this elegant wood-panelled restaurant celebrates the rich flavours of Burgundy. Immortal Loiseau recipes include snail ragout.

Café Constant
Bistro €€

(Map p230; www.cafeconstant.com; 139 rue Ste-Dominique, 7e; 2-/3-course menus €16/23; ⊙lunch & dinner Tue-Sun; Ⓜ École Militaire or RER Port de l'Alma) Take a former Michelin-star chef and a dead-simple corner cafe and what do you get? This jam-packed ad dress with original mosaic floor, wooden tables and huge queues every meal time. The pride and joy of Christian and Catherine Constant, it doesn't take reservations but you can enjoy a drink at the bar (or on the pavement outside) while you wait.

Cuisine is creative bistro, mixing old-fashioned grandma staples like *purée de mon enfance* (mashed potato from my childhood) with Sunday treats like foie-gras-stuffed quail and herb-roasted chicken. **Les Cocottes** (p228), a couple of doors down on the same street, is another Constant hit.

Brasserie Thoumieux
Traditional French €€

(Map p230; 📞 01 47 05 49 75; www.thoumieux. com; 79 rue St-Dominique; mains €20-23; ⊙noon-midnight; Ⓜ La Tour Maubourg) An old-school institution, Thoumieux was founded in 1923, and has been worshipped by generations of diners ever since for its menu of duck thighs, veal and snails and its smooth-as-silk service.

Boulangerie-Pâtisserie Stéphane Secco
Boulangerie €

(Map p230; 20 rue Jean Nicot, 7e; ⏰8am-8.30pm Tue-Sat; Ⓜ️La Tour-Maubourg) Don't miss Stéphane Secco's signature *Paris-Brest* (wheel-shaped choux pastry with butter cream and almonds, which was created in 1891 to commemorate the bicycle race between Paris and Brest in Brittany), delicate *madeleines* (traditional lemon-flavoured shell-shaped cakes) and 0% fat cheesecake (yes, really).

Rue Cler
Market €

(Map p230; rue Cler, 7e; ⏰8am-7pm Tue-Sat, 8am-noon Sun; Ⓜ️École Militaire) Pick up fresh bread, sandwich fillings, pastries and wine for a picnic along the lively market street rue Cler, which buzzes with local shoppers, especially on weekends.

Marché Raspail
Market €

(Map p230; bd Raspail btwn rue de Rennes & rue du Cherche Midi, 6e; ⏰regular market 7am-2.30pm Tue & Fri, organic market 9am-3pm Sun; Ⓜ️Rennes) A traditional open-air market on Tuesday and Friday, Marché Raspail is especially popular on Sundays when it's filled with organic produce.

Poissonnerie du Bac
Seafood €

(Map p230; 69 rue du Bac, 7e; ⏰9am-1pm & 4-7.30pm Tue-Sat, 9.30am-1pm Sun; Ⓜ️Rue du Bac) Self-caterers shouldn't miss this superb aquamarine- and cobalt-tiled fishmonger.

Montparnasse
Le Dôme
Brasserie €€€

(Map p238; ☎️01 43 35 25 81; 108 bd du Montparnasse, 14e; mains €37-49, seafood platters €54; ⏰lunch & dinner; Ⓜ️Vavin) A 1930s art deco extravaganza, Le Dôme is a monumental place for a meal service of the formal white-tablecloth and bow-tied waiter variety. It's one of the swishest places around for shellfish platters piled high with fresh oysters, king prawns, crab claws and so on, followed by traditional creamy home-made *millefeuille* for dessert, wheeled in on a trolley and cut in front of you.

La Closerie des Lilas
Brasserie €€

(Map p238; ☎️01 40 51 34 50; www.closeriedes lilas.fr; 171 bd du Montparnasse, 6e; restaurant mains €23-49, brasserie mains €23-27; ⏰restaurant lunch & dinner, brasserie noon-1am, piano bar 11am-1am; Ⓜ️Vavin or RER Port Royal) As anyone who has read Hemingway knows,

Brasserie Lipp (p227)

what is now the American Bar at the 'Lilac Enclosure' is where Papa did a lot of writing (including much of *The Sun Also Rises*), drinking and oyster slurping. Brass plaques tell you exactly where he and luminaries such as Pablo Picasso, Guillaume Apollinaire, Man Ray, Jean-Paul Sartre and Samuel Beckett stood, sat or fell.

La Closerie des Lilas is split into a late-night piano bar, chic restaurant and more lovable (and cheaper) brasserie with a hedged-in pavement terrace.

🍷 Drinking & Nightlife

St-Germain's Carrefour de l'Odéon has a cluster of lively bars and cafes. Rue de Buci, rue St-André des Arts and rue de l'Odéon enjoy a fair slice of night action with their arty cafes and busy pubs, while place St-Germain des Prés buzzes with the pavement terraces of fabled literary cafes.

St-Germain

Les Deux Magots   Cafe
(Map p222; www.lesdeuxmagots.fr; 170 bd St-Germain, 6e; ⏰7.30am-1am; Ⓜ St-Germain des Prés) If you're feeling decadent, order this iconic literary cafe's famous shop-made hot chocolate, served in porcelain jugs. The name refers to the two *magots* (grotesque figurines) of Chinese dignitaries at the entrance.

Au Sauvignon   Wine Bar
(Map p222; 80 rue des Saints Pères, 7e; ⏰8.30am-10pm; Ⓜ Sèvres-Babylone) There's no more authentic *bar à vin* than this. Grab a table in the evening sun or head to the quintessential bistro interior, with an original zinc bar, tightly packed tables and hand-painted ceiling celebrating French viticultural tradition. Order a plate of *casse-croûtes au pain Poilâne* – toast with ham, pâté, terrine, smoked salmon, foie gras and so on.

Left: Exterior of Café de Flore; **Below:** Diners outside Les Deux Magots

(LEFT) DANITA DELIMONT/GETTY IMAGES ©; (BELOW) LONELY PLANET/GETTY IMAGES ©

Brasserie O'Neil
Microbrewery

(Map p222; www.oneilbar.fr; 20 rue des Canettes, 6e; ☺noon-2am; Ⓜ St-Sulpice or Mabillon) Paris' first microbrewery was opened by a French restaurateur and French brewer over two decades ago, and still brews four fabulous beers (blond, amber, bitter brown and citrusy white) on the premises. Soak them up with thin-crusted *flammekueches* (Alsatian pizzas).

Café de Flore
Cafe

(Map p222; www.cafedeflore.fr; 172 bd St-Germain, 6e; ☺7am-1.30am; Ⓜ St-Germain des Prés) The red upholstered benches, mirrors and marble walls at this art deco landmark haven't changed much since the days when Jean-Paul Sartre and Simone de Beauvoir essentially set up office here, writing in its warmth during the Nazi occupation. It also hosts a monthly English-language philocafé session.

Prescription Cocktail Club
Cocktail Bar

(Map p222; www.prescriptioncocktailclub.com; 23 rue Mazarine, 6e; ☺7pm-1am Mon-Thu, to 4am Fri & Sat; Ⓜ Odéon) With bowler and flat-top hats as lampshades and a 1930s speakeasy New York air to the place, this cocktail club (one in a trio run by the same massively successful team as **Curio Parlor** (p207) and **Experimental** (p112)) is very Parisian-cool. Getting past the doorman can be tough, but once in it's friendliness and old-fashioned cocktails all round. Watch its Facebook page for events such as Sunday afternoon Mad Hatters pyjama parties.

Les Invalides

Alain Milliart
Juice Bar

(Map p230; ☎01 45 55 63 86; www.alain-milliat. com; 159 rue de Grenelle, 7e; ☺10am-10pm Tue-Sat; Ⓜ La Tour Maubourg) Alain Milliart's fruit juices, bottled in the south of France, were

235

until recently reserved for ultra-exclusive hotels and restaurants. But the opening of his Parisian juice bar/bistro means you can pop in to buy one of 33 varieties of juices and nectars, or sip them in house. Milliart's jams and compotes are equally lush.

Montparnasse

Le Batofar
Nightclub

(www.batofar.org; opp 11 quai François Mauriac, 13e; ⏰9pm-midnight Mon & Tue, to 4am or later Wed-Sun; Ⓜ Quai de la Gare or Bibliothèque) This incongruous, much-loved, red-metal tugboat has a rooftop bar that's terrific in summer, and a respected restaurant, while the club underneath provides memorable underwater acoustics between its metal walls and portholes. Le Batofar is known for its edgy, experimental music policy and live performances, mostly electro-oriented but also incorporating hip-hop, new wave, rock, punk or jazz. Hours can vary.

Le Select
Cafe

(Map p238; 99 bd du Montparnasse, 6e; ⏰7am-2.30am; Ⓜ Vavin) Dating from 1923, this Montparnasse institution was the first of the area's grand cafes to stay open late into the night, and it still draws everyone from beer-swigging students to whisky-swilling politicians. Open sandwiches made with Poilâne bread are a speciality.

✪ Entertainment

Cinéma La Pagode
Cinema

(Map p230; ☎01 45 55 48 48; www.etoile-cinema.com; 57bis rue de Babylone, 7e; Ⓜ St-François-Xavier) This 19th-century Japanese pagoda was converted into a cinema in the 1930s and remains the most atmospheric spot in Paris to catch arthouse and classic films. Don't miss a moment or two in its bamboo-enshrined garden.

🛍 Shopping

Art and antique dealers congregate within the **Carré Rive Gauche** (www.carre rivegauche.com; Ⓜ Rue du Bac or Solférino). Bounded by quai Voltaire and rues de l'Université, des St-Pères and du Bac, this 'Left Bank square' is home to more than 120 specialised merchants. Antiques fairs

Le Batofar nightclub on the banks of the Seine

re usually held in spring, while exhibitions take place during the year.

To the east, meandering the art galleries on rue Mazarine, rue Jacques Callot, rue des Beaux Arts and rue de Seine is a real feast for the designer soul.

Adam Montparnasse   Art Supplies

(Map p238; www.adamparis.com; 11 bd Edgar Quinet, 14e; ☺9.30am-12.30pm & 1.30-7pm Mon, 9.30am-7pm Tue-Sat; MⒺdgar Quinet) If Paris' glorious art galleries have awoken your inner artist, pick up paint brushes, charcoals, pastels, sketchpads, watercolours, oils, acrylics, canvases and all manner of art supplies at this historic shop. Picasso, Brancusi and Giacometti were among Édouard Adam's clients.

Another seminal client was Yves Klein, with whom Adam developed the ultramarine 'Klein blue' – the VLB25 Klein Blue' varnish is sold exclusively here.

Cire Trudon   Home, Garden

(Map p222; www.ciretrudon.com; 78 rue de Seine, 6e; ☺10-7pm Mon-Sat, closed Mon Aug; MOdéon) Claude Trudon began selling candles here in 1643, and the company – which officially supplied Versailles and Napoleon with light – is now the world's oldest candle-maker (look for the plaque to the left of the shop's awning). A rainbow of candles and candlesticks fill the shelves inside.

Le Bon Marché   Department Store

(Map p230; www.bonmarche.fr; 24 rue de Sèvres, 7e; ☺10am-8pm Mon-Wed & Fri, to 9pm Thu & Sat; MSèvres Babylone) Built by Gustave Eiffel as Paris' first department store in 1852, Le Bon Marché translates as 'good market' but also means 'bargain', which it isn't. But it is the epitome of style, with a superb concentration of men's and women's fashions, beautiful homewares, stationery and a good range of books and toys as well as chic dining options.

The icing on the cake is its glorious food hall, **La Grande Épicerie de Paris**.

Art & Antique Streets

The northern wedge of the 6e between Église St-Germain des Prés and the Seine is a dream to mooch around with its bijou art galleries, antique shops, stylish vintage clothes, and fashion boutiques (PennyBlack, Vanessa Bruno, Joseph, Isabel Marant et al). St-Germain des Prés' natural style continues along the western half of bd St-Germain and rue du Bac – two streets with a striking collection of contemporary furniture, kitchen and design shops.

La Grande Épicerie de Paris   Food, Drink

(Map p230; www.lagrandeepicerie.fr; 36 rue de Sèvres, 7e; ☺8.30am-9pm Mon-Sat; MSèvres Babylone) Among other edibles, Le Bon Marché's magnificent food hall sells vodka-flavoured lollipops with detoxified ants inside and fist-sized Himalayan salt crystals to grate over food. Its fantastical displays of chocolates, pastries, biscuits, cheeses, fresh fruit and vegetables and deli goods are a sight to behold.

Au Plat d'Étain   Games, Hobbies

(Map p222; 16 rue Guisarde, 6e; ☺11am-12.30pm & 2-7pm Tue & Thu-Sat; MOdéon) Nail-sized tin (étain) and lead soldiers, snipers, cavaliers, military drummers and musicians (great for chessboard pieces) cram this fascinating boutique. In business since 1775, the shop itself is practically a collectable.

Hermès   Concept Store

(Map p222; www.hermes.com; 17 rue de Sèvres, 6e; ☺10.30am-7pm Mon-Sat; MSèvres-Babylone) A stunning art deco swimming pool now houses luxury label Hermès' first-ever concept store. Retaining its original mosaic tiles and iron balustrades and adding enormous timber pod-like 'huts', the vast, tiered space showcases new directions in home furnishings including fabrics and wallpaper, as well as classic lines including its signature scarves.

Montparnasse

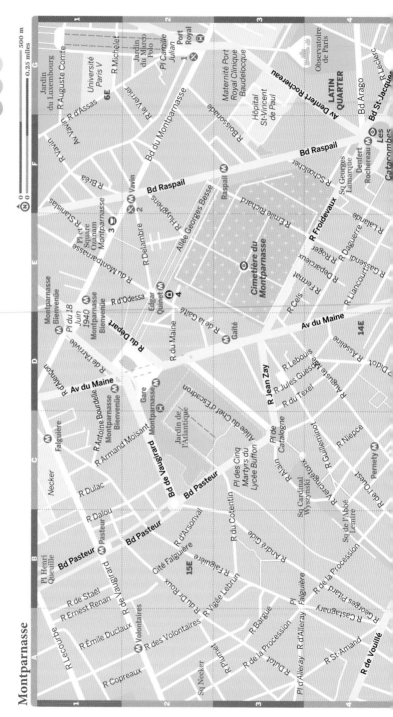

500 m
0.25 miles

6E

Jardin du Luxembourg
R Auguste Comte
Université Paris V
R Michelet
Jardin du Marco Polo
Pl Camille Julian
Port Royal
Av Vavin
R d'Assas
R Verrier
Maternité Port Royal Clinique Baudelocque
Bd du Montparnasse
R Boissonade
Hôpital St-Vincent de Paul
Av Denfert Rochereau
LATIN QUARTER
Observatoire de Paris
Bd Arago
Bd St-Jacques - R Leclerc

R Vavin
R Bréa
R Stanislas
Pl et Square Ozanam
Montparnasse
Vavin
Bd Raspail
R du Montparnasse
R Huyghens
R Émile Richard
Raspail
Bd Raspail
R Schoelcher
Sq Georges Lamargue
Denfert Rochereau
Les Catacombes

Montparnasse Bienvenüe
Pl du 18 Juin 1940
Montparnasse Bienvenüe
R Delambre
R d'Odessa
Edgar Quinet
Cimetière du Montparnasse
R Froidevaux
R Lalande
R Daguerre
R Roger
R Gassendi
R Liancourt
R Depardieu
R Fermat
R Cels

R de l'Arrivée
R d'Alençon
Av du Maine
R Antoine Bourdelle
R Armand Moisant
Gare Montparnasse
Montparnasse Bienvenüe
R du Départ
Pl de la Gaîté
R de la Gaîté
R du Maine
Av du Maine
14E
R Asseline
R Didot

Falguière
Necker
R Dulac
R Dalou
Bd de Vaugirard
Jardin de l'Atlantique
Allée du Chef d'Escadron
Pl des Cinq Martyrs du Lycée Buffon
R du Cotentin
Sq Cardinal Wyszynski
Sq de l'Abbé Lemire
R Jean Zay
Pl de Catalogue
R du Châtel
R Lebouis
R Jules Guesde
R du Texel
R Auguste Mie
R Guilleminot
R Vercingétorix
R Niepce
Pernety
R de l'Ouest

Pl Henri Queuille
Bd Pasteur
Pasteur
R de Staël
R Ernest Renan
R du Dr Roux
R de Vaugirard
Bd Pasteur
Bd Pasteur
R d'Arsonval
R Falguière
Cité Falguière
15E
R André Gide
Bd Pasteur

R Lecourbe
R Émile Duclaux
Volontaires
R des Volontaires
R Copreaux
Sq Necker
R Plumet
R Vigée Lebrun
R de la Procession
Pl de Falguière
R de la Procession
R Bargue
R Dutot
R d'Alleray
R d'Alleray
R Georges Pitard
R Castagnary
R St-Amand
R de Vouillé

Montparnasse

Alexandra Sojfer   Accessories

(Map p222; www.alexandrasojfer.fr; 218 bd
St-Germain, 7e; ⏰9.30am-6.30pm Tue-Sat;
Ⓜ St-Germain des Prés) Become Parisian
chic with a frivolous, frilly, fantastical or frightfully fashionable *parapluie*
(umbrella), parasol or walking cane,
handcrafted by Alexandra Sojfer at this
parapluie-packed St-Germain boutique,
in the trade since 1834.

Le Bain Rose   Home, Garden

(Map p222; www.le-bain-rose.fr; 11 rue d'Assas,
6e; ⏰10am-7pm Mon-Sat; Ⓜ Rennes) The
antique and retro mirrors, perfume
spritzers, soap dishes, mirrors (hand-
held and on stands) and even basins and
tapware at this long-established shop
can transform your bathroom into a belle
epoque sanctum.

Quatrehomme   Food, Drink

(Map p230; 62 rue de Sèvres, 6e; ⏰8.45am-1pm
& 4-7.45pm Tue-Thu, 8.45am-7.45pm Fri & Sat;
Ⓜ Vanneau) Buy the best of every French
cheese you can find, many with an original take (eg Epoisses boxed in chestnut
leaves, Mont d'Or flavoured with black
truffles, spiced honey and Roquefort
bread etc), at this king of *fromageries*. The
smell alone as you enter is heavenly.

A La Recherche
De Jane   Accessories

(Map p222; http://alarecherchedejane.word
press.com; 41 rue Dauphine, 6e; ⏰11.30am-
7.30pm Tue-Sat, 12.30-7pm Sun; Ⓜ St-Germain
des Prés) This *chapelier* (milliner) has liter-

239

ally thousands of handcrafted hats on hand for both men and women, and can also make them to order. Hours can vary.

JB Guanti — Accessories

(Map p222; www.jbguanti.fr; 59 rue de Rennes, 6e; ⊙10am-7pm Mon-Sat; MSt-Sulpice or Mabillon) For the ultimate finishing touch, the men's and women's gloves at this specialist boutique, are the epitome of both style and comfort, whether unlined, silk lined, cashmere lined, lambskin lined or trimmed with rabbit fur.

La Dernière Goutte — Food, Drink

(Map p222; www.ladernieregoutte.net; 6 rue du Bourbon le Château, 6e; ⊙10am-1.30pm & 3.30-8.30pm; MMabillon) 'The Last Drop' is the brainchild of Cuban-American sommelier Juan Sánchez, whose tiny wine shop is packed with exciting French *vins de pro-priétaires* (estate-bottled wines) made

Discount Designer Outlets & Secondhand Chic

For previous seasons' collections, surpluses, prototypes and seconds by name-brand designers, save up to 70% off men's, women's and kids' fashions at outlet stores along **rue d'Alésia** (MAlésia), 14e, particularly between av de Maine to rue Raymond-Losserand. For slashed prices on *grandes marques* (big names) under one roof, head to the 15e's **Mistigriff** (www.mistigriff.fr; 83-85 rue St-Charles, 15e; MCharles Michels), near the Place Charles Michels. Pick up current designer and vintage cast-offs at *dépôt-vente* (secondhand) boutiques. A superb place to start is **Chercheminippes** (Map p230), which has five boutiques, including menswear and childrenswear, on one street.

by small independent producers. Check the website for its program of talks and tastings.

Pierre Hermé — Food, Drink

(Map p222; www.pierreherme.com; 72 rue Bonaparte, 6e; ⊙10am-7pm Sun-Fri, to 8pm Sat; MOdéon or RER Luxembourg) It's the size of a chocolate box but once in, your tastebuds will go wild. Pierre Hermé is one of Paris' top chocolatiersand this boutique is a veritable feast of perfectly presented petits fours, cakes, chocolate, nougats, *macarons* and jam.

Sonia Rykiel — Fashion

(Map p222; www.soniarykiel.com; 175 bd St-Germain, 6e; ⊙10.30am-7pm Mon-Sat; MSt-Germain des Prés) In the heady days of May 1968 amid Paris' student uprisings, Sonia Rykiel opened her inaugural Left Bank boutique here, and went on to revolution-ise garments with inverted seams, 'no hems' and 'no lining'. Her diffusion labels (including children's wear) are housed in separate boutiques nearby, with other outlets around Paris.

La Maison du Chocolat — Food, Drink

(Map p222; www.lamaisonduchocolat.com; 19 rue de Sèvres, 6e; ⊙10am-7.30pm Mon-Sat, to 1pm Sun; MSèvres-Babylone) Pralines, ganaches and fruit chocolates are the hallmark of this exquisite chocolatier. Other treats in-clude *macarons* inspired by its signature chocolates, such as Rigoletto (choco-late and salted caramel) and Salvador (chocolate and raspberry), as well as sinful éclairs.

Fragonard Boutique — Perfume

(Map p222; ☎01 42 84 12 12; 196 bd St-Germain; ⊙11am-9pm Mon-Sat, 2-7.30pm Sun; MRue du Bac or St-Germain des Prés) The bd St-Germain boutique of perfumer maker Fragonard (which runs Paris' **perfume museum** (p72)) stocks a heady range of souvenirs – from scarves to cookbooks – evoking the sights, scents and flavours of France.

Patricia Wells' Culinary Shopping Secrets

Cookery teacher and author of *The Food Lover's Guide to Paris*, American Patricia Wells (www.patriciawells.com) has lived, cooked and shopped in Paris since 1980, and is considered to have truly captured the soul of French cuisine.

What is it that makes Paris so wonderful for culinary shopping?
The tradition, the quality, the quantity, the atmosphere and physical beauty!

Where do you buy your weekly groceries?
All over: the Sunday organic market at Rennes, Marché Raspail (p233) – I love the dried fruits and nuts; Poilâne (p228) for bread; Quatrehomme (p239) for cheese; and Poissonnerie du Bac (p233) for fish.

What about for an extraspecial gourmet meal?
I shop regularly at Le Bon Marché's La Grande Épicerie de Paris (p237) because it is right down the street from me. But for special meals I always order things in advance and go from shop to shop – La Maison du Chocolat (p240) and Pierre Hermé (p240) for chocolate and cakes, and La Dernière Goutte (p240) for wine. That is the fun of Paris, and of France.

Your top food shopping tip?
If you live in Paris, become a *client fidèle* so they reach in the back and give you the best stuff. If you only go once in a while, just smile and be friendly.

A perfect culinary souvenir from Paris?
Fragonard (p240), the perfume maker, has a great shop on bd St-Germain. They have a changing litany of *great* things for the home, such as fabulous vases with an Eiffel Tower theme, lovely embroidered napkins with a fish or vegetable theme, great little spoons with a cake or pastry theme. Nothing is very expensive and the offerings change every few months, so you have to pounce when you find something you love. The gift wrapping in gorgeous Fragonard bags is worth it alone!

🟢 Sports & Activities

École Le Cordon Bleu Cooking
(☎ 01 53 68 22 50; www.cordonbleu.edu; 8 rue Léon Delhomme, 15e; Ⓜ Vaugirard or Convention) Learn how to impress dinner party guests at this venerable 1895-established culinary school. Short courses start from €41 for two hours.

Patricia Wells Cooking
(www.patriciawells.com) Five-day moveable feast from the former *International Herald Tribune* food critic.

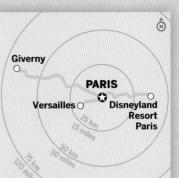

Day Trips

Versailles (p244)

When it comes to over-the-top opulence, the colossal Château de Versailles is in a class of its own, even for France.

Disneyland Resort Paris (p249)

The 'party never stops' at Europe's Disneyland theme park and Walt Disney Studios Park, which bring film, animation and TV production to life.

Giverny (p250)

Art and/or garden lovers shouldn't miss Giverny's Maison de Claude Monet, the former home and flower-filled garden of the impressionist master.

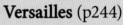

Château de Versailles (p244)
RIGOULET GILLES/HEMIS.FR/GETTY IMAGES IMAGES ©

Don't Miss
Versailles

Louis XIV transformed his father's hunting lodge into the monumental Château de Versailles in the mid-17th century, and it remains France's most famous palace. Intended to house his court of 6000 people, during its construction entire hills were flattened, marshes drained and forests moved to create the seemingly endless gardens, ponds and fountains. The baroque château was the political capital and seat of the royal court from 1682 up until the fateful events of 1789 when Revolutionaries massacred the palace guard and dragged Louis XVI and Marie Antoinette back to Paris.

22km southwest of Paris

☎ 01 30 83 78 00

www.chateau
versailles.fr

admission passport (estate-wide access) €18, with musical events €25, palace €15

⊙8am-6pm Tue-Sat, 9am-6pm Sun Apr-Oct, 8.30am-5.30pm Tue-Sat, 9am-5.30pm Sun Nov-Mar

The Estate

Situated in the prosperous, leafy suburb of Versailles and sprawling over 900 hectares, the estate is divided into four main sections: the palace; the gardens, canals and pools to the west; two smaller palaces, the **Grand Trianon** and the **Petit Trianon**, to the northwest; and the **Queen's Hamlet**.

Château de Versailles

Few alterations have been made to the château since construction, though most of the interior furnishings disappeared during the Revolution and some rooms were rebuilt by Louis-Philippe (r 1830–48).

To access areas that are otherwise off limits, take a 90-minute **guided tour** (☏01 30 83 77 88; €16; ☺English-language tours 9.30am & 2pm Tue-Sun). Tour tickets include access to the most famous parts of the palace, such as the **Hall of Mirrors** and the **King's and Queen's State Apartments**.

The Gardens

Don't miss a stroll through the château's magnificent **gardens**. Fountains include the 17th-century *Bassin de Neptune* (Neptune's Fountain), a dazzling mirage of 99 spouting fountains north of the palace, and the *Bassin d'Apollon* (Apollo's Fountain), at the eastern end of the Grand Canal.

Planning for Versailles

By noon ticket queues spiral out of control: arrive early in the morning and avoid Tuesday and Sunday, the busiest days. Save time by pre-purchasing tickets on the château's website or at **Fnac** (www.fnac.com).

The estate is so vast that the only way to see it all is to hire an **electric car** (per hr €30) or hop aboard the **shuttle train** (www.train versailles.com; adult/child €6.70/5); you can also rent a **bike or boat** (per hr €6.50/15).

Getting There & Away

◗ **Bus** RATP bus 171 (€1.70, 35 minutes) links Paris' Pont de Sèvres metro station (15e) with the place d'Armes at least every 15 minutes between 5am and 1am.

◗ **Train** RER Line C5 (€3.20, 45 minutes, frequent) runs from Left Bank RER stations to Versailles-Rive Gauche station.

Don't Miss List

BY SYLVAIN POSTOLLE, OFFICIAL GUIDE, CHÂTEAU DE VERSAILLES

1 **KING'S PRIVATE APARTMENT**
This is the most fascinating part of the palace as it shows the king as a man and very much reflects his daily life in the 18th century. Of the 10 or so rooms, the most famous is his bedroom – where he not only slept, but also held ceremonies. He had lunch here each day at 1pm and also supper, which up to 150 courtiers and people invited from outside the court would watch! By the 1780s, the king's life had become more private – he had an official supper just once a week, on Sunday.

2 **HERCULES SALON**
I love one particular perspective inside the palace: from the Hercules Salon you can see all the rooms comprising the King's State Apartment, and to the right, through the gallery leading to the opera house. The salon served as a passageway for the king to go from his state apartment to the chapel to celebrate daily Mass.

3 **THE ROYAL CHAPEL**
This is an exquisite example of the work of a very important architect of the time, Jules Hardouin-Mansart (1646–1708). The paintings, very representative of art fashions at the end of the reign of Louis XIV, are also stunning: they evoke the idea that the French king was chosen by God and as such was his lieutenant on earth. This is the chapel where, in 1770, the future king Louis XVI wed Marie Antoinette – the beginning of the French Revolution.

4 **ENCELADE GROVE**
Versailles' gardens are extraordinary; my favourite spot has to be this grove, typical of the gardens created for Louis XIV by André Le Nôtre. A gallery of trellises surrounds a pool with a statue of Enceladus, chief of the Titans, who was punished for his pride by the gods from Mount Olympus. When the fountains are on, it's impressive.

245

A Day in Versailles

Visiting Versailles – even just the State Apartments – may seem overwhelming at first, but think of it as a house where people ate, drank, worked, slept and conspired and you'll be on the right path.

Some two decades into his long reign, Louis XIV began turning his father's hunting lodge into a palace large enough to house his entire court (to keep closer tabs on the 6000-strong army of courtiers). Sparing no expense, the Sun King employed the greatest artists and craftspeople of the day and by 1682 he'd created the most extravagant dormitory in history.

The royal schedule was as accurate and predictable as a Swiss watch. By following this itinerary of rooms you can recreate the king's day, starting with the **King's Bedchamber** ❶ and the Queen's Bedchamber ❷, where the royal couple was roused at about the same time. The royal procession then leads through the **Hall of Mirrors** ❸ to the **Royal Chapel** ❹ for morning Mass and returns to the **Council Chamber** ❺ for late-morning meetings with ministers. After lunch the king might ride or hunt or visit the **King's Library** ❻. Later he could join courtesans for an 'apartment evening' starting from the **Hercules Drawing Room** ❼ or play billiards in the Diana **Drawing Room** ❽ before supping at 10pm.

VERSAILLES BY NUMBERS

Rooms 700 (11 hectares of roof)

Windows 2153

Staircases 67

Gardens and parks 800 hectares

Trees 200,000

Fountains 50 (with 620 nozzles)

Paintings 6300 (measuring 11km laid end to end)

Statues and sculptures 2100

Objets d'art and furnishings 5000

Visitors 5.3 million per year

CHRISTOPHE LEHENAFF/PHOTOLIBRARY ©

Queen's Bedchamber
Chambre de la Reine
The queen's life was on constant public display and even the births of her children were watched by crowds of spectators in her own bedchamber. **DETOUR »** The Guardroom, with a dozen armed men at the ready.

Lunch Break

Diner-style food at Sister's Café, crêpes at Le Phare St-Louis or picnic in the park.

Guardroom

South Wing

King's Library
Bibliothèque du Roi
The last resident, bibliophile Louis XVI, loved geography and his copy of *The Travels of James Cook* (in English, which he read fluently) is still on the shelf here.

GIANNI DAGLI ORTI/ALAMY ©

Savvy Sightseeing

Avoid Versailles on Monday (closed), Tuesday (Paris' museums close, so visitors flock here) and Sunday, the busiest day. Also, book tickets online so you don't have to queue.

Hall of Mirrors
Galerie des Glaces
The solid-silver candelabra and furnishings in this extravagant hall, devoted to Louis XIV's successes in war, were melted down in 1689 to pay for yet another conflict. DETOUR» The antithetical Peace Drawing Room, adjacent.

King's Bedchamber
Chambre du Roi
The king's daily life was anything but private and even his *lever* (rising) at 8am and *coucher* (retiring) at 11.30pm would be witnessed by up to 150 sycophantic courtiers.

Council Chamber
Cabinet du Conseil
This chamber, with carved medallions evoking the king's work, is where the monarch met his various ministers (state, finance, religion etc) depending on the days of the week.

Hall of Mirrors

Apollo Drawing Room

Marble Courtyard

Entrance

North Wing

To Royal Opera

Diana Drawing Room
Salon de Diane
With walls and ceiling covered in frescos devoted to the mythical huntress, this room contained a large billiard table reserved for Louis XIV, a keen player.

Royal Chapel
Chapelle Royale
This two-storey chapel (with gallery for the royals and important courtiers, and the ground floor for the B-list) was dedicated to St Louis, patron of French monarchs. DETOUR» The sumptuous Royal Opera.

Hercules Drawing Room
Salon d'Hercule
This salon, with its stunning ceiling fresco of the strong man, gave way to the State Apartments, which were open to courtiers three nights a week. DETOUR» Apollo Drawing Room, used for formal audiences and as a throne room.

Versailles

0 ————— 500 m
0 ————— 0.25 miles

Allée du Rendez-Vous

Hameau de la Reine

Domaine de Marie-Antoinette (Marie-Antoinette Estate)

Jardins du Petit Trianon

R des Sports

Bd Saint Antoine

R de Versailles

R de l'Ermitage

Angelina

Parc du Grand Trianon

Grand Trianon

Allée des Deux Trianons

Av de Trianon

Allée de St-Antoine

Petite Allée du Saint Antoine

Parc de Versailles

Allée de la Reine

Allée des Matelots

Allée d'Apollon

R du Maréchal Gallieni

R Berthier

R d'Angiviller

Allée de Bailly

Allée du Petit Pont

Bd de la Reine

Château Bike Hire

Grand Canal

Château Bike Hire

Allée de Cérès et de Flore

Bassin de Neptune

Boat Hire

Bassin d'Apollon

R des Réservoirs

R Carnot

Pl Hoche

Le Tapis Vert

Allée des Matelots

Allée d'Apollon

Bassin du Miroir

Château de Versailles

Entrance A

Av de Saint Cloud

Shuttle Train

Allée du Mail

Electric Car Hire

Louis XIV Statue

Grandes Écuries

Route de St Cyr

Parterre du Midi

Av Rockefeller

Académie du Spectacle Équestre

Orangerie

Salle de Jeu de Paume

Petites Écuries

R de l'Orangerie

R du Vieux Versailles

Av de Sceaux

R du Général Leclerc

R des Tournelles

Allée du Mail

Pièce d'Eau des Suisses

Allée du Potager

Potager du Roi

R d'Anjou

Allée des Mortemets

Parc Balby

R du Maréchal Joffre

R St Honoré

R Royale

JOHN SONES SINGING BOWL MEDI/GETTY IMAGES ©

✅ Don't Miss
Disneyland Resort Paris

It took almost €4.6 billion to turn the beet fields east of Paris into Europe's first Disney theme park. What started out as Euro-Disney in 1992 sees families pour into the park to share a fiesta of magical moments with Mickey and his mates

The resort comprises three areas. The traditional **Disneyland Park** has five themed 'lands': Main Street USA; Frontierland; Adventureland (home to the Pirates of the Caribbean ride); Fantasyland, crowned by Sleeping Beauty's castle; and the high-tech Discoveryland with massive-queue rides such as Space Mountain: Mission 2.

Film-oriented **Walt Disney Studios Park** has behind-the-scenes tours, larger-than-life characters and spine-tingling rides like the Twilight Zone Tower of Terror.

Adjacent to both is the hotel-, shop- and restaurant-filled **Disney Village**. And the kids – and kids at heart – can't seem to get enough.

One-day admission includes unlimited access to attractions in either Disneyland Park or Walt Disney Studios Park. The latter includes entry to Disneyland Park three hours before it closes. A multitude of multiday passes, special offers and packages is always available. Devote a good hour on the website planning your day, and buy tickets in advance wherever possible to avoid ticket queues.

Picnics aren't allowed but there are ample themed restaurants. Most have meal coupons for adults/children (€28/15). The resort's seven American-styled hotels are linked by free shuttle bus to the parks. Rates vary hugely.

Marne-la-Vallée/Chessy, Disneyland's RER station, is served by line A4; trains run frequently from central Paris (€7.10).

NEED TO KNOW

32 km east of Paris; 📞 hotel booking 01 60 30 60 30, restaurant reservations 01 60 30 40 50; www.disneylandparis.com; one-day admission adult/child €59/53; ⏰ hours vary; Ⓜ Marne-la-Vallée/Chessy

Giverny

Giverny's two main draws, the Musée des Impressionismes Giverny and, especially, Monet's former home, the Maison de Claude Monet, are only open from April to October (as are most places to eat, drink and sleep). If you're here during these months however, the Maison de Claude Monet's gardens are magnificent, so factor in plenty of time to enjoy them.

Getting There & Away

Travel time 45 minutes by train to Vernon, then 20 minutes by bus (or by taxi or bike).

Train From Paris' Gare St-Lazare SNCF, trains run to Vernon (€13.30, 1¼ hours).

Bus Seasonal shuttle buses (€4 return, from April to October) link Vernon's station with Giverny.

Taxi A taxi from Vernon's station to Giverny costs about €15 one way. Call ☎ 02 32 51 10 24.

Bike Hire a bike from Bar-Restaurant du Chemin de Fer (€12 per day), opposite Vernon's station, or 800m northeast at **Cyclo News** (7 cours du Marché aux Chevaux; per day €12.20; ⏰8:30am-7.30pm Tue-Sat).

Need to Know

- **Location** 74km northwest of Paris
- **Tourist Office** The closest tourist office – and the transport springboard for Giverny – is in Vernon, 7km to the northwest. See www.vernon-visite.org for more information

Sights

Musée des Impressionnismes Giverny
Art Museum

(☎ 02 32 51 94 65; www.mdig.fr; 99 rue Claude Monet; adult/child €6.50/3; ⏰10am-5.30pm Apr-Oct) About 100m northwest of the Maison de Claude Monet is the Giverny Museum of Impressionisms. Set up in partnership with the Musée d'Orsay, among others, the pluralised name reinforces its coverage of all aspects ofim pressionism and related movements. In homage to the Maison de Claude Monet, the museum is surrounded by fabulous flowering gardens and meadows.

Until 2009 the museum was known as the Musée d'Art Américain (American Art Museum), which focused on a fine collection of works by American impressionist painters who flocked to France in the late 19th andearly 20th centuries; the new museum covers impressionists and their works both home-grown and abroad, while still exhibiting American works.

Reserve ahead for two-hour **art workshops** offering an introduction to watercolour, drawing, sketching or pastels (high season only). Lectures, readings, concerts and documentaries also take place regularly – check the program on the website.

Eating & Drinking

Auberge du Vieux Moulin
Traditional French €€

(☎ 02 32 51 46 15; www.vieuxmoulingiverny.com; 21 rue de la Falaise; salads €12, lunch menus €15-18, dinner menus €24-35; ⏰lunch daily, dinner Fri & Sat Apr-Oct, lunch Fri-Sun Nov-Mar) The lovely little 'Old Mill Inn', a couple of hundred metres east of the Maison de Claude Monet, is an excellent place for lunch and has a lovely terrace.

La Musardière
Hotel €€

(☎ 02 32 21 03 18; www.lamusardiere.fr; 123 rue Claude Monet; d €83-97; ⏰hotel Feb–mid-Dec, restaurant daily Apr-Oct; P 📶) Dining at the crêperie-oriented restaurant of this 1880-established hotel, evocatively called the 'Idler', is a pleasure. It's set amid a lovely garden less than 100m northeast of the Maison de Claude Monet.

PETER GROENENDIJK/GETTY IMAGES ©

✓ Don't Miss
Maison de Claude Monet

The prized drawcard of tiny Giverny is the home and flower-filled garden of the seminal impressionist painter and his family, who lived here from 1883 to 1926. It was here that Monet painted some of his most famous series, including *Décorations des Nymphéas* (Waterlilies).

Unfortunately, Monet's hectare of land has become two distinct areas, cut by the Chemin du Roy, a small railway line that has been converted into the D5 road.

The northern area of the property is **Clos Normand**, where Monet's famous pastel-pink-and-green house and the **Atelier des Nymphéas** (Waterlilies Studio) stand. These days the studio is the entrance hall, adorned with precise reproductions of his works and ringing with cash-register bells from the busy gift shop. Outside are the symmetrically laid-out gardens. From early to late spring, daffodils, tulips, rhododendrons, wisteria and irises appear, followed by poppies and lilies. By June, nasturtiums, roses and sweet peas are in blossom. Around September, there are dahlias, sunflowers and hollyhocks.

From the Clos Normand's far corner a foot tunnel leads under the D5 to the **Jardin d'Eau** (Water Garden). Having bought this piece of land in 1895 after his reputation (and bank account) had swelled, Monet dug a pool, planted water lilies and constructed the famous Japanese bridge (since rebuilt). Draped with purple wisteria, the bridge blends into the asymmetrical foreground and background, creating the intimate atmosphere for which the 'Painter of Light' was famous.

NEED TO KNOW

📞 02 32 51 28 21; www.fondation-monet.com; 84 rue Claude Monet; adult/7-12yr/under 7yr €9/5/ free; ⏰9.30am-6pm Apr-Oct

Paris
In Focus

The Champs-Élysées
PHOTOGRAPHER: MARTIN CHILD/GETTY IMAGES ©

Paris Today

Eiffel Tower (p52) and Parc du Champ de Mars (p54)

Europe's mythical 'City of Light' continues its urban rejuvenation and renewal

living in Paris
(% of population by area)

80
Outer Arrondissements

20
Central Paris

if Paris were 100 people

86 would be French

14 would be foreign

population per sq km

👤 ≈ 100 people

FRANCE   PARIS

While the elegance, depth and extraordinary spirit of the Paris of Haussmann, Hugo and Toulouse-Lautrec will never disappear, Europe's mythical 'City of Light' continues its urban rejuvenation and renewal, and the arts scene has never been more exciting. Parisians themselves, moreover, are in the mood for change: 2012 presidential elections ushered in France's first Socialist president in 17 years.

Reinvention & Innovation

The city today is about reinvention and innovation. From community based-projects like turning an art-nouveau market into a sports centre in the Haut-Marais, or gargantuan developments like the overhaul of the Forum des Halles, Paris is not resting on its laurels. At Les Halles, it's out with the tired 1970s concrete and in with a designer garden crowned with a futuristic, rainforest-inspired canopy in glass (by 2016). The same goes for the historic Gare d'Austerlitz and the Seine-side quarter around

JOSE FUSTE RAGA/CORBIS ©

In central Paris, place de la République will be a dramatically different place once the car-jammed roundabout is dumped on the scrapheap of history and replaced with a pedestrian zone. Similarly, a 2.3km-long stretch of riverbank on the Left Bank will be pedestrianised to create a riverside footpath between the Musée d'Orsay and Eiffel Tower. Floating gardens on the Seine will complete the picturesque ensemble, part of the larger Berges de Seine initiative aimed at greening-up the riverbanks. Work started in 2012.

When the Paris Council adopted a new Plan de Biodiversité at the end of 2011, it did not ignore its urban rooftops. The goal is to double the 3.7 hectares currently planted green with vegetal roofs and roof gardens by 2020.

ne train station where builders are eavering away on yet another renais- ance fashioned out of glass (and lurid ne-green, in the case of the fashionable ocks en Seine).

At the Musée du Louvre, meanwhile, e opening of brand new Islamic art alleries in Cour Visconti – a splendid ece of 21st-century architecture – only rthers the musuem's iconic standing s a place of essential pilgrimage for art vers the world over.

Growing Green Space

reating more green space for Parisians promenade in peace is the big driver r urban planners. Enter Île Seguin, an ventive project in Boulogne-Bilancourt n Paris' western fringe, which will see an bandoned car factory morphed into a sionary eco-city with a cultural centre, arterside gardens, tree-lined espla- ades, restaurants and play spaces.

A Boost to Morale

Unemployment in the Paris region re- mained at a disconcerting 8.1% in 2012. Yet cultural morale runs high. Art lovers are bursting with excitement over the reopening, after months of painstaking renovation, of both the Picasso museum in the Marais and the Comédie Française where Molière trod the boards at the Palais Royal. Building work on Paris' new €336 million philharmonic concert hall, to open in 2014, is back on track (after being stalled in 2010 for lack of funding), and then there's Frank Gehry's dazzling glass crystal of a contemporary art gal- lery in the Bois de Bologne, an architec- tural redefinition of style. Cinema goers are celebrating Oscar wins by favourite Parisian actors and directors, while promised new restaurant openings by Guy Savoy (inside the Seine-side Hôtel de la Monnaie) and Anne-Sophie Pic (on rue du Louvre) are titillating the taste- buds of Parisian gourmets. *Bon appétit!*

History

Bedroom in the Grand Trianon, Versailles (p245)

FRENCH SCHOOL /GETT

As the national capital, Paris is the administrative, business and cultural centre of France. Since before the French Revolution, it has been what urban planners call a 'hypertropic city' – the enlarged head of a nation-state's body – and virtually everything of importance in the republic starts, finishes or is currently taking place here. Throughout the city's (and the country's) illustrious history, political rebellion has remained a constant theme.

The Beginnings to the Renaissance

Paris was born in the 3rd century BC, when a tribe of Celtic Gauls known as th Parisii settled on what is now the Île de la Cité. Centuries of conflict between the Gauls and Romans ended in 52 BC, wher Julius Caesar's legions crushed a Celtic revolt. Christianity was introduced in the 2nd century AD, and Roman rule ended in the 5th century with the arrival of the

3rd century BC
Celtic Gauls called Parisii arrive in the Paris area and set up huts on what is now the Île de la Cité and engage in fishing and trading.

Germanic Franks. In 508 Frankish king Clovis I united Gaul and made Paris his seat.

France's west coast was beset in the 9th century by Scandinavian Vikings (also known as Norsemen and, later, as Normans). Three centuries later, the Normans started pushing towards Paris, which had risen rapidly in importance: construction had begun on the cathedral of Notre Dame in the 12th century, the Louvre began life as a riverside fortress around 1200, the beautiful Ste-Chapelle was consecrated in 1248 and the Sorbonne opened in 1253.

The Vikings' incursions heralded the Hundred Years' War between Norman England and Paris' Capetian dynasty, bringing French defeat in 1415 and English control of the capital in 1420. In 1429 the 17-year-old Jeanne d'Arc (Joan of Arc) rallied the French troops to defeat the English at Orléans. With the exception of Calais, the English were eventually expelled from France in 1453.

The Renaissance helped Paris get back on its feet in the late 15th century. Less than a century later, however, turmoil ensued as clashes between Huguenot (Protestant) and Catholic groups culminated in the St Bartholomew's Day massacre in 1572.

The Best...
Historical Sights

1 **Musée d'Art et d'Histoire du Judaïsme** (p148)

2 **Cimetière du Père Lachaise** (p144)

3 **Les Catacombes** (p226)

4 **Château de Versailles** (p244)

The Revolution to a New Republic

A five-year-old Louis XIV (later known as the Sun King) ascended the throne in 1643 and ruled until 1715, virtually emptying the national coffers with his ambitious battling and building, including the construction of his extravagant palace at Versailles. The excesses of this grandiose king and his heirs, including Louis XVI and his Vienna-born queen Marie Antoinette, eventually led to an uprising of Parisians on 14 July 1789, kick-starting the French Revolution. Within four years, the Reign of Terror was in full swing.

The unstable postrevolutionary government was consolidated in 1799 under Napoleon Bonaparte, who declared himself First Consul. In 1804 he had the Pope crown him emperor of the French, and went on to conquer most of Europe before his eventual defeat at Waterloo in present-day Belgium in 1815. He was exiled to St Helena, and died in 1821.

France struggled under a string of mostly inept rulers until a coup d'état in 1851 brought Emperor Napoleon III to power. At his behest, Baron Haussmann razed

AD 845–86
Paris is repeatedly raided by Vikings for more than four decades.

1682
Louis XIV, the 'Sun King', moves his court from the Palais des Tuileries in Paris to Versailles.

14 July 1789
The French Revolution begins when a mob storms the prison at Bastille.

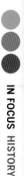

The Best...
Historic Nightlife

1 **Comédie Française**
(p114)

2 **Moulin Rouge**
(p136)

3 **Palais Garnier**
(p77)

4 **Au Lapin Agile**
(p136)

whole tracts of the city, replacing them with sculptured parks, a hygienic sewer system and – strategically – boulevards too broad for rebels to barricade. Napoleon III embroiled France in a costly war with Prussia in 1870, which ended within months with the French army's defeat and the capture of the emperor. When the masses in Paris heard the news, they took to the streets, demanding a republic.

20th Century History

Out of WWI's conflict came increased industrialisation, confirming Paris' place as a major commercial, as well as artistic, centre and establishing its reputation among freethinking intellectuals.

This was halted by WWII and the Nazi occupation of 1940. During Paris' occupation, almost half the population evacuated, including General Charles de Gaulle, France's undersecretary of war, who fled to London and set up a government-in-exile. In a radio broadcast he appealed to French patriots to continue resisting the Germans, and established the Forces Françaises Libres (Free French Forces) to fight the Germans alongside the Allies. Following Paris' liberation, de Gaulle set up a provisional government, but resigned in 1946; he formed his own party (Rassemblement du Peuple Français) and remained in opposition until 1958, when he was brought back to power. He was succeeded as president in 1969 by Gaullist leader Georges Pompidou.

After the war, Paris regained its position as a creative nucleus and nurtured a revitalised liberalism that peaked with the student-led uprisings of May 1968 – the Sorbonne was occupied, the Latin Quarter blockaded and a general strike paralysed the country.

Under centre-right President Jacques Chirac's watch, the late 1990s saw Paris seize the international spotlight with the rumour-plagued death of Princess Di in 1997, and France's first-ever World Cup victory in July 1998.

The New Millenium

In May 2001 Socialist Bertrand Delanoë was elected mayor, becoming widely popular for making Paris more liveable through improved infrastructure and green spaces. Chirac (himself a former Paris mayor) named Dominique de Villepin as prime minister in 2005. In October that year, the deaths of two teenagers who were electrocuted while allegedly hiding from police in an electricity substation sparked riots that quickly

1889
The Eiffel Tower is completed in time for the opening of the Exposition Universelle (World Fair).

25 August 1944
Spearheaded by Free French units, Allied forces liberate Paris and the city escapes destruction.

1968
Paris is rocked by student led riots that bring the nation and the city to the brink of civil war.

The French Resistance

Despite the infamy of 'la France Résistante' (the French Resistance), the underground movement never actually included more than 5% of the population. Resistance members engaged in railway sabotage, collected intelligence for the Allies, helped Allied airmen who had been shot down and published anti-German leaflets, among other activities. The impact of their pursuits might have been modest but the Resistance served as an enormous boost to French morale – not to mention fresh fodder for numerous literary and cinematic endeavours.

spread across Paris, and then across France. One of Villepin's first efforts – the introduction of two-year work contracts for workers under 26 years old – was met by street protests and transport strikes by sympathetic unions around the country, sparking comparisons with May '68. Backed by a reputed 70% of the French public, Chirac overrode Villepin, scrapping the week-old law.

Chirac retired in 2007. His centre-right successor, Nicolas 'Sarko' Sarkozy, defeated Socialist Ségolène 'Ségo' Royal in the 2007 presidential elections. Sarkozy's win was widely attributed to his platform of economic reform, with many French claiming it was time for 'modernisation'. Following his election, however, many voters were unimpressed at the media hype surrounding the presidency, notably Sarkozy's divorce, whirlwind romance and marriage to actress/model/singer Carla Bruni. Many people believe this contributed to the subsequent defeat of the right at France's March 2008 municipal elections, including left-wing Delanoë's comfortable re-election as mayor.

Recent History

Presidential elections in May 2012 pitted incumbent right-wing president Nicolas Sarkozy against left-wing candidate François Hollande, resulting in France's first Socialist president since 1988. Hollande had campaigned to reduce unemployment (which was at a 12-year high), clear the country's debts by 2017, raise income tax on top-end salaries and steer France though Europe's biggest economic crisis in decades. Some voters, fed up with austerity and desperate for change, welcomed this approach. Legislative elections held a month later sealed the left's grip on power: the Socialists won a comfortable majority (273 seats) in France's 577-seat lower-house National Assembly, paving the way for the new president to enact many of his promised reforms.

1994
Eurostar trains link Waterloo in London with the Gare du Nord in Paris in just over three hours. Gare du Nord

2004–05
The French electorate rejects the EU Constitution; Arab and African youths riot in Parisian suburbs.

DAVID BANK /GETTY IMAGES ©

Family Travel

BETHUNE CARMICHAEL/GETTY IMA

Parisians adore les enfants *(children) and welcome them with open arms just about everywhere. The French are great believers in doing things* en famille *(as a family), and children are active participants in many aspects of social life, including visiting museums and dining out. And central Paris' residential make-up means you'll find playground equipment in parks all over the city.*

Sights & Activities

In addition to playgrounds, Paris' parks also have a host of children's activities. Among the best are the toy boats, *marionettes* (puppets), pony rides and carousel of the Jardin du Luxembourg (p218); the new millennium playgrounds of Parc de la Villette (p128), adjacent to the fabulous interactive science museum Cité des Sciences (p128); the Jardin des Plantes (p196)' *ménagerie* (zoo), with snow panthers, pandas and art deco snake and monkey houses, which neighbours the kid-friendly Musée National d'Histoire Naturelle (p196) (Museum of Natural History); and the Bois de Boulogne's adorable Jardin d'Acclimatation amusement park (p61).

The shark tank inside the Cinéaqua (p55) aquarium is another winner with animal-mad kids, while a trip to the Louvre (p90) can be a treat, particularly following thematic trails such as hunting for lions or galloping horses.

Further afield, you might consider a day trip to Disneyland Resort Paris (p249).

Eating Out

Many restaurants accept little diners (confirm ahead), but they're expected to behave (bring crayons/books). Children's menus are common, but most restaurants don't have highchairs. Department-store cafeterias and chain restaurants, such as **Flunch** (**www.flunch.fr**), offer kid-friendly fare, as do a new wave of gourmet pizza, pasta and burger restaurants throughout the city. In fine weather, good options include picking up sandwiches and crêpes from a street stall or packing a market-fresh picnic and heading to parks and gardens where kids can play to their hearts' content.

Need to Know

- **Cots/cribs** Available upon request in many midrange and top-end hotels
- **Highchairs** Rare; bring your own screw-on seat
- **Children's menus** Available in many restaurants
- **Nappies (diapers)** Widely available in supermarkets and pharmacies
- **Changing facilities** Rare; bring a towel and improvise (no one minds)
- **Strollers (pushchairs)** A strict no-no inside Château de Versailles; bring a baby sling

Way to Go

Paris' narrow streets and metro stairways are a trial if you have a stroller (pram or pushchair) in tow; buses offer an easier, scenic alternative. Car-rental firms have children's safety seats for hire at a nominal cost; book in advance. Children under four years of age travel free on public transport and generally receive free admission to sights. For older kids, discounts vary from place to place – anything from a euro off for over fours to free entry up to the age of 18.

The choice of baby food, infant formula, soy and cow's milk, nappies (diapers) and the like in French supermarkets is similar to that in any developed country, but remember that opening hours may be more limited. Pharmacies – of which a handful are open 24/7, and others open for at least a few hours on a Sunday – also sell baby paraphernalia.

Bedtime

When booking accommodation, check availability and costs for a *lit bébé* (cot/crib). Weekly magazine *L'Officiel des Spectacles* advertises *gardes d'enfants* (babysitting) services.

Various types of *fromage* (cheese)

Some cities rally around local sports teams, but Parisians rally around la table *– and everything on it. Food is not fuel here; it's the reason you get up in the morning. The freshness of ingredients and reliance on natural flavours combined with refined, often very complex cooking methods – and, of course, wine – means you are in a gourmet's paradise.*

Capital Cuisine

Paris doesn't have its own 'local' cuisine but is the crossroads for the regional flavours of France. Dishes from the hot south favour olive oil, garlic and tomatoes; the cooler, pastoral northern regions turn to cream and butter; and coastal areas concentrate on seafood.

Regional French specialities you'll encounter in the capital include the following:

○ **Burgundy** A culinary trinity of beef, red wine and Dijon mustard. Savour *bœuf bourguignon* (beef marinated and cooked in young red wine with mushrooms, onions, carrots and bacon) or snails.

○ **The Dordogne** Black truffles and poultry, especially ducks and geese, whose fattened livers are turned into *pâté de foie gras* (duck- or goose-liver pâté).

Lyon An age-old repertoire of distinctive dishes like breaded fried tripe, *andouillettes* (pig-intestine sausage) and lighter *quenelles* (poached dumplings).

Loire Valley The cuisine refined in the kitchens of the Loire Valley's châteaux in the 16th century became what's often now considered 'quintessentially French': *coq au vin* (chicken in red wine), *cuisses de grenouilles* (frogs legs) and *tarte tatin* (upside-down apple tart).

Alsace The brasserie, which means 'brewery' in French, originated in Alsace, and brasserie menus often include classic Alsatian dishes like *choucroute alsacienne* – sauerkraut flavoured with juniper berries and served hot with sausages, bacon, pork and/or ham knuckle.

Provence Sun-ripened fruit and vegetables abound; *à la Provençal* means anything dosed with garlic-seasoned tomatoes. Bouillabaisse, Marseille's mighty fish stew, is Provence's most famous dish.

Brittany Best known for seafood, and sweet, wheat flour *crêpes* and savoury buckwheat *galettes* paired with *une bolée* (a small bowl) of apple-rich Breton cider.

Auvergne Traditional dishes include *aligot* (puréed potato with garlic and Tomme cheese) and *truffade* (sliced potatoes with Cantal cheese). Another speciality is the *lentille verte de Puy* (green Puy lentil).

Languedoc Famed for *cassoulet*, an earthy cockle-warming stew of white beans and meat.

Basque Country Essential ingredients of Basque cooking include deep-red Espelette chillies and Bayonne ham.

Prix-Fixe Menus

In addition to the *carte* (menu), most Parisian restaurants offer daily *formules* or *menus* (fixed-price menus), which typically include two- to four-course meals. In some cases, particularly at market-driven neobistros, there is no *carte* – only a selection of *menus*.

Lunch *menus* are often a fantastic deal and allow you to enjoy *haute cuisine* at very affordable prices. In this guide, the price for a lunch *menu* generally corresponds to a two-course meal served Monday to Friday. The price for a dinner *menu* generally corresponds to a three-course meal, available every day.

Cheese

France counts upwards of 500 varieties of *fromage* (cheese) made from raw or pasteurised milk, or from *petit-lait* (the whey left over after the milk fats and solids have been curdled with rennet).

Cheeses at the Paris' enticing *fromageries* (cheese shops) are split into five main categories: *fromage de chèvre* (goat's cheese), *fromage à pâte persillée* (veined or blue cheese), *fromage à pâte molle* (soft cheese), *fromage à pâte demi-dure* (semihard cheese) and *fromage à pâte dure* (hard cheese). The selection here or at a Parisian market can be overwhelming – ask to sample before buying.

You can also taste cheese with wine at wine bars, or enjoy it instead of (or as well as) dessert at simple through to celebrated restaurants across the capital.

Charcuterie

Traditionally charcuterie was made only from pork, though other meats – from beef and veal to chicken and goose – are now used in making sausages, blood puddings, hams, and other cured- and salted-meat products.

Every region in France produces standard charcuterie favourites as well as its own specialities. Pâtés, terrines and *rillettes* – potted meat (or fish) that is shredded, seasoned, mixed with fat and spread cold, like pâté, over bread or toast – are essentially charcuterie. They're all often nibbled on with wine, some of the most popular are *jambon* (ham, either smoked or salt-cured), *saucisse* (usually a small fresh sausage, boiled or grilled), *saucisson* (usually a large salami eaten cold) and *saucisson sec* (air-dried salami).

Bread & Bakery Treats

Few things are as tantalising – or prevalent – as the smell of freshly-baked buttery croissants wafting from a bakery door. There are roughly 1200 *boulangeries* (bakeries) in Paris – or 11.5 per sq km. As you'll notice in the extravagant display windows, bakeries not only bake baguettes and croissants but also éclairs, quiches and an astounding array of pastries and cakes.

If it's *pain* (bread) you're after, try to familiarise yourself with the varieties on sale while you're standing in the queue. Most Parsians today will ask for a *baguette tradition* (traditional-style baguette, with a coarse, handcrafted surface and pointy tips). Other breads you'll commonly see include *boules* (round loaves), *pavés* (flattened rectangular loaves) and *ficelles* (skinny loaves that are half the weight of a baguette).

Need to Know

○ **Price Ranges** The following symbols indicate the cost for a two-course meal:

€	under €20
€€	€20-40
€€€	more than €40

○ **Reservations** Advisable for midrange restaurants (especially dinner) and essential for top-end restaurants (sometimes up to two months in advance).

○ **Vegetarians and vegans** Options are emerging but still rare; see www.happycow.net for a decent guide.

○ **The Bill** The French consider it rude to bring *l'addition* (the bill) immediately – you have to be persistent.

○ **Tipping** A *pourboire* (tip) is not necessary as service is included, but it's not uncommon to round up the bill for good service.

Pastries & Chocolates

Patisseries (pastry shops) are similar to but generally more sophisticated than *boulangeries*. Although they sell different varieties, they're often known for a particular speciality – Ladurée (p73) and Pierre Hermé (p240) do *macarons*, Gérard Mulot (p228) does cakes and *tartes*, and so on. *Chocolatiers* (chocolate specialists) typically sell chocolates measured in 100g increments in mouth-watering flavours like pistachio, lavender and ginger.

Wine

In Paris you'll find wine from dozens of wine-producing regions throughout France, including the seven principal ones: Burgundy, Bordeaux, the Rhône and

Loire valleys, Champagne, Languedoc, Provence and Alsace. Wines are generally named after the location of the vineyard rather than the grape varietal. Organic and biodynamic wines are increasingly popular.

The best French wines are Appellation d'Origine Contrôlée (AOC), meaning they meet stringent regulations governing where, how and under what conditions they are grown, fermented and bottled. Some regions, such as Alsace, only have a single AOC; others, like Burgundy, have scores. About a third of all French wine carries that AOC hallmark of guarantee.

Specialist wine shops and wine bars are the best places to sample the varieties, or consider a wine-tasting course.

Market-Stall Streets

1 Rue Montorgueil, 2e

2 Rue Mouffetard, 5e

3 Rue Cler, 7e

4 Rue de Seine & Rue de Buci, 6e

Architecture

Detail of Notre Dame cathedral (p178)

ELIO CIOL/CE

Several key eras are woven into Paris' contemporary architectural fabric. *Magnificent cathedrals and palaces took hold from the 11th century. Baron Haussmann created broad boulevards lined by neoclassical buildings. Later additions centred on French presidents' bold* grands projets. *Modern and historic complement each other, even if additions take a while to fully appreciate – the now-iconic Eiffel Tower was originally derided as the 'metal asparagus'.*

Romanesque

A religious revival in the 11th century led to the construction of a large number of *roman* (Romanesque) churches, so-called because their architects adopted many architectural elements (eg vaulting) from Gallo-Roman buildings still standing at the time. Romanesque buildings typically have round arches, heavy walls, few (and small) windows that let in very little light, and a lack of ornamentation that borders on the austere. The Église St-Germain des Prés, built in the 11th century on the site of the Merovingian ruler Childeric's 6th-century abbey, has been altered many times over the centuries, but the Romanesque bell tower over the west entrance has changed little since AD 1000.

Gothic – Radiant to Flamboyant

In the 14th century, the Rayonnant – or Radiant – Gothic style developed, named after the radiating tracery of the rose windows. Light was welcomed into interiors by broad windows and translucent stained glass. One of the most influential Rayonnant buildings was Ste-Chapelle, whose stained glass forms a curtain of glazing on the 1st floor. The two transept façades of the Cathédrale de Notre Dame de Paris are another fine example.

By the 15th century, decorative extravagance led to what is now called Flamboyant Gothic, so named because the wavy stone carving made the towers appear to be blazing or flaming *(flamboyant)*.

Early Renaissance

The Early Renaissance style of the 15th and early 16th centuries, in which a variety of classical components and decorative motifs (columns, tunnel vaults, round arches, domes etc) were blended with the rich decoration of Flamboyant Gothic, is best exemplified in Paris by the Église St-Eustache. The Marais remains the best area for spotting reminders of the Renaissance in Paris proper, with some fine *hôtels particuliers* (private mansions) from this era, such as Hôtel Carnavalet, which houses part of the Musée Carnavalet.

Baroque

During the baroque period – which lasted from the end of the 16th to the late 18th centuries – painting, sculpture and classical architecture were integrated to create structures and interiors of great subtlety, refinement and elegance. With the advent of the baroque, architecture became more pictorial, with the painted ceilings in churches illustrating the Passion of Christ to the faithful, and palaces invoking the power and order of the state.

Salomon de Brosse, who designed Paris' Palais du Luxembourg in the Jardin du Luxembourg in 1615, set the stage for prominent early baroque architect François Mansart, designer of the Église Notre Dame du Val-de-Grâce.

Neoclassicism

Neoclassical architecture, which emerged in about 1740 and remained popular in Paris until well into the 19th century, had its roots in the renewed interest in classical forms. Neoclassicism was more profoundly a search for order, reason and serenity through the adoption of the forms and conventions of Graeco-Roman antiquity: columns, simple geometric forms and traditional ornamentation. Neoclassicism really came into its own under Napoleon, who used it extensively for monumental architecture intended to embody the grandeur of imperial France and its capital.

The Best...
Architectural Icons

1 **Arc de Triomphe** (p68)

2 **Opéra Bastille** (p152)

3 **Musée du Quai Branly** (p59)

4 **Centre Pompidou** (p96)

The Best...
Neoclassical Sights

Haussman

Baron Haussman's late 19th-century renovation of the medieval city's disease-ridden streets demolished more than 20,000 homes, making way for wide boulevards lined by 40,000 new apartments in neoclassical creamy stone, grey-roofed buildings. And the turn-of-the-century art nouveau movement, which emerged in Europe and the USA in the second half of the 19th century under various names (Jugendstil, Sezessionstil, Stile Liberty), caught on quickly in Paris. It was characterised by sinuous curves and flowing, asymmetrical forms reminiscent of creeping vines, water lilies, the patterns on insect wings and the flowering boughs of trees. Influenced by the arrival of exotic objets d'art from Japan, its French name came from a Paris gallery that featured works in the 'new art' style. In Paris, it ushered in signature sights including the Musée d'Orsay, Grand Palais and Paris' ornate brasseries and wrought-iron metro entrances – and, of course, the Eiffel Tower.

Contemporary

Additions to the cityscape in the late 20th century centred on French presidents' *grand projets* (huge public edifices through which French leaders sought to immortalise themselves). President Georges Pompidou's Centre Pompidou, unveiled in 1977, prompted a furore, as did President François Mitterand's Louvre's glass pyramid in 1989. However, both are now widely admired and considered iconic Paris landmarks. Mitterand oversaw a slew of other costly *projets,* including the Opéra Bastille. In 1995 the presidential baton shifted to Jacques Chirac – his pet *projet,* the Musée du Quai Branly, opened in a Jean Nouvel–designed structure in 2006. The *grand projet* of Chirac's successor, Nicolas Sarkozy, is a national history museum, the Maison de l'Histoire de France (www.maison-histoire.fr), due to open in the Marais in 2016. Watch this space for projects from new president François Hollande.

The Oath of the Horatii by Jacques Louis David

CIRCLE OF JACQUES LOUIS DAVID/GETTY IMAGES ©

If there's one thing that rivals a Parisian's obsession with food, it's art. Over 200 museums pepper the city, and whether you prefer the classicism of the Louvre, the impressionists of the Orsay or detailed exhibits of French military history, you can always be sure to find something new just around the corner. Viewing art is an integral part of Parisians' leisure time, which accounts for their keen aesthetic sensibility.

Painting

While art in Paris today means anything and everything – metro installations, monumental frescoes, mechanical sculpture, suburban tags and bicycles strung on walls – the city's art heritage is rooted in the traditional genres of painting and sculpture.

Baroque to Neoclassicism

According to philosopher Voltaire, French painting proper began with baroque painter Nicolas Poussin (1594–1665), the greatest representative of 17th-century classicism who frequently set scenes from classical mythology and the Bible in ordered landscapes bathed in golden light. It's not a bad starting point; many of Poussin's finest works now hang in the Louvre.

Modern still life pops up on the canvases of Jean-Baptiste Chardin (1699–1779), who

The Best...
Art & Sculpture Museums

1 **Musée du Louvre** (p90)

2 **Musée Rodin** (p225)

3 **Musée d'Orsay** (p216)

4 **Musée Marmottan Monet** (p60)

brought the domesticity of the Dutch masters to French art. A century later, in 1785, neoclassical artist Jacques Louis David (1748–1825) became one of the leaders of the French Revolution and was made official state painter by Napoleon Bonaparte. Many of his works, including the famous *Oath of the Horatii*, can be viewed in the Louvre.

David's pupil Jean-Auguste-Dominique Ingres (1780–1867) continued in the neoclassical tradition, devoting most of his life to historical pictures such as Oedipus and the Sphinx, the 1808 version of which is in the Louvre. Ingres played the violin for enjoyment; the phrase *violon d'Ingres* now means 'hobby' in French.

Romanticism to Realism

One of the Musée du Louvre's most gripping paintings, the *Raft of the Medusa* by Théodore Géricault (1791–1824), hovers on the threshold of romanticism. If Géricault had not died early he likely would have become a leader of the movement, along with his friend Eugène Delacroix (1798–1863), who has his own museum in Paris as well as works at the Louvre and frescoes in St-Sulpice.

Édouard Manet (1832–1883) used realism to depict the life of the Parisian middle classes, incorporating numerous references to the Old Masters. He was pivotal in the transition from realism to impressionism.

Impressionism

Paris' Musée d'Orsay is the crown jewel of impressionist (and postimpressionist) art. Claude Monet (1840–1926) is generally considered the founder of the genre; other impressionists showcased at the Musée d'Orsay include Alfred Sisley (1839–99), Camille Pissarro (1830–1903) and Pierre-Auguste Renoir (1841–1919). The impressionists' main aim was to capture the effects of fleeting light; unusually for the time, they almost always painted in the open air. The term comes from the title of Monet's 1874 experimental painting, *Impression: Soleil Levant* (Impression: Sunrise), displayed at the Musée Marmottan Monet.

Other artists you'll see at the Musée d'Orsay include Edgar Degas (1834–1917) a fellow traveller of the impressionists who preferred painting cafe life and ballet studios, Henri de Toulouse-Lautrec (1864–1901), best known for his posters and lithographs, who chose 'lower' subject including people in the bistros, brothels and music halls of Montmartre; and Paul Cézanne (1839–1906) and Paul Gauguin (1848–1903), who are usually referred to as postimpressionists, encompassing the diverse styles that flowed from impressionism.

20th Century & Beyond

Twentieth-century French painting was characterised by a bewildering diversity of styles, including fauvism, named after the slur of a critic who compared the exhibitors at the 1905 Salon d'Automne (Autumn Salon) in Paris with fauves (wild animals) because of their wild brushstrokes and radical use of intensely bright colours. Among these 'beastly' painters was Henri Matisse (1869–1954); the Centre Pompidou's Musée National d'Art Moderne houses a fabulous collection of his works.

The Literary Arts

Flicking through a street directory reveals just how much Paris honours its literary history, with listings including places Colette and Victor Hugo, avs Marcel Proust and Émile Zola, and rue Balzac. The city has nurtured countless French authors over the centuries, who, together with expat writers from Dickens onwards – including the Lost Generation's Hemingway, Fitzgerald and Joyce – have sealed Paris' literary reputation.

You can leaf through Paris' literary heritage in atmospheric bookshops, hang out in cafes and swish literary bars, visit writers' former-homes-turned-museums, sleep in hotels where they holed up and pay your respects at cemeteries.

Cubism, which deconstructs the subject into a system of intersecting planes and presents various aspects simultaneously, was effectively launched in 1907 with *Les Demoiselles d'Avignon* by Spanish prodigy Pablo Picasso; the Musée Picasso has an astonishing collection of his works.

In the 1920s and '30s the so-called École de Paris (School of Paris) was formed by a group of expressionists including Italian Amedeo Modigliani and Russian Marc Chagall, whose works combined fantasy and folklore.

Dada, a literary and artistic movement of revolt, started in Zürich in 1915. The most influential proponent was Spanish-born Salvador Dalí, who arrived in Paris in 1929 and painted some of his most seminal works here; you can view some at the Espace Dalí in Montmartre.

Artists in the late 20th century turned to the minutiae of everyday urban life to express social and political angst, using media other than paint to let rip – the Musée National d'Art Moderne offers a great insight (as does the building itself). The museum also points to Paris' artistic present – and future.

Sculpture

By the 14th century, sculpture was increasingly commissioned by the nobility for their extravagant, monumental tombs, while in the 15th century Jean Goujon created the stunning *Fontaine des Innocents*. The later baroque style is exemplified by Guillaume Coustou's *Horses of Marly* at the entrance to the Champs-Élysées.

In the mid-19th century, memorial statues in public places came to replace sculpted tombs – the Jardin du Luxembourg is today studded with over 100 sculptures. Jean-Baptiste Carpeaux began as a romantic, but his works – such as *The Dance* on the Palais Garnier and his fountain in the Jardin du Luxembourg – look back to the flamboyance of the baroque era. At the end of the 19th century Auguste Rodin's work overcame the conflict between neoclassicism and romanticism. One of Rodin's most gifted pupils was his lover Camille Claudel, whose work can be seen along with Rodin's in the Musée Rodin.

Among the most influential sculptors to emerge in Paris before WWII was the Romanian-born Constantin Brancusi, whose work can be seen at the Centre Pompidou. Ossip Zadkine was another sculptor who lived and worked in Paris and has a museum.

The Best...
Museums For 20th & 21st Century Art

1 **Musée National d'Art Moderne** (p97)

2 **Palais de Tokyo** (p54)

3 **Dalí Espace Montmartre** (p126)

4 **La Défense** (p55)

In 1936 France put forward a bill providing for 'the creation of monumental decorations in public buildings' by allotting 1% of all building costs to public art. It didn't really get off the ground for another half-century, until Daniel Buren's *Les Deux Plateaux* sculpture was commissioned at Palais Royal. The concept mushroomed, and artwork started to appear everywhere in Paris, including in the Jardin des Tuileries (*The Welcoming Hands*) and even the metro.

The Art of Travel

Metro stations increasingly incorporate artistic themes, including the following:

o **Abbesses** Hector Guimard's finest glass-canopied, twin wrought-iron lampposts illuminating the dark-green-on-lemon-yellow *Metropolitain* sign.

o **Arts et Métiers** (line 11 platform) Jules Verne-inspired copper panelling.

o **Bastille** (line 5 platform) Revolution-era newspaper-engraving frescoes.

o **Cluny-La Sorbonne** (line 10 platform) A mosaic replicates the signatures of Latin Quarter intellectuals including Molière, Rabelais and Robespierre.

o **Concorde** (line 12 platform) Lettered tiles spell out the Déclaration des Droits de l'Homme et du Citoyen (Declaration of the Rights of Man and of the Citizen).

o **Louvre-Rivoli** (line 1 platform & corridor) Statues and bas-reliefs.

o **Palais Royal-Musée du Louvre** Contemporary twist on Guimard's entrances incorporating 800 colourful glass balls.

Drinking & Nightlife

Cocktails at Experimental Cocktail Club (p112)

OWEN FRANKEN/CORBIS ©

For Parisians, drinking and eating go together like wine and cheese, and the line between a café, salon de thé (tearoom), bistro, bar and even a bar à vins (wine bar) is blurred, while the line between drinking and clubbing is often nonexistent – a cafe that's quiet midafternoon might have DJ sets in the evening and dancing later on. And with legendary venues to choose from, live performances in Paris are a treat.

Drinking

Drinking in Paris as Parisians do could mean anything, from downing a coffee at a zinc counter with locals, getting a fruit juice vitamin fix, sipping Japanese *gyokuro* (green tea) in a sleek *salon de thé* (tearoom) or meeting friends after work for *une verre* (a glass), to savouring a cheese platter with a glass of sauvignon on a pavement terrace, debating existentialism over an early-evening *apéritif* in the same literary cafes that Sartre and de Beauvoir did, dancing on tables to bossa nova beats, swilling martinis on a dark leather couch while listening to jazz, or partying aboard floating clubs on the Seine...and much, much more.

The Best...
Drinking Spots

1 **Le Baron Rouge** (p161)

2 **Experimental Cocktail Club** (p112)

3 **Le Batofar** (p236)

4 **Kong** (p113)

5 **Harry's New York Bar** (p113)

6 **Chez Prune** (p135)

Nightlife

From sipping cocktails in swanky bars to grooving at hip clubs, rocking to live bands, being awed by spectacular operas, ballets and classical concerts, entertained by films, dazzled by high-kicking cabarets, intrigued by avant-garde theatre productions or listening to smooth jazz or stirring *chansons*, a night out in Paris promises a night to remember.

Nightclubs

Paris' residential make-up means nightclubs aren't ubiquitous. Lacking a mainstream scene, clubbing here tends to be underground and extremely mobile, making blogs, forums and websites the savviest means of keeping apace with what's happening. The best DJs and their followings have short stints before moving on, and the scene's hippest *soirées clubbing* (clubbing events) float between venues – including the city's many dance-driven bars.

But the beat is strong. Electronic music is of particularly high quality in Paris' clubs, with some excellent local house and techno, laced with funk and groove. The Latin scene is huge; salsa dancing and Latino music nights pack out plenty of clubs. R & B and hip-hop pickings are decent, if less represented than in many other European capitals.

Entertainment

Paris became Europe's most important jazz centre after WWII and the city has some fantastic jazz clubs as well as *chansons* (heartfelt, lyric-driven music typified by Édith Piaf) venues.

Whirling lines of high-kicking dancers at cabarets like the Moulin Rouge are a quintessential fixture on Paris' entertainment scene – for everyone but Parisians. Still, the dazzling sets, costumes and dancing guarantee an entertaining evening (or matinée).

France's national opera and ballet companies perform at the Palais Garnier and Opéra Bastille opera houses. Virtually all theatre productions are in French but increasingly project English-language subtitles.

The city hosts dozens of orchestral, organ and chamber-music concerts each week. In addition to theatres and concert halls, Paris' beautiful, centuries-old stone churches have magnificent acoustics and provide a meditative backdrop for classical music concerts.

Shopping

BRIGITTE MERLE/GETTY IMAGES ©

Paris has it all: broad boulevards lined with international chains, luxury avenues studded with designer fashion houses, famous department stores and fabulous markets. But the real charm of Parisian shopping lies in strolling through the backstreets, where tiny speciality shops and quirky boutiques selling everything from strawberry-scented Wellington boots to heaven-scented candles are wedged between cafes, galleries and churches.

Fashion

Fashion shopping is Paris' forte. Yet although its well-groomed residents make the city at times look and feel like a giant catwalk, fashion here is about style and quality first and foremost, rather than status or brand names. A good place to get an overview of Paris fashion is at department stores like Le Bon Marché, Galeries Lafayette and Le Printemps.

Parisian fashion doesn't have to break the bank. Paris' twice-yearly *soldes* (sales) usually last around six weeks, starting in mid-January and again in mid-June, and can yield discounts of up to 80%. Year-round, there are fantastic bargains at vintage and secondhand boutiques (generally, the more upmarket the area, the better quality the cast-offs), along with outlet shops selling previous seasons' collections, surpluses and seconds by name-brand designers.

The Best...
Parisian
Shops

Markets

Many street markets also sell clothes, accessories, homewares and more.

Bric-a-brac, antiques, retro clothing, jewellery, cheap brand-name clothing, footwear, African carvings, DVDs, electronic items and much more are laid out at the city's flea markets. Watch out for pickpockets!

The website www.paris.fr (in French) lists every market by *arrondissement*, including speciality markets such as flower markets.

Art, Antiques & Homewares

From venerable antique dealers to edgy art galleries, there is a wealth of places in this artistic city to browse and buy one-off conversation pieces and collectibles. Paris also has some unique home and garden shops selling colourful, quirky innovations to brighten your living and/or working environment.

Books

Paris' literary heritage has inspired atmospheric bookshops, including English-language bookshops that are a magnet for writers and that host readings, workshops and other literary events. *Bandes dessinées* (comics), known as *le neuvième art* (the ninth art), are big business in France, with dozens of specialist shops.

Top Shopping Tips

◦ Dating from the 19th century, Paris' glass-roofed covered passages, such as the Passage des Panoramas (p115), are treasure chests of small, exquisite boutiques.

◦ The most exclusive designer boutiques require customers to buzz to get in – don't be shy about ringing the bell.

◦ Particularly in smaller shops, shopkeepers may not like you touching the merchandise until invited to do so.

◦ Clothing sizes aren't standardised among European countries – head to a *cabine d'essayage* (fitting room) or www.onlineconversion.com/clothing.

◦ If you're happy browsing, tell sales staff *'Je regarde'* – 'I'm just looking'.

◦ Practically all shops offer free (and beautiful) gift wrapping – ask for *un paquet cadeau*.

◦ Greet/farewell shopkeepers and sales staff, with '*Bonjour* (*bonsoir* at night)/*Au revoir*'.

◦ Bargaining is only acceptable at flea markets.

◦ Food, wine and tea shops make for mouthwatering shopping – see **Gourmet Food Shops** (p29) for more.

Survival Guide

Iconic French brands
PHOTOGRAPHER: CARLOS SANCHEZ PEREYRA/JAI/CORBIS ©

Sleeping

Paris has a huge choice of accommodation, from hostels through to deluxe hotels, some of which rank among the finest in the world. Although the city has more than 150,000 beds in over 1500 establishments, you'll still need to book well ahead during the warmer months (April to October) and for all public and school holidays.

Accommodation Types

Hotels

Hotels in Paris are inspected by government authorities and classified into six categories – from no star to five stars. The vast majority are two- and three-star hotels, which are generally excellent value. All hotels must display their rates, including TVA (*taxe sur la valeur ajoutée;* valued-added tax).

Paris' hotel rooms tend to be small by international standards – a family of four will probably need two connecting rooms; if children are too young to stay in their own room, it's possible to make do with triples, quads or suites in some places.

Cheaper hotels may not have lifts/elevators and/or air conditioning. Some don't accept credit cards.

Breakfast is rarely included in hotel rates; heading to a cafe often works out to be better value.

Hostels

Paris is awash with hostels, and standards are improving. Rates often include basic breakfast.

More institutional hostels have daytime lock-outs and curfews; some have a maximum three-night stay. Only the official *auberges de jeunesse* (youth hostels) require guests to present Hostelling International (HI) cards or their equivalent.

B&Bs & Homestays

Bed-and-breakfast accommodation (*chambres d'hôte* in French) is increasingly popular. The city of Paris has inaugurated a scheme called Paris Quality Hosts (Hôtes Qualité Paris) to foster B&Bs – not just to offer an alternative choice of accommodation, but also to ease the isolation of some Parisians, half of whom live alone. There's often a minimum stay of three or four nights.

Apartments

Families – and anyone wanting to self-cater – should consider renting a short-stay apartment. Paris has a number of excellent apartment hotels, such as the international chain **Apart'hotels Citadines** (www.citadines.com/Apart_hotels).

For an even more authentic Parisian experience, apartment rental agencies offer furnished residential apartments for stays of a few days to several months. Apartments often include facilities such as wi-fi

Need to Know

PRICE RANGES

In this book, the following price ranges apply for a double room with en suite bathroom in high season (breakfast not included).

- **€**   under €110
- **€€**   €110–€200
- **€€€**   over €200

TAXE DE SÉJOUR

The city of Paris levies a *taxe de séjour* (tourist tax) of between €0.20 (campgrounds, 'NN' or un-classified hotels) and €1.50 (five-star hotels) per person per night on all forms of accommodation.

INTERNET ACCESS

Most hotels and hostels in Paris have some form of internet access available. Increasingly, wi-fi (pronounced wee-fee in French) is free of charge. In some older hotels, the higher the floor, the less reliable the wi-fi connection.

SMOKING

Smoking is now officially banned in all Paris hotels.

nd washing machines, and an be superb value. Beware of irect-rental scams.

Useful Websites

Lonely Planet (www. lonelyplanet.com/hotels) accommodation reviews; book directly online.

Paris Hotel Service (www. parishotelservice.com)

Specialises in boutique hotel gems.

Paris Hotel (www.hotels-paris. fr) Well-run hotel booking site with lots of user reviews.

Paris Quality Hosts (www. hqp.fr) B&B accommodation in the city.

Guest Apartment Services (www.guestapartment.com)

Romantic apartment rentals on and around Paris' islands.

Room Sélection (www. room-selection.com) Select apartment rentals centred on the Marais.

Paris Attitude (www. parisattitude.com) Thousands of apartment rentals, professional service and reasonable fees.

Where to Stay

NEIGHBOURHOOD	FOR	AGAINST
EIFFEL TOWER & LA DÉFENSE	Close to Paris' iconic tower and museums. Upmarket area with quiet residential streets.	Limited nightlife. Short on budget and midrange accommodation options.
CHAMPS-ÉLYÉES & GRANDS BOULEVARDS	Luxury hotels, famous boutiques and department stores, gastronomic restaurants, great nightlife.	Some areas extremely pricey. Nightlife hotspots can be noisy.
LOUVRE & LES HALLES	Central location, excellent transport links, major museums, shopping galore.	Not many bargains. Ongoing Forum des Halles construction work may be noisy/ inconvenient.
MONTMARTRE & NORTHERN PARIS	Village atmosphere and some lively multicultural areas. Many places have views across Paris.	Hilly, further out than some areas, some parts very touristy. Red light district around Pigalle, although well-lit and safe, won't appeal to some travellers.
LE MARAIS & BASTILLE	Buzzing nightlife, hip shopping, great range of eating options. Excellent museums. Lively gay and lesbian scene. Busier on Sundays than most areas. Very central.	Can be seriously noisy in areas where bars and clubs are especially concentrated. Some Bastille areas slightly out of the way.
THE ISLANDS	As geographically central as it gets. Almost all accommodation situated on the peaceful, romantic Île St-Louis.	No metro station on the Île St-Louis. Limited self-catering options, zero nightlife.
LATIN QUARTER	Energetic student area, stacks of eating and drinking options, late-opening bookshops.	Popularity with students and visiting academics makes rooms hardest to find during conferences and seminars from March to June and in October.
ST-GERMAIN, LES INVALIDES & MONTPARNASSE	Stylish, central location, superb shopping, sophisticated dining, proximity to the Jardin du Luxembourg. Montparnasse area has few tourists and excellent links to both airports.	Budget accommodation is seriously short changed. Some Montparnasse areas slightly out of the way.

Best Places to Stay

NAME		REVIEW
HÔTEL SEZZ €€€	Eiffel Tower & La Défense	Zen-spirited design- and technology-heavy boutique bonanza punning on the number of its posh arrondissement, 16 (*seize* in French).
GENTLE GOURMET €€	Eiffel Tower & La Défense	Extras at this small vegan B&B include vegan dinners (reservations essential). Book well in advance.
HIDDEN HOTEL €€€	Champs-Élysées & Grands Boulevards	Serene, stylish and reasonably spacious, with earth-coloured natural pigments (there's no paint), handmade wooden furniture and stone basins.
W PARIS – OPÉRA €€€	Champs-Élysées & Grands Boulevards	Don't sell yourself short with a Cozy or Wonderful room what you want is a Spectacular room or Wow suite.
HÔTEL LANGLOIS €€	Champs-Élysées & Grands Boulevards	Built in 1870, Hôtel Langlois has kept its charm, from the tiny caged elevator to original bathroom fixtures and tiles.
HÔTEL CRAYON €€	Louvre & Les Halles	The pencil (*le crayon*) is the theme – line drawings by French artist Julie Gauthron bedeck the walls and doors
HÔTEL TIQUETONNE €	Louvre & Les Halles	Spick-and-span rooms over seven floors with varying decor; some have Sacré-Cœur or Eiffel Tower views.
LE PRADEY €€€	Louvre & Les Halles	Exclusive new address with art books in the chic lounge and individually themed suites like Cabaret and Opéra.
HÔTEL VIVIENNE €	Louvre & Les Halles	While these 45 rooms are not huge, they have all the mod cons; some even boast little balconies.
LE CITIZEN HOTEL €€	Montmartre & Northern Paris	Twelve alluring minimalist-design rooms with iPads and filtered water. Artwork is from Oakland's Creative Growth Art Center for disabled artists.
HÔTEL DU NORD – LE PARI VÉLO €	Montmartre & Northern Paris	This particularly charming place has 24 personalised rooms decorated with flea-market antiques in a prized location near place République.
HÔTEL AMOUR €€	Montmartre & Northern Paris	Planning a romantic Paris escapade, free of TV? The inimitable black-clad Amour features original design and artwork in every room.
HÔTEL PARTICULIER MONTMARTRE €€€	Montmartre & Northern Paris	This hidden 18th-century mansion is like staying in a modern art collector's residence, with rotating exhibitions and five artist-designed suites.
MANOIR DE BEAUREGARD €€	Montmartre & Northern Paris	If you ever dreamt of staying in an 18th-century French townhouse, this would certainly be your pick.
TERRASS HÔTEL €€€	Montmartre & Northern Paris	For the ultimate Parisian experience, choose room 608 for stunning Eiffel Tower and Panthéon views.

PRACTICALITIES	BEST FOR
📞 01 56 75 26 26; www.hotelsezz.com; 6 av Frémiet,16e; d €353, ste €428-910; ❄ @ 🛜 🏊; M Passy	Pampering.
📞 01 45 00 46 55; www.gentlegourmetbandb.com; 21 rue Duret,16e; s €135-155, d €160-200; 🛜; M Argentine	Wholesome food and hospitality.
📞 01 40 55 03 57; www.hidden-hotel.com; 28 rue de l'Arc de Triomphe, 17e; r from €376; ❄ @ 🛜; M Charles de Gaulle-Étoile	Ecofriendly credentials.
📞 01 77 48 94 94; www.wparisopera.fr; 4 rue Meyerbeer, 9e; d €340-500; ❄ @; M Chaussée d'Antin–La Fayette	Haussmann style and modern design.
📞 01 48 74 78 24; www.hotel-langlois.com; 63 rue St-Lazare, 9e; s €110-120, d €140-150; ❄ @ 🛜; M Trinité	Belle époque ambiance.
📞 01 42 36 54 19; www.hotelcrayon.com; 25 rue du Bouloi, 1er; s €129-249, d €149-299; ❄ 🛜; M Les Halles or Sentier	Creative, retro design.
📞 01 42 36 94 58; www.hoteltiquetonne.com; 6 rue Tiquetonne, 2e; d €65, with shared shower €45 ; 🛜; M Étienne Marcel	Vintage charm.
📞 01 42 60 31 70; www.lepradey.com; 5 rue St-Roch, 1er; d from €220; ❄ @ 🛜; M Tuileries	Designer luxury.
📞 01 42 33 13 26; www.hotel-vivienne.com; 40 rue de Marivaux, 2e; d €102-150, tr & q €150-190; @ 🛜; M Grands Boulevards	Style on a budget.
📞 01 83 62 55 50; www.lecitizenhotel.com; 96 quai de Jemmapes, 10e; d €177-275, q €450; 🛜; M Gare du Nord	Canal St-Martin creative spirit.
📞 01 42 01 66 00; www.hoteldunord-leparivelo.com; 47 rue Albert Thomas, 10e; s/d/q €71/85/110; 🛜; M République	Cyclists.
📞 01 48 78 31 80; www.hotelamourparis.fr; 8 rue Navarin, 9e; s €105, d €155-215; 🛜; M St-Georges or Pigalle	Adventurous romantics.
📞 01 53 41 81 40; http://hotel-particulier-montmartre.com; 23 av Junot, 18e; ste €390-590; ❄ 🛜; M Lamarck-Caulaincourt	Art aficionados.
📞 01 42 03 10 20; manoir-de-beauregard-paris.com; 43 rue des Lilas,19e; rooms €135-250; 🛜; M Danube	Period style.
📞 01 46 06 72 85; www.terrass-hotel.com; 12 rue Joseph de Maistre, 18e; s & d €285-345; ❄ 🛜; M Blanche	Views, views, views!

NAME		REVIEW
HÔTEL ELDORADO €	Montmartre & Northern Paris	A great find, with 23 colourfully decorated rooms and a garden. Cheaper singles have washbasin only.
MAMA SHELTER €	Le Marais & Bastille	These 170 designer rooms have iMacs, concrete walls and microwaves, plus a rooftop terrace and pizzeria.
HÔTEL JEANNE D'ARC €	Le Marais & Bastille	Games to play, a rocking chair for tots in the lounge and knick-knacks everywhere create a 'family home' air.
LE PAVILLON DE LA REINE €€€	Le Marais & Bastille	On Paris' most beautiful square, you can sleep as Queen Anne of Austria did at this sumptuous address.
HÔTEL DU 7E ART €€	Le Marais & Bastille	The 'seventh art' (ie cinema) has jaunty retro movie posters and cinematic black-and-white bathroom tiling.
HÔTEL DU PETIT MOULIN €€€	Le Marais & Bastille	Scrumptious 17-room hotel – a bakery at the time of Henri IV – designed from head to toe by Christian Lacroix
HÔTEL ST-LOUIS EN l'ÎLE €€	The Islands	A pristine taupe façade and a perfectly polished interior. The stone-cellar breakfast room is a gem.
HÔTEL HENRI IV €	The Islands	Much-loved budget hotel with freshly renovated, rooms and wonderful views. Phone reservations only.
FIVE HOTEL €€€	Latin Quarter	Choose from one of five perfumes to scent your room at this contemporary romantic sanctum.
HÔTEL LES DEGRÉS DE NOTRE DAME €€	Latin Quarter	A block from the Seine with a winding timber staircase (no lift). Rooms 47 and 501 have Notre Dame views.
HÔTEL RÉSIDENCE HENRI IV €€€	Latin Quarter	Generously sized rooms (minimum 17 sq metres), two-room apartments (minimum 25 sq metres) equipped with kitchenettes (hot plates, fridge, microwave)
L'HÔTEL €€€	St-Germain, Les Invalides & Montparnasse	The stuff of romance, Parisian myths and urban legends: in 1900, Oscar Wilde died in room 16. Live music bar.
L'APOSTROPHE €€	St-Germain, Les Invalides & Montparnasse	This art hotel's 16 dramatically different rooms pay homage to the written word (eg spray-painted graffiti tags in room U ('urbain').
LE BELLECHASSE €€	St-Germain, Les Invalides & Montparnasse	Fashion (and, increasingly, interior) designer Christian Lacroix's entrancing room themes evoke larger-than-life oil paintings. Mod cons include 200 TV channels.
HÔTEL PERREYVE €€	St-Germain, Les Invalides & Montparnasse	Warmly welcoming 1920s hotel that's superb value given its coveted location, with cosy, carpeted rooms and a gold-hued breakfast room.
HÔTEL D'ANGLETERRE €€€	St-Germain, Les Invalides & Montparnasse	The Treaty of Paris ending the American Revolution was prepared here in 1783, and Hemingway and Charles Lindbergh lodged here.
HÔTEL ST-ANDRÉ DES ARTS €	St-Germain, Les Invalides & Montparnasse	A veritable bargain in the centre of the action. Rooms are basic and there's no lift, but rates include breakfast.

PRACTICALITIES	BEST FOR
☎ 01 45 22 35 21; www.eldoradohotel.fr; 18 rue des Dames, 17e; s €39-65, d €58-85, tr €75-93; 🛜; Ⓜ Place de Clichy	Bohemian budget travellers.
☎ 01 43 48 48 48; www.mamashelter.com; 109 rue de Bagnolet, 20e; r €80-200; ❄ @ 🛜; 🖵 76, Ⓜ Alexandre Dumas or Gambetta	Haven-seeking hipsters.
☎ 01 48 87 62 11; www.hoteljeannedarc.com; 3 rue de Jarente, 4e; s €65, d €81-96, tr €149, q €164; 🛜; Ⓜ St-Paul	Value for money.
☎ 01 44 59 80 40; www.pavillondelareine.com; 28 place des Vosges, 3e; d from €330; Ⓜ Chemin Vert	Royal treatment, including a spa.
☎ 01 44 54 85 00; www.paris-hotel-7art.com; 20 rue St-Paul, 4e; s €75, d €100-180, tr €180, q €200; 🛜; Ⓜ St-Paul	Film fans.
☎ 01 42 74 10 10; www.hoteldupetitmoulin.com; 29-31 rue du Poitou, 3e; d €190-350; Ⓜ Filles du Calvaire	Haut Marais style.
☎ 01 46 34 04 80; www.saintlouisenlisle.com; 75 rue St-Louis en l'Île, 4e; d €169-199, with balcony €239-259, tr €279; ❄ @ 🛜; Ⓜ Pont Marie	Luxury island living.
☎ 01 43 54 44 53; www.henri4hotel.fr; 25 place Dauphine, 1er; s/d/tr from €67/72/88; Ⓜ Pont Neuf or Cité	Budget island living.
☎ 01 43 31 74 21; www.thefivehotel-paris.com; 3 rue Flatters, 5e; d €202-342; ❄ 🛜; Ⓜ Les Gobelins	Romance.
☎ 01 55 42 88 88; www.lesdegreshotel.com; 10 rue des Grands Degrés, 5e; d incl breakfast €115-170; 🛜; Ⓜ Maubert-Mutualité	Old-school charm.
☎ 01 44 41 31 81; www.residencehenri4.com; 50 rue des Bernadins, 5e; d €260-330; ❄ @ 🛜; Ⓜ Maubert-Mutualité	Families.
☎ 01 44 41 99 00; www.l-hotel.com; 13 rue des Beaux Arts, 6e; d €285-795; ❄ @ 🛜 ⌧; Ⓜ St-Germain des Prés	Literary history.
☎ 01 56 54 31 31; www.apostrophe-hotel.com; 3 rue de Chevreuse, 6e; d €150-350; ❄ @ 🛜; Ⓜ Vavin	Design fiends.
☎ 01 45 50 22 31; www.lebellechasse.com; 8 rue de Bellechasse, 7e; d from €161; ❄ 🛜; Ⓜ Solférino	Lavish luxury.
☎ 01 45 48 35 01; www.hotel-perreyve.com; 63 rue Madame, 6e; d €145-165; ❄ 🛜; Ⓜ Rennes	Jardin du Luxembourg proximity.
☎ 01 42 60 34 72; www.hotel-dangleterre.com; 44 rue Jacob, 6e; s €160, d €220-260; @ 🛜; Ⓜ St-Germain des Prés	History buffs.
☎ 01 43 26 96 16; 66 rue St-André des Arts, 6e; s/d/tr/q incl breakfast €75/95/119/132; 🛜; Ⓜ Odéon	Budget St-Germain living.

Transport

●●●
Getting To Paris

Few roads *don't* lead to Paris, one of the most visited destinations on earth. Practically every major airline flies though one of its three airports, and most European train and bus routes cross it.

Paris is the central point in the French rail network, Société Nationale des Chemins de Fer Français (SNCF), with six train stations that handle passenger traffic to different parts of France and Europe. Each is well connected to the Paris public transportation system, the Régie Autonome des Transports Parisiens (RATP). To buy onward tickets from Paris, visit a station or go to **Voyages SNCF** (www.voyages-sncf. com). Most trains – and all Trains à Grande Vitesse (TGV) – require advance reservations. As with most tickets, the earlier you book, the better your chances of securing a discounted fare. Mainline stations in Paris have left-luggage offices and/or *consignes* (lockers).

On public transport, children under four travel free and those aged between four

and nine (inclusive) pay half-price; exceptions are noted.

Flights, tours and rail tickets can be booked online at www.lonelyplanet.com/bookings.

✈ Charles de Gaulle Airport

Most international airlines fly to **Charles de Gaulle (CDG; www.aeroportsdeparis. fr)**, 28km northeast of central Paris; in French the airport is commonly referred to as 'Roissy', after the suburb in which it is located.

Metro & RER Networks
CDG is served by the RER B line (€9.10, approximately 35 minutes, every 10 to 15 minutes), which serves the Gare du Nord, Châtelet–Les Halles and St-Michel–Notre Dame stations in the city centre. Trains run from 5am to 11pm; there are fewer trains on weekends.

Taxi
A taxi to the city centre takes approximately 40 minutes, assuming no traffic jams. During the day, expect to pay around €50; the fare increases 15% between 5pm and 10am and on Sundays. Only take taxis at a clearly marked rank. Never follow anyone who approaches you at the airport and claims to be a driver.

Bus
There are six main bus lines.

Air France bus 2 (€15, 45 minutes, every 20 minutes, 6am to 11pm) Links the airport with the Arc de Triomphe. Children aged two to 11 pay half-price.

Air France bus 4 (€16.50, every 30 minutes, 6am to 10pm from CDG, 6am to 9.30pm from Paris) Links the airport with Gare de Lyon (50 minutes) in eastern Paris and Gare Montparnasse (55 minutes) in southern Paris. Kids aged two to 11 pay half-price.

Roissybus (€10, 45 to 60 minutes, every 15 minutes, 5.30am to 11pm) Links the airport with the Opéra.

RATP bus 350 (€5.10 or three metro tickets, one hour, every 30 minutes, 5.30am to 11pm) Links the airport with Gare de l'Est in northern Paris.

RATP bus 351 (€5.10 or three metro tickets, 50 minutes, every 30 minutes, 5.30am to 11pm) Links the airport with place de la Nation in eastern Paris.

Noctilien bus 140 & 143 (€7.60, hourly, 12.30am to 5.30pm) Part of the RATP night service, Noctilien has two buses that go to CDG: bus 140 from Gare de l'Est, and 143 from Gare de l'Est and Gare du Nord.

✈ Orly Airport
Orly (ORY; ☎ 01 70 36 39 50; www.aeroportsdeparis.fr) is located 19km south of central Paris but, despite being closer than CDG, it is not used as often by international airlines and public transportation options aren't as easy. If you have heavy luggage or young kids in tow, consider a taxi.

Taxi
A taxi to the city centre takes roughly 30 minutes, assuming no traffic jams. During the

...ay, expect to pay around €45; the fare increases 15% between 5pm and 10am and on Sundays. Only take a taxi at a clearly marked rank. Never follow anyone who approaches you at the airport and claims to be a driver.

Metro & RER Networks

There is no direct train to/from Orly; you'll need to change transport halfway. Note that while it is possible to take a shuttle to the RER C line, this service is quite long and not recommended.

RER B (€10.75; 35 minutes, every four to 12 minutes) This line connects Orly with the St-Michel–Notre Dame, Châtelet–Les Halles and Gare du Nord stations in the city centre. In order to get from Orly to the RER station (Antony), you must first take the Orlyval automatic train. The service runs from 6am to 11pm; there are fewer trains on weekends. You only need one ticket to take the two trains.

Bus

There are several bus lines that serve Orly; only the most practical are listed here.

Air France bus 1 (€11.50, every 20 minutes, 5am to 10.20pm from Orly, 6am to 11.20pm from Invalides) This bus runs to/from the Gare Montparnasse (35 minutes) in southern Paris, Invalides in the 7e, and the Arc de Triomphe. Children aged two to 11 pay half-price.

Orlybus (€6.90, 30 minutes, every 15 minutes, 6am to 11.20pm from Orly, 5.35am to 11.05pm from Paris) This bus runs to/from the metro station Denfert Rochereau in southern Paris, making several stops en route.

✈ Beauvais Airport

Beauvais (BVA; ☎ 08 92 68 20 66; www.aeroportbeauvais.com) is 75km north of Paris and a few low-cost flights go through here – but before you snap up that bargain, consider if the post-arrival journey is worth it.

Bus

Shuttle (€15, 1¼ hours) The Beauvais shuttle links the airport with the metro station Porte de Maillot in western Paris. See the airport website for details.

🚆 Gare du Nord

Eurostar (www.eurostar.com) The London–Paris line runs from St-Pancras International to Gare du Nord. Voyages take 2¼ hours.

Thalys (www.thalys.com) Thalys trains pull into Paris' Gare du Nord from Brussels, Amsterdam and Cologne.

●●● Getting Around

Getting around Paris is comparatively easy for a big city. Most visitors combine the vast and efficient metro with walking – few cities can match Paris for scenic strolls – and the city's communal bike-share scheme, Vélib'.

Ⓜ Train

Paris' underground network is run by **RATP** (www.ratp.fr) and consists of two separate but linked systems: the metro and the RER suburban train line. The metro has 14 numbered lines; the Réseau Express Régional (RER) has five main lines (but you'll probably only need to use A, B and C). When giving the names of stations in this book, the term 'metro' is used to cover both the metro and the RER within Paris proper. At the time of writing, there were five concentric transportation zones rippling out from Paris (five being the furthest); if you travel from Charles de Gaulle airport to Paris, for instance, you will have to buy a zone 1–5 ticket.

Metro

Metro lines are identified by both their number (eg ligne 1; line 1) and their colour, listed on official metro signs and maps.

Signs in metro and RER stations indicate the way to the correct platform for your line. The *direction* signs on each platform indicate the terminus. On lines that split into several branches (such as lines 7 and 13), the terminus of each train is indicated on the cars and on signs on each platform giving the number of minutes until the next and subsequent train.

Signs marked *correspondance* (transfer) show how to reach connecting trains. At stations with many intersecting lines, like Châtelet and Montparnasse Bienvenüe, walking from one platform to the next can take a very long time.

Different station exits are indicated by white-on-blue

sortie (exit) signs. You can get your bearings by checking the *plan du quartier* (neighbourhood maps) posted at exits.

Each line has its own schedule, but trains usually start at around 5.30am, with the last train beginning its run between 12.35am and 1.15am (2.15am on Friday and Saturday).

RER

The RER is faster than the metro but the stops are much further apart.

If you're going out to the suburbs (eg Versailles or Disneyland), ask for help on the platform – finding the right train can be confusing. Also make sure your ticket is for the correct zone.

Tickets & Fares

The same RATP tickets are valid on the metro, the RER (for travel within the city limits), buses, trams and the Montmartre funicular.

A ticket – white in colour and called *Le Ticket t+* – costs €1.70 (half-price for children aged four to nine years) if bought individually and €12.70 for adults for a *carnet* (book) of 10.

Tickets are sold at all metro stations: ticket windows accept most credit cards; however, automated machines *do not* accept North American credit cards.

One ticket lets you travel between any two metro stations (no return journeys) for a period of 1½ hours, no matter how many transfers are required. You can also use it on the RER for travel within zone 1, which encompasses all of central Paris.

A single ticket can be used to transfer between buses, but not to transfer from the metro to bus or vice-versa. Transfers are not allowed on Noctilien buses.

Always keep your ticket until you exit from your station or risk a fine.

Tourist Passes

The Mobilis and Paris Visite passes are valid on the metro, RER, SNCF's suburban lines, buses, night buses, trams and Montmartre funicular railway. No photo is needed, but write your card number on the ticket. Passes are sold at larger metro and RER stations, SNCF offices in Paris, and the airports.

Mobilis allows unlimited travel for one day and costs €6.40 (two zones) to €14.20 (five zones). Buy it at any metro, RER or SNCF station in the Paris region. Depending on how many times you plan to hop on/off the metro in a day, a *carnet* might work out cheaper.

Paris Visite allows unlimited travel (including to/ from airports) as well as discounted entry to certain museums and other discounts and bonuses. Passes are valid for either three or five zones. The zone 1 to 3 pass costs €9.75/15.85/21.60/31.15 for one/two/three/five days. Children aged four to 11 years pay half-price.

Navigo Découverte (Navigo Discovery) card (www.navigo. fr; €5) may be useful if you'll be in Paris a week or more.

 ## Bicycle

Vélib'

The **Vélib' bike share** (http://en.velib.paris.fr) scheme has revolutionised how Parisians get around. There are some 1800 stations throughout the city, each with anywhere from 20 to 70 bike stands. The bikes are accessible round the clock.

To get a bike, you first need to purchase a one-/seven-day subscription (€1.70/8). There are two ways to do this: either at the terminals found at docking stations, or online (best for North American credit card holders).

After you authorise a deposit (€150), you'll receive an ID number and PIN code and you're ready to go.

Bikes are rented in 30-minute intervals: the 1st half-hour is free, the 2nd is €2, the 3rd and each additional half-hour are €4. If you return a bike before a half-hour is up and then take a new one, you will not be charged.

If the station you want to return your bike to is full, log in to the terminal to get 15 minutes for free to find another station.

Bikes are geared to cyclists aged 14 and over, and are fitted with gears, an antitheft lock with key, reflective strips and front/rear lights. Bring your own helmet, though!

Rentals

Most rental places will require a deposit. Take ID and credit card.

Au Point Vélo Hollandais (☏ 01 43 45 85 36; www.pointvelo.com; 83 bd St-Michel, 5e; per day €15; ☉ 10am-7.30pm Mon-Sat; Ⓜ Cluny-La Sorbonne or RER Luxembourg)

🚌 Bus

Paris' bus system, operated by RATP, runs from 5.30am to 8.30pm Monday to Saturday; after that, certain evening-service lines continue until between midnight and 12.30am. Services are drastically reduced on Sunday and public holidays, when buses run from 7am to 8.30pm.

The RATP runs 47 night bus lines known as **Noctilien** (www.noctilien.fr), which depart hourly from 12.30am to 5.30pm. You pay a certain number of standard €1.70 metro/bus tickets, depending on the distance. If you don't have a ticket, the driver can sell you one for €1.90. If you have a Mobilis or Paris Visite pass, flash it at the driver when you board.

🚢 Boat

Batobus (www.batobus.com; 1-/2-/5-day pass €15/18/21; ☉ 10am-9.30pm Apr-Aug, to 7pm rest of year) runs a ferry down the Seine, docking at eight stops: Eiffel Tower, Champs-Élysées, Musée d'Orsay, Musée du Louvre, St-Germain des Prés, Hôtel de Ville, Notre Dame and Jardin des Plantes.

Buy tickets online, at ferry stops or at tourist offices. You can also buy a 2-/3-day ticket in conjunction with the L'Open Tour buses for €43/46.

🚕 Taxi

The *prise en charge* (flagfall) is €2.40. Within the city limits, it costs €0.96 per kilometre for travel between 10am and 5pm Monday to Saturday (*Tarif A*; white light on taxi roof and meter).

At night (5pm to 10am), on Sunday from 7am to midnight, and in the inner suburbs the rate is €1.21 per km (*Tarif B*; orange light).

Travel in the outer suburbs is at *Tarif C*, €1.47 per kilometre (blue light).

There's a €2.95 surcharge for taking a fourth passenger, but drivers sometimes refuse for insurance reasons. The first piece of baggage is free; additional pieces over 5kg cost €1 extra. When tipping, round up to the nearest €1 or so.

Flagging down a taxi in Paris can be difficult; it's best to find an official taxi stand.

To order a taxi, call or reserve online with **Taxis G7** (☏ 01 41 27 66 99; www.taxisg7.fr), **Taxis Bleus** (☏ 01 49 36 10 10; www.taxis-bleus.com) or **Alpha Taxis** (☏ 01 45 85 85 85; www.alphataxis.com).

Climate Change & Travel

Every form of transport that relies on carbon-based fuel generates CO_2, the main cause of human-induced climate change. Modern travel is dependent on aeroplanes, which might use less fuel per kilometre per person than most cars but travel much greater distances. The altitude at which aircraft emit gases (including CO_2) and particles also contributes to their climate change impact. Many websites offer 'carbon calculators' that allow people to estimate the carbon emissions generated by their journey and, for those who wish to do so, to offset the impact of the greenhouse gases emitted with contributions to portfolios of climate-friendly initiatives throughout the world. Lonely Planet offsets the carbon footprint of all staff and author travel.

🚗 Car & Motorcycle

Driving in Paris is defined by the triple hassle of navigation, heavy traffic and parking. It doesn't make sense to use a car to get around, but if you're heading out of the city on an excursion, then your own set of wheels can certainly be useful. If you plan on hiring a car, it's best to do it online and in advance. In December 2011, Paris launched the world's first electric-car-share programme, **Autolib'** (www.autolib.eu).

A-Z
Directory

Tours

Bicycle & Scooter

Fat Tire Bike Tours (Map p56; ☑ 01 56 58 10 54; www.fattirebiketours.com) Daytime bike tours of the city (€28; four hours) start at 11am daily from mid-February to early January, with an additional departure at 3pm from April to October. Night bicycle tours depart at 7pm from April to October and 6pm (not always daily) in low season. Other tours go to Versailles, Monet's garden in Giverny and the Normandy beaches.

Paris à Vélo, C'est Sympa! (☑ 01 48 87 60 01; www.parisvelosympa.com; ☉ Apr-Oct) Four guided bike tours (€34; three hours), including an evening cycle and a sunrise tour.

Left Bank Scooters (☑ 06 82 70 13 82; www.leftbankscooters.com) If you'd rather not pedal, sign up for a scooter tour around Paris or Versailles (€150/250).

🚢 Boat

A boat cruise down the Seine is the most relaxing way to watch the city glide by. If it's your first time in Paris, it's also a good way to get a quick introduction to the city's main monuments.

Bateaux-Mouches (Map p74; ☑ 01 42 25 96 10; www.bateauxmouches.com; Port de la Conférence, 8e; adult/4-12yr €11/5.50; ☉ Apr-Dec; Ⓜ Alma Marceau) The largest river cruise company in Paris and a favourite with tour groups. Cruises (70 minutes) run regularly from 10.15am to 11pm April to September and 13 times a day between 11am and 9pm the rest of the year. Commentary is in French and English. It's located on the Right Bank, just east of the Pont de l'Alma.

🚌 Bus

L'Open Tour (Map p80; www.pariscityrama.com; 2-day passes adult/child €32/15) This hop-on, hop-off bus tour runs open-deck buses along four circuits (central Paris; Montmartre–Grands Boulevards; Bastille–Bercy; and Montparnasse–St-Germain) daily year-round. You can jump on and off at main sites, making them very convenient for whirlwind tours of the city. Cityrama, which owns the buses, has a host of other packages as well.

🏃 Walking

Paris Greeter (www.parisiendunjour.fr; by donation) See Paris through local eyes with these two- to three-hour city tours. Volunteers lead groups (maximum six people) to their favourite spots in the city. Minimum two weeks' advance notice needed.

Paris Walks (www.pariswalks.com; adult/child €12/8) Long established and highly rated by our readers, Paris Walks offers thematic tours (fashion, chocolate, the French Revolution).

Business Hours

The following list shows *approximate* standard opening hours for businesses. Many businesses close for the entire month of August for summer holidays.

Banks 9am-1pm & 2-5pm Mon-Fri, some Sat morning

Bars & Cafes 7am-2am

Museums 10am-6pm, closed Mon or Tue

Post Offices 8am-7pm Mon-Fri & Sat till noon

Restaurants Lunch noon-2pm, dinner 7.30-10.30pm

Shops (clothing) 10am-7pm Mon-Sat, occasionally closed in the early afternoon for lunch

Shops (food) 8am-1pm & 4-7.30pm, closed Sun afternoon & sometimes Mon

Discount Cards

Almost all museums and monuments in Paris have discounted tickets (*tarif réduit*).

for students and seniors (generally over 60 years), provided you have a valid ID. Children often get in free, though the cut-off age for 'child' can be anywhere between six and 18 years.

EU citizens under 26 years get in for free at national monuments and museums.

Paris Museum Pass (www.parismuseumpass.fr; 2/4/6 days €39/54/69) Gets you into some 38 venues in the city and 22 more outside the city; also allows you to bypass long ticket queues.

Electricity

230V/50Hz

Emergency

Ambulance (SAMU) (15)

Fire (📞18)

Police (📞17)

●●●
Internet Access

Wi-fi (pronounced 'wee-fee' in French) is available at most hotels in Paris, and is increasingly free.

Wi-fi is available at 400 public hotspots, mainly parks but also libraries and municipal buildings. Participating parks have a purple 'Zone Wi-Fi' sign posted near the gate. To connect, look for the Orange network and log in. You'll have two hours of consecutive use. There is also free wi-fi on Paris' metro and at some museums.

You'll probably find at least one internet cafe in your immediate neighbourhood. Expect to pay about €4 for one hour.

●●●
Medical Services
Hospitals

There are some 50 hospitals in Paris, including the following:

American Hospital of Paris (📞 01 46 41 25 25; www.american-hospital.org; 63 bd Victor Hugo, Neuilly-sur-Seine; Ⓜ Pont de Levallois) Private hospital offering emergency 24-hour medical and dental care.

Hertford British Hospital (📞 01 47 59 59 59; www.ihfb.org; 3 rue Barbès, Levallois; Ⓜ Anatole France) A less expensive private English-speaking option than the American Hospital.

Hôpital Hôtel Dieu (📞 01 42 34 82 34; www.aphp.fr; 1 place du Parvis Notre Dame, 4e; Ⓜ Cité) One of the city's main government-run public hospitals; after 8pm use the emergency entrance on rue de la Cité.

Pharmacies

There will always be at least one *pharmacie* in your neighbourhood with extended hours.

Pharmacie Bader (📞 01 43 26 92 66; 12 bd St-Michel, 5e; 🕐 9am-9pm; Ⓜ St-Michel)

Pharmacie de la Mairie (📞 01 43 54 23 99; 9 rue des Archives, 4e; 🕐 9am-8pm; Ⓜ Hôtel de Ville)

Pharmacie Les Champs (📞 01 45 62 02 41; 84 av des Champs-Élysées, 8e; 🕐 24hr; Ⓜ George V)

●●●
Money

France uses the euro (€). For updated currency exchange rates, check www.xe.com.

ATMs

You'll find ATMs throughout Paris. To change money, bureaux de change are usually more efficient, open longer hours and give better rates than most banks.

Credit Cards

Visa is the most widely accepted credit card, followed by MasterCard. American Express and Diners Club cards are accepted only at more exclusive establishments. Some restaurants don't accept credit cards. Many

289

automated services, such as ticket machines, require a chip-and-PIN credit card. Ask your bank for advice before you leave.

Tipping

French law requires that restaurant, cafe and hotel bills include a service charge (usually between 12% and 15%). Taxi drivers expect small tips of between 5% and 10% of the fare, though the usual procedure is to round up to the nearest €1 regardless of the fare.

Police

Police in France are here are to maintain order; assisting tourists is not part of their job description. They have wide powers of search and seizure; you are expected to have photo ID on you at *all* times.

Do not leave baggage unattended; suspicious objects will be summarily blown up.

Public Holidays

In France a *jour férié* (public holiday) is celebrated strictly on the day on which it falls. Thus if May Day falls on a Saturday or Sunday, no provision is made for an extra day off.

The following holidays are observed in Paris:

New Year's Day *(Jour de l'An)*
1 January

Easter Sunday & Monday
(Pâques & Lundi de Pâques)
Late March/April

May Day *(Fête du Travail)*
1 May

Victory in Europe Day
(Victoire 1945) 8 May

Ascension Thursday
(L'Ascension) May (celebrated on the 40th day after Easter)

Whit Monday *(Lundi de Pentecôte)* Mid-May to mid-June (seventh Sunday and Monday after Easter)

Bastille Day/National Day
(Fête Nationale) 14 July

Assumption Day
(L'Assomption) 15 August

All Saints' Day *(La Toussaint)*
1 November

**Armistice Day/
Remembrance Day** *(Le Onze Novembre)* 11 November

Christmas *(Noël)*
25 December

Safe Travel

In general, Paris is a safe city and random street assaults are rare. The city is generally well lit and there's no reason not to use the metro at night.

Metro stations that are best avoided late at night include Châtelet–Les Halles and its seemingly endless corridors, Château Rouge in Montmartre, Gare du Nord, Strasbourg St-Denis, Réaumur Sébastopol and Montparnasse Bienvenüe. *Bornes d'alarme* (alarm boxes) are located in the centre of each metro/RER platform and in some station corridors.

Nonviolent crime such as pickpocketing and thefts from handbags and packs is a problem wherever there are crowds, especially of tourists.

Take the usual precautions: don't carry more money than you need, and keep your credit cards, passport and other documents in a concealed pouch, a hotel safe or a safe-deposit box.

Taxes & Refunds

France's value-added tax (VAT) is known as TVA *(taxe sur la valeur ajoutée)* and is 19.6% on most goods except medicine and books, for which it's 5.5%. Prices that include TVA are often marked TTC *(toutes taxes comprises;* literally 'all taxes included').

If you're not an EU resident, you may be entitled to a TVA refund on certain purchases – for more information contact the **customs information centre** (☎ 08 11 20 44 44; www.douane.minefi.gouv.fr; ⏰ 8.30am-6pm Mon-Fri).

Telephone

France's country code is 33.There are no area codes in France – you always dial the 10-digit number.

To call abroad from Paris, dial France's international access code (00), the country code, the area code (usually without the initial '0', if there is one) and the local number.

Mobile Phones

Check with your service provider about using your mobile phone in France, but beware of roaming costs, especially for data.

Rather than staying on your home network, it is usually more convenient to buy a local SIM card from a French provider such as **Orange** (www.orange.fr), which will give you a local phone number. In order for this to work, however, you'll need to ensure your phone is 'unlocked', which means you can use another service provider while abroad.

Phonecards

Public telephones in Paris usually require a *télécarte* (phonecard; €7.50/15 for 50/120 calling units), which can be purchased at post offices, *tabacs,* supermarkets, SNCF ticket windows, metro stations and anywhere you see a blue sticker reading *'télécarte en vente ici'* (phonecard for sale here).

You can buy prepaid phonecards in France such as **Allomundo** (www.allomundo. com) that are up to 60% cheaper for calling abroad than the standard *télécarte*.

⬤⬤⬤
Time

France uses the 24-hour clock in most cases, with the hours usually separated from the minutes by a lower-case 'h'. Thus, 15h30 is 3.30pm, 00h30 is 12.30am and so on.

France is on Central European Time (like Berlin and Rome), which is one hour ahead of GMT. When it's noon in Paris it's 11am in London, 3am in San Francisco, 6am

in New York and and 9pm in Sydney.

Daylight-saving time runs from the last Sunday in March to the last Sunday in October.

⬤⬤⬤
Toilets

Public toilets in Paris are signposted *toilettes* or *WC*. The self-cleaning cylindrical toilets you see on Parisian pavements are open 24 hours, reasonably clean and are free of charge. Look for the words *libre* ('available'; green-coloured) or *occupé* ('occupied'; red-coloured).

In older cafes and bars, you may find a *toilette à la turque* (Turkish-style toilet), the French term for a squat toilet.

Cafe owners do not appreciate you using their facilities if you are not a paying customer. Major department stores and big hotels are good bets. Take advantage of the facilities when visiting museums.

There are free public toilets in front of Notre Dame cathedral, near the Arc de Triomphe, east down the steps at Sacré Cœur and at the northwestern entrance to the Jardins des Tuileries.

⬤⬤⬤
Tourist Information

The main branch of the **Paris Convention & Visitors Bureau** (Office de Tourisme et de Congrès de Paris; ☎ 08 92 68 30 00; www.parisinfo. com; 25-27 rue des Pyramides, 1er; ☺ 9am-7pm Jun-Oct, shorter hours rest of year;

Ⓜ Pyramides) is about 500m northwest of the Louvre.

The bureau maintains a handful of centres elsewhere in Paris, most of which are listed here (telephone numbers and websites are the same as for the main office). There are also information desks at Charles de Gaulle Airport, where you can pick up maps and brochures.

Paris Convention & Visitors Bureau (opposite 72 blvd Rochechouart, 18e; ☺ 10am-6pm; Ⓜ Anvers) At the foot of Montmartre.

Paris Convention & Visitors Bureau (Place du 11 Novembre 1918, 10e; ☺ 8am-7pm Mon-Sat; Ⓜ Gare de l'Est) In the arrivals hall for TGV trains.

Paris Convention & Visitors Bureau (Hall d'Arrivée, 20 blvd Diderot, 12e; ☺ 8am-6pm Mon-Sat; Ⓜ Gare de Lyon) In the arrivals hall for mainline trains.

Paris Convention & Visitors Bureau (18 rue de Dunkerque, 10e; ☺ 8am-6pm; Ⓜ Gare du Nord) Under the glass roof of the Île de France departure and arrival area at the eastern end of the station.

Syndicate d'Initiative de Montmartre (☎ 01 42 62 21 21; 21 place du Tertre, 18e; ☺ 10am-7pm; Ⓜ Abbesses) This locally run tourist office and shop is in Montmartre's most picturesque square and is open year-round. It sells maps of Montmartre and organises tours in July and August.

Travellers with Disabilities

Paris is an ancient city and therefore not particularly well equipped for *les handicapés* (people with a disability): kerb ramps are few and far between, older public facilities and budget hotels usually lack lifts, and the metro, dating back more than a century, is mostly inaccessible for those in a wheelchair *(fauteuil roulant)*. But efforts are being made and early in the new millennium the tourist office launched its 'Tourisme & Handicap' initiative in which museums, cultural attractions, hotels and restaurants that provided access or special assistance or facilities for those with physical, mental, visual and/or hearing disabilities would display a special logo at their entrances. For a list of the places qualifying, visit the tourist office's website (www.parisinfo.com) and click on 'Practical Paris'.

For information on accessibility on all forms of public transport in the Paris region, get a copy of the *Guide Practique à l'Usage des Personnes à Mobilité Réduite* (Practical Usage Guide for People with Reduced Mobility) from the Syndicate des Transports d'Île de France. Its **Info Mobi** (www.infomobi. com) is especially useful.

For information about what cultural venues in Paris are accessible to people with disabilities, visit the website of **Accès Culture** (www.accesculture.org).

Access in Paris, a 245-page guide to the French capital for people with a disability, is available online from **Access Project** (www.accessinparis. org; 39 Bradley Gardens).

Visas

There are no entry requirements for nationals of EU countries. Citizens of Australia, the USA, Canada and New Zealand do not need visas to visit France for up to 90 days. Except for people from a handful of other European countries (including Switzerland), everyone, including citizens of South Africa, needs a Schengen Visa, named after the Schengen Agreement that has abolished passport controls among 22 EU countries and has also been ratified by the non-EU governments of Iceland, Norway and Switzerland. A visa for any of these countries should be valid throughout the Schengen area, but it pays to double-check with the embassy or consulate of each country you intend to visit. Note that the UK and Ireland are not Schengen countries.

Check www.france. diplomatie.fr for the latest visa regulations and the closest French embassy to your current residence.

a b c

Language

The sounds used in spoken French can almost all be found in English. There are a couple of exceptions: nasal vowels (represented in our pronunciation guides by 'o' or 'u' followed by an almost inaudible nasal consonant sound 'm', 'n' or 'ng'), the 'funny' *u* sound ('ew' in our guides) and the deep-in-the-throat *r*. Bearing these few points in mind and reading our pronunciation guides below as if they were English, you'll be understood just fine.

To enhance your trip with a phrasebook, visit **lonelyplanet.com**. Lonely Planet iPhone phrasebooks are available through the Apple App store.

BASICS

Hello./Goodbye.
Bonjour./Au revoir.   bon·zhoor/o·rer·vwa
How are you?
Comment allez-vous?   ko·mon ta·lay·voo
I'm fine, thanks.
Bien, merci.   byun mair·see
Excuse me./Sorry.
Excusez-moi./Pardon.   ek·skew·zay·mwa/par·don
Yes./No.
Oui./Non.   wee/non
Please.
S'il vous plaît.   seel voo play
Thank you.
Merci.   mair·see
That's fine./You're welcome.
De rien.   der ree·en
Do you speak English?
Parlez-vous anglais?   par·lay·voo ong·glay
I don't understand.
Je ne comprends pas.   zher ner kom·pron pa
How much is this?
C'est combien?   say kom·byun

ACCOMMODATION

I'd like to book a room.
Je voudrais réserver   zher voo·dray ray·zair·vay
une chambre.   ewn shom·brer
How much is it per night?
Quel est le prix par nuit?   kel ay ler pree par nwee

EATING & DRINKING

I'd like ..., please.
Je voudrais ...,   zher voo·dray ...
s'il vous plaît.   seel voo play
That was delicious!
C'était délicieux!   say·tay day·lee·syer
Bring the bill/check, please.
Apportez-moi l'addition,   a·por·tay·mwa la·dee·syon
s'il vous plaît.   seel voo play

I'm allergic (to peanuts).
Je suis allergique   zher swee a·lair·zheek
(aux cacahuètes).   (o ka·ka·wet)
I don't eat ...
Je ne mange pas de ...   zher ner monzh pa de ...
  fish   *poisson*   pwa·son
  (red) meat   *viande (rouge)*   vyond (roozh)
  poultry   *volaille*   vo·lai

EMERGENCIES

I'm ill.
Je suis malade.   zher swee ma·lad
Help!
Au secours!   o skoor
Call a doctor!
Appelez un médecin!   a·play un mayd·sun
Call the police!
Appelez la police!   a·play la po·lees

DIRECTIONS

I'm looking for (a/the) ...
Je cherche ...   zher shairsh ...
  bank
  une banque   ewn bongk
  ... embassy
  l'ambassade de ... lam·ba·sahd der ...
  market
  le marché   ler mar·shay
  museum
  le musée   ler mew·zay
  restaurant
  un restaurant   un res·to·ron
  toilet
  les toilettes   lay twa·let
  tourist office
  l'office de tourisme lo·fees der too·rees·mer

Behind the Scenes

Author Thanks

CATHERINE LE NEVEZ

Un grand merci to my co-authors Chris and Nicola – it's a pleasure working with you. *Merci mille fois* to Julian, and to all of the innumerable Parisians who offered insights and inspiration. Thanks too to those interviewed in this book, including Elise Maillard at the Louvre, and to Jo Cooke, Annelies Mertens and everyone at Lonely Planet. And *merci encore* to my parents, brother and *belle-sœur* for instilling in me and sustaining my lifelong love of Paris.

Acknowledgments

Cover photographs:
Front: The lena bridge and the Eiffel Tower Photographer: Bertrand Gardel/Getty Images ©
Back: People relaxing beside steps at Basilique du Sacré-Coeur Photographer: John Sones Singing Bowl Media/Hemis ©

This Book

This 2nd edition of Lonely Planet's Discover Paris guidebook was researched and written by Catherine Le Nevez, Christopher Pitts and Nicola Williams. The previous edition was written by Caroline Sieg, Steve Fallon, Catherine Le Nevez, Christopher Pitts and Nicola Williams. This guidebook was commissioned in Lonely Planet's London office, and produced by the following:

Commissioning Editor Joanna Cooke
Coordinating Editor Samantha Forge
Coordinating Cartographer Karusha Ganga
Coordinating Layout Designer Lauren Egan
Managing Editors Annelies Mertens, Bruce Evans
Managing Cartographers Anita Banh, Anthony Phelan
Managing Layout Designer Chris Girdler
Assisting Editors Peter Cruttenden, Kate Mathews, Tracy Whitmey
Cover Research Naomi Parker
Internal Image Research Aude Vauconsant
Illustrator Javier Zarracina
Language Content Branislava Vladisavljevic

Thanks to Ryan Evans, Jouve India, Anna Lorincz, Trent Paton, Raphael Richards, Rebecca Skinner, Gerard Walker

SEND US YOUR FEEDBACK

We love to hear from travellers – your comments keep us on our toes and help make our books better. Our well-travelled team reads every word on what you loved or loathed about this book. Although we cannot reply individually to postal submissions, we always guarantee that your feedback goes straight to the appropriate authors, in time for the next edition. Each person who sends us information is thanked in the next edition, the most useful submissions are rewarded with a selection of digital PDF chapters.

Visit **lonelyplanet.com/contact** to submit your updates and suggestions or to ask for help. Our award-winning website also features inspirational travel stories, news and discussions.

Note: We may edit, reproduce and incorporate your comments in Lonely Planet products such as guidebooks, websites and digital products, so let us know if you don't want your comments reproduced or your name acknowledged. For a copy of our privacy policy visit lonelyplanet.com/privacy.

NOTES

Index

See also separate subindexes for:
- 🍴 **Eating p306**
- 🍷 **Drinking & Nightlife p308**
- ☆ **Entertainment p308**
- 🔒 **Shopping p309**
- ➕ **Sports & Activities p310**

Sights 000
Map pages 000

Sights 000
Map pages 000

⊖ Drinking & Nightlife

Sights 000
Map pages 000

★ Entertainment

🛍 Shopping

Sights 000
Map pages 000

How to Use This Book

These symbols will help you find the listings you want:

- ◉ Sights
- ✖ Eating
- 🍷 Drinking & Nightlife
- ✪ Entertainment
- 🛍 Shopping
- ⚽ Sports & Activities

Look out for these icons:

- **FREE** No payment required
- 🌿 A green or sustainable option

Our authors have nominated these places as demonstrating a strong commitment to sustainability – for example by supporting local communities and producers, operating in an environmentally friendly way, or supporting conservation projects.

These symbols give you the vital information for each listing:

- ☏ Telephone Numbers
- ☺ Opening Hours
- P Parking
- ⊖ Nonsmoking
- ❋ Air-Conditioning
- @ Internet Access
- 🛜 Wi-Fi Access
- 🏊 Swimming Pool
- 🥗 Vegetarian Selection
- 📖 English-Language Menu
- 👪 Family-Friendly
- 🐾 Pet-Friendly
- 🚌 Bus
- ⛴ Ferry
- Ⓜ Metro
- Ⓢ Subway
- ⊖ London Tube
- 🚊 Tram
- 🚆 Train

Reviews are organised by author preference.

Map Legend

Sights
- 🏖 Beach
- 🛕 Buddhist
- 🏰 Castle
- ✝ Christian
- 🕉 Hindu
- ☪ Islamic
- ✡ Jewish
- ❶ Monument
- 🏛 Museum/Gallery
- 🏚 Ruin
- 🍷 Winery/Vineyard
- 🦓 Zoo
- ◉ Other Sight

Sports & Activities
- 🤿 Diving/Snorkelling
- 🛶 Canoeing/Kayaking
- 🎿 Skiing
- 🏄 Surfing
- 🏊 Swimming/Pool
- 🚶 Walking
- 🏄 Windsurfing
- ⚽ Other Sports & Activities

Eating
- ✖ Eating

Drinking & Nightlife
- 🍷 Drinking
- ☕ Cafe

Entertainment
- ✪ Entertainment

Shopping
- 🛍 Shopping

Sleeping
- 🛏 Sleeping
- ⛺ Camping

Information
- 🏤 Post Office
- ❶ Tourist Information

Transport
- ✈ Airport
- ⊗ Border Crossing
- 🚌 Bus
- 🚠 Cable Car/Funicular
- 🚲 Cycling
- ⛴ Ferry
- 🚝 Monorail
- P Parking
- Ⓢ S-Bahn
- 🚕 Taxi
- 🚉 Train/Railway
- 🚊 Tram
- ⊖ Tube Station
- Ⓤ U-Bahn
- Ⓜ Underground Train Station
- ✳ Other Transport

Routes
- Tollway
- Freeway
- Primary
- Secondary
- Tertiary
- Lane
- Unsealed Road
- Plaza/Mall
- Steps
-)═(Tunnel
- Pedestrian Overpass
- Walking Tour
- Walking Tour Detour
- Path

Boundaries
- — — — International
- ------ State/Province
- — — Disputed
- — — Regional/Suburb
- Marine Park
- Cliff
- Wall

Geographic
- 🛖 Hut/Shelter
- 🗼 Lighthouse
- 👓 Lookout
- ▲ Mountain/Volcano
- 🌴 Oasis
- 🏞 Park
-)(Pass
- 🧺 Picnic Area
- 💧 Waterfall

Hydrography
- River/Creek
- Intermittent River
- Swamp/Mangrove
- Reef
- Canal
- Water
- Dry/Salt/Intermittent Lake
- Glacier

Areas
- Beach/Desert
- Cemetery (Christian)
- Cemetery (Other)
- Park/Forest
- Sportsground
- Sight (Building)
- Top Sight (Building)

Our Story

A beat-up old car, a few dollars in the pocket and a sense of adventure. In 1972 that's all Tony and Maureen Wheeler needed for the trip of a lifetime – across Europe and Asia overland to Australia. It took several months, and at the end – broke but inspired – they sat at their kitchen table writing and stapling together their first travel guide, *Across Asia on the Cheap*. Within a week they'd sold 1500 copies. Lonely Planet was born.

Today, Lonely Planet has offices in Melbourne, London and Oakland, with more than 600 staff and writers. We share Tony's belief that 'a great guidebook should do three things: inform, educate and amuse'.

Our Writers

CATHERINE LE NEVEZ

Coordinating Author Catherine first lived in Paris aged four and she's been returning here at every opportunity since, completing her Doctorate of Creative Arts in Writing, Masters in Professional Writing, and post-grad qualifications in Editing and Publishing along the way. Catherine's writing on Paris includes numerous Lonely Planet guides to the city. Revisiting her favourite Parisian haunts and uncovering new ones is a highlight of this (and every) book. As well as newspaper and radio reportage covering Paris' literary scene, Catherine has authored, co-authored and contributed to dozens of Lonely Planet guidebooks throughout France, Europe and beyond. Wanderlust aside, Paris remains her favourite city on earth.

CHRISTOPHER PITTS

Eiffel Tower & La Défense, Champs Élysées & Grands Boulevards, Montmartre & Northern Paris, Le Marais & Bastille Christopher Pitts has lived in Paris since 2001. He first started writing about the city as a means to buy baguettes – and to impress a certain Parisian (it worked, they're now married with two kids). Over the past decade he has written for various publications, in addition to working as a translator and editor.

NICOLA WILLIAMS

Louvre & Les Halles, Le Marais & Bastille, The Islands British writer and editorial consultant Nicola Williams has lived in France and written about it for more than a decade. From her hillside house on the southern shore of Lake Geneva, it's an easy hop to Paris where she has spent endless years revelling in its extraordinary art, architecture and cuisine. Resisting the urge to splurge in every boutique she passed while walking the streets of the Marais was this trip's challenge.

Published by Lonely Planet Publications Pty Ltd
ABN 36 005 607 983
2nd edition – March 2013
ISBN 978 1 74220 568 7
© Lonely Planet 2013   Photographs © as indicated 2013
10 9 8 7 6 5 4 3 2
Printed in China